WITNESS FOR MY FATHER

A WORLD WAR II STORY OF LOSS, HOPE, AND DISCOVERY

HOW A JEWISH SURVIVOR AND A BLACK LIEUTENANT PREVAILED AGAINST GENOCIDE AND RACISM

BARBARA BERGREN

First paperback edition January 2020

Design by Vanessa Mendozzi

ISBN 978-1-7342444-0-3 (paperback)
ISBN 978-1-7342444-1-0 (ebook)

Published in the United States by SandKey Press
barbarabergren.com

For Dad, my hero.

For John, my other hero.

Note from the Author

This is a narrative non-fiction story. The main characters are real and the events are factual, recounted to the best of my knowledge. Some names are changed and scenes adjusted for narrative format. Dialogue, individual thoughts, and viewpoints from my father's childhood are derived from our discussions, the interview with Bryan Gruley, interviews with his hometown friends, testimony from witnesses, travel to Germany, Poland and Israel, and historic research.

We cannot direct the wind,
But we can adjust the sails.

—Thomas S. Monson

"If anything can, it is memory that will save humanity."

—Elie Wiesel, 1986 Nobel Lecture

INTRODUCTION

Children are brought up on stories. I know I was. My mother would read to me before my naps: animal tales like *Bambi* and *The Ugly Duckling*; lighthearted accounts of the mischievous *Max and Moritz*, two little boys and their pranks. Those were the fanciful books that kept me company and informed my early childhood. But my father was the real keeper of stories. He was the one who'd tuck me in at night, who'd ease me into bedtime with his tales. The accounts were his own, mostly about his workday. I remember him coming home in his military uniform, an owl insignia sewn to his sleeve. He'd tell me about the people he met and the birds he saw, who he ate lunch with on any given day. And he'd talk to me about the motors he fixed, how he'd puzzle over each one until he figured out what was wrong. My father was a problem solver, good with his hands, and when he'd talk about bringing an old engine back to life, his face would light up, satisfied with a job well done.

Sitting on the edge of my bed, Papa would brush my bangs away from my face or stroke the top of my head. He'd pull the bedcovers up to my neck, making sure I was warm. His words felt special, as if they were intended only for me. It might have been the soft, rounded vowels of his Polish accent. Maybe it was the fact of just the two of us alone with the world of his stories. But those moments were everything to me. I'd drift off to sleep, clutching his forearm, keeping him close.

When I think back on those years as a young girl—I remember how safe and warm I felt, how I knew without question that I was loved, that I was safe. Our nightly dinner routine was my favorite time. When Papa was late coming home, I'd sit on the front stoop of our house in Mishmar HaShiv'a, waiting for him to pull up in his jeep. Seven o'clock was late for a four-year-old, but I didn't care. I loved sitting at the table like a grown-up, listening to my mother and father talk. Kohlrabi was a bargain at the market. Beef was only for special occasions. And you couldn't just move anywhere in the world. You had to plan. You had to have papers. I didn't understand any of it, just that my parents had a dream.

My life was beautiful and complete. Our tight little circle didn't seem strange to me until years later when I went to school in America and was asked about my family tree for a social studies class. It had always been the three of us and that had been enough. I had met my mother's family when I was four. I don't remember much, other than a delicious apple strudel and my Oma taking me to the butcher shop.

As for my father's family—he told me little. He was orphaned at sixteen. He met my mother after the war ended. He was twenty-one when I was born. He had a sister once. Klara with a K. I sat very still when my father talked to me about his childhood, hanging on to every precious word. I knew not to ask for more. I accepted my father's reluctance in talking about his life *before*. With a child's instinct, I knew that when his face would tighten, when his eyes would soften as if he was looking at ghosts, it was time to stop asking questions. My father wanted me to have only a brief summary of his life—that much was clear. For the longest time, it seemed enough.

PART ONE

CHAPTER ONE

CONNECTICUT 2003

"Where do you want to sit, Dad?" I asked, coming up behind him and planting a kiss on his cheek. "Inside or out?"

"Let's sit on the deck," he said.

The upper deck was shaded, private. A fitting backdrop. "Perfect," I said.

Dad paused at the sliding glass door, looking out at the backyard. Blood-red geraniums stood out in the flower garden, startling in their brilliance. Green-and blue-leaf hostas circled the base of two sturdy oak trees. As if on cue, two robins swooped in for birdseed, chirping their secret language. Dad smiled. He loved *the nature*, as he called it.

"Ed," I called to my brother. "Dad wants to sit outside."

"Okay, sure. Whatever he wants," he replied, picking up his camera equipment.

Turning to Jeff, I said, "Can you move the chairs to the shady side near the house?"

"No problem, Mom." Jeff was like my father, his Opa—soft-spoken, smart, kind. I needed him here today.

Ed wanted to videotape the interview. Dad said it was okay. I wasn't sure. Would it be too much for him?

The doorbell rang. It was Bryan Gruley. "Hello Barbara, good to see you again."

"You too—come in, come in. We're setting up out back." I waved him to follow me.

"How's your dad doing?" he asked.

"He seems fine," I said. "I'm the one who's nervous."

Dad greeted Bryan, shaking his hand. "Hello," he said. "Sorry you have to work today."

"Are you kidding? You're the one that has to do all the hard stuff."

I filled the coffee mugs as we sat down in our deck chairs.

Dad inhaled, taking his first sip. "Dat smells good."

Despite their physical differences—at over six feet tall, Bryan towered over my father—both men held themselves with a natural authority, something I think each recognized in the other.

Bryan flipped open his spiral notebook, pen in hand. Ed started rolling the videotape. My heart beat faster.

"Martin, you grew up in Poland in a town called Starachowice," Bryan began. "Is that correct?

"Well, yes," he replied. "We lived in the section called Wierzbnik …"

NEW YEAR'S EVE, 1938

STARACHOWICE, POLAND

Isaak and Sonia Wajgenszperg's two-story house caught the fresh morning sun. Their fashionable address at 38 Pilsudskiego Street was typical of the affluent homes lining the long riverside road. This was the heartbeat of the Jewish district of Wierzbnik, the place where families did their shopping, where children amused themselves in the marketplace while their mothers bought groceries and chatted with friends. Small shops surrounded the bustling square and every day a line of women would spill outside the bakery door, eager to purchase braided challah and plump fresh bagels. In the butcher's window, sides of beef hung above a handwritten sign that advertised hot soup. On one side stood a shoemaker. On the other, a newsagent that sold small bars of bitter chocolate along with copies of Polish and Hebrew newspapers.

December 1938 had been frigid but bright. When early evening came, the sun dropped like a white porcelain plate, flooding the town with gray light before disappearing behind the forest skyline. There was less snowfall this winter, but it was still bitterly cold.

The Wajgenszpergs and their children, Mietek and Klara, were preparing to celebrate the New Year at the home of their close friends and neighbors. Sonia rushed to box bottles of dark beer and cover her hard salami sandwich platter with cheesecloth. Darting around her kitchen, she checked that everything was packed. Satisfied, she untied her apron and headed upstairs to change into her long black skirt and favorite flowered blouse. With a sigh of relief, she sat down at her vanity table.

Sonia brushed her soft brown hair, letting the loose curls fall down her shoulders; her high cheekbones glowed, accentuated by her natural blush. Rummaging for her clips on the silver tray that held her brushes, she pulled back her long hair, pinning it on each side at the nape of her neck. She jumped when her ten-year-old flew into the room.

“Mama, can I bring my stamp collection and the jelly candies to share at the party?”

Such a good boy. “Why not? But you haven’t combed your hair or finished dressing. We’re almost ready to go.”

Isaak came in to wash up. “Mietek, what are you waiting for? Go and get ready.”

The boy dashed out of the room.

Isaak turned to his wife. “You look beautiful.”

“I will never get tired of hearing this,” Sonia said.

Isaak removed his shirt, revealing a hint of brown from his summer tan. Sonia watched him shyly, still enamored with his strong body. He dipped a soft cloth into the ceramic water bowl to wipe his face. He buttoned his stiff white shirt, then put on his tie and suit jacket. “Let’s go toast the New Year,” he said. “We deserve it.”

“Can you please check on Klara? I told her we were leaving at eight.” Sonia said. “But you know, she needs a gentle push.”

She was sitting on the floor of her room playing with her favorite doll. Isaak sighed. “Are you ready?” Klara turned her head, her chubby cheeks pronounced as she flashed the coy smile her father couldn’t resist.

“I’m all done, Papa.”

Together they walked downstairs and grabbed their coats and scarves. Mietek picked up the wrapped plates of food. Isaak cradled the beer and champagne bottles as he ushered his family out.

Despite the short walk, only two houses away, Mietek and Klara shivered while waiting in front of the Laks’ front door. Pola greeted them with hugs.

Isaac Laks took their coats and called his daughter downstairs. “Renia, our neighbors are here.”

“Put the food over there,” said Pola. “And thank you for all your help,” she whispered to her friend. Sonia tried to make herself available to Pola, whose arthritic hands were knobby and stiff.

The festive dining table was set with champagne, crystal glasses, beer bottles, and a huge basket of fruit. Early guests had already helped themselves to cheese and bread. Renia held Klara’s hand and led her upstairs, with Mietek close behind.

The party was in full swing. Urish Helstein opened his violin case and warmed up on a cabaret piece he’d heard at the packed Café George, just one of many thriving night clubs in Warsaw. Henryk Gold’s Orchestra led with the trumpet and violins, setting the stage for their tenor singer. His seductive voice romanced the patrons: *Because It Usually Starts Like This—Bo to sie zwykle tak zaczyna.*

Isaak reached in his pocket for his wooden flute. Relaxing his lips, he centered the mouthpiece, and tuned up with Urish. First he played “Song of the Golden Land,” picking up the rhythm by stomping his foot. Then he blended into a softer, folksier song,“Reyzele,” without effort. Sonia and Pola clapped their hands with the music. Others joined in.

Everyone piled their plates with food; drinks flowed all evening. Moniek Zuckerman raised his bottle of beer: “May this year bring prosperity to Poland and to our industrialized little town. Hear, hear.”

“And may our forestry business flourish—I hope you can hear me across town Henry.” Isaak grinned, saluting his brother who managed the business with him. But not all talk was cheery.

“We can’t ignore what’s happening,” Moniek said, biting his lower lip. “Just a few weeks ago the Nazis attacked the Jews and their stores and businesses.”

“It’s been downhill ever since Hitler stripped the German Jews of their rights. That was four years ago," declared Abraham. "The anti-Jewish campaign is escalating. We should have seen this coming."

"For God's sake, they declared Jews a separate race," replied Moniek. "Can you imagine?"

Isaac Laks interrupted quickly, "Let's keep this evening free of politics, please."

Everyone nodded, as if they only just remembered they were at a party.

Mietek and Klara fell asleep after playing all evening. But Renia stayed with the adults as the hour grew late, arguing that her two older sisters were still out celebrating so it was only fair that she got to stay up too. Then it was time to watch the clock for the New Year's countdown. A few minutes before midnight, Isaac Laks poured the drinks. Sonia picked up her glass, held it high above her head, flashed her enchanting smile, and toasted, "To a happy and healthy New Year. We are so grateful for our family and dearest friends. *L'chaim.*"

To Life!

New Year's Eve, 1938

CHAPTER TWO

Isaak rose early. The smell of freshly brewed coffee greeted him in the kitchen as Sonia poured the last cup of boiling water over the steeping coffee grinds. Isaak was to meet the president of the local bank that morning, to access his line of credit. Luckily for Isaak, that was his father.

"Don't you dare leave without having the eggs I made for you."

"I'm in a hurry, Sonia." He grabbed two bites to appease her. "Bank first, then we're filling a new order for the furniture company. It's a good sign for the new year."

"You'll need your heavy boots; it snowed all night."

"Yes, Sonia."

"Tell your father that we accept their invitation for dinner on Saturday."

"Yes, Sonia."

"Oh—I almost forgot. The Lakses asked us over for a card game on Sunday afternoon. I think we can make it."

"Yes, Sonia."

"Is that all you have to say, my husband?"

Isaak burst out laughing and took his wife in his arms. "Yes, yes, yes, Sonia. That is all I have to say. That—and I adore you."

With Isaak having left for work, Sonia cooked another batch

of eggs for the children, lathering rye bread slices with goose fat and raspberry jam.

"Mama," yelled Mietek rushing down the stairs. "I can't believe how much it snowed. Jakub will be here soon—we're skiing to school—I have to hurry."

"Your snow pants are hanging in the closet," she yelled back.

Mietek wrapped his woolen scarf around his neck and sprinted out the door within ten minutes. He and Jakub met up with another group of his classmates to head to their school—public school. His parents and their close friends worshipped in a progressive temple and chose not to send their children to Hebrew school full time. The family was stalwart in their faith, but they chose to be integrated with their community. They learned to read and write in Polish and honored holidays with their Christian friends.

Klara came down barefoot but dressed. "I'm ready Mama," she said with pride. Her sweater was inside out, but Sonia gave her credit for being on time. She grabbed her for a hug, then pointed to sit down.

"Renia and her sister are picking you up today," said Sonia putting Klara's plate on the table. "Did you pack your writing homework?"

"I did Mama. I love my story."

"I do too. Where did you come up with the idea for a secret flower garden?"

"It's so much fun to plant flower seeds with you—and to watch them grow. I thought, what if they just grow and grow so that I can hide behind the sunflowers after they get big!" She thrust her hand above her head.

Klara's writing talents shone through at an early age. Barely able to talk, she'd beg Sonia and sometimes Mietek to read her stories. Fanciful tales about fairies and gardens were her favorites, and her little face would light up when pixies and changelings would come onto the page. It didn't take her long to come up with her own versions.

"I want you to read your story at your grandparents' dinner this Saturday. They'll love it!"

"Really Mama?" Klara squealed. She smiled broadly, the picture of pride.

Mietek slid his arms out of his backpack. Flush from the chilly winds, he pulled out his math book and slide rule, then slid into his desk seat.

"Morning Alex."

"Hi Mietek. You ready to take the test?"

"As ready as I'll ever be." He felt a mutual respect with Alex. They helped each other with tough equations, sometimes even staying after school.

"Good morning Mrs. Adamski," the class chorused as their teacher entered. She waved and had them sit down.

"Let's get started. First, let us pray."

Alex and the others made the sign of the cross and folded their hands. "Our Father, which art in Heaven, hollowed be thy name."

Mietek and his six Jewish classmates sat silently waiting for the prayer to end, a ritual they'd repeat at the end of the day. He sharpened his pencil and positioned his slide rule on the desk. Mrs. Adamski handed out the test papers. Hungry to answer, Mietek delved in, setting up his first division question. He slowed down when he realized he would be first to finish. He didn't like standing out.

Class was dismissed. Mietek gathered his books and headed to the history room, eager to catch up with Renia. They were studying World War I and how it ended with peace treaties.

"Can you believe we weren't an independent country until the end of the war?" Mietek asked Renia.

"Mr. Olinski says all the trouble we're hearing about from Germany is because they're still mad about us having our own country. I can't imagine Poland any different, can you?"

"No. It seems that it's all about independence and having rights."

Mr. Olinski entered the room with a stack of history books under his arm. "Good morning class. We're finally at the end of studying the war. Today you'll learn about the Treaty of Versailles, which ended this chapter in history."

The Germans had been blamed for causing tremendous loss of life and damage to other countries. They would lose land and have to pay reparations. This was a major blow to them. They needed to rebuild their country, create jobs, feed their people. For Germany, the peace treaty was an expensive end to the war. For the rest of the world, it would be a prelude to another.

CHAPTER THREE

SUMMER 1939

Pilsudskiego Street was bustling with shoppers, but the real excitement was inside the Wajgenszperg's house. It was July 11th. Mietek's eleventh birthday.

Mietek ran in and out of the kitchen as his mother tended to the pot simmering on the stove. Sonia had told her oldest that she would make him his favorite meal. It may have been a scorching hot day, but a promise made was a promise kept. Mietek breathed in the sweet smell of sautéed onions and garlic. He loved the way the sliced potatoes exploded as they were dropped into the steaming pot, the way his mother flour-dusted her rolling pin to spread the dough, thinning it to her satisfaction. And he loved to watch her hands as she sliced ripe strawberries, then sprinkled them with white confection sugar before scooping them into the pie crusts for baking. This would be a feast.

Sitting on the front stoop, eight-year-old Klara moved her tongue back and forth as she finished wrapping her artwork. She carefully folded a shiny gold sheet of paper around her drawing, letting the string attached at the top of her gift hang free. She used leftover twine to tie a bow around the wrapping.

“Mietek!” she yelled toward the kitchen window. “Come here!”

“What is it, Klara?” he asked, running outside. He was often annoyed when his sister called for his attention, but not today. Not on his birthday.

“This is for you,” she said, thrusting the offering at him. “I made it myself!” She handed Mietek the package. He carefully untied the bow, unfolding the wrap.

“It’s a marker for your books because you always read to me. Happy birthday!”

Mietek looked at his sister, her pixie haircut framing her soft round face. “Oh … this is perfect, Klara. Just perfect.” He scanned the fancy *M* surrounded by flowers she’d carefully drawn. “I love it!”

Soon Mietek’s soccer team arrived, the neighbors too. The grown-ups settled into chairs on the porch, picking at sandwich platters while the boys ran to take their positions in the yard. Mietek won the toss to kick off the game. After taking one step back, he booted his new soccer ball, passing it to his left. With the ball in play, everyone sprinted back and forth. Mietek zigzagged the ball up the field.

“Pass it to me!” screamed his teammate. Two passes and they spiked the ball past the goalie. “Score!” he and his team roared. Their audience cheered them on until both sides were red-faced and out of breath, with beads of sweat running down their cheeks.

After the games were played, after the presents were opened, and the pie devoured, Mietek sat next to his father, recounting the highlights of the day.

“Did you see when I made that goal? I slipped it right past Josef.”

“I did indeed, son. That was some terrific footwork. Great ball control.”

"Do you think I might be a soccer player when I grow up? Play for the Polish Football Union?"

"You never know. If you practice hard and stay serious about playing, you might just become a member of the league." He bumped his son's arm with a fist. "But you're young and love mathematics too—always keep your options open, son. Look at me, I studied electronics, and now I market timber all over the country."

Sonia finished washing the last pot, untying her apron.

"Are we done, Mama?" asked Klara.

"Yes, you were a great help. Wash your hands and we'll go sit with Papa and Mietek."

Klara grabbed her doll and scurried out the front, letting the door slam. She plopped down on the stairs, propping her doll next to her.

Pulling her hair up in a bun, Sonia came out and kissed the top of her son's head. "Happy birthday, my Mietek."

Two weeks later, before the birthday party had even faded from memory, the Wajgenszpergs prepared to leave for their summer house in the country. It was a pleasant getaway and the family joked that they didn't know what they were getting away from, as many of their neighbors and indeed their relatives had houses on the same lake. Mietek loved this annual trip—two weeks with no school or chores, just swimming and sun and trees. Lots of trees. He'd packed his duffel bag and knapsack: two bathing trunks, sleeveless tee shirts, four short-sleeve shirts, shorts, a jacket, underwear. Nothing but easy summer outfits. He loaded his knapsack with two books and a small chess board. His cousin Eitan would come to play on rainy afternoons. They both agreed that they needed the practice. A pad and pencil for writing and drawing fit neatly in the front pouch. Just one more thing … he scoured his room before heading to the top of the stairs.

"Have you seen my deck of cards? I can't find them," he hollered to his mother. Klara came out of her room, her hand over her mouth, holding up the deck.

"You little—"

Klara screamed. Mietek chased her down the stairs, leaping two steps at a time, beating his sister to the bottom. "Stop taking my stuff!"

"Enough you two," shouted Sonia. "Enough. Have you finished your chores?"

Klara grudgingly finished sweeping the kitchen floor before putting the broom away. Mietek stacked wood for the kitchen stove, placing it in perfect piles the way his father had taught him. Then the two children raced to their rooms to check their knapsacks in case they'd forgotten anything.

The horses were fed and harnessed. Nevertheless, when Isaak arrived home from work at noon, he checked on them again. That done, he put the last piece of luggage on the cart as Mietek and Klara climbed into their carriage.

"Are you sure you want to leave today?" Isaak teased as he pulled on the reins.

"Yes!" the children shouted. The carriage jerked forward and they were on their way.

Yellow shades of evening sky illuminated the vast lake. Hovering over treetops, the sun invited the dimming of the day. The horses clip-clopped over crushed stone as they reached the last road leading to their thatched roof cottage. Mietek was first to climb off the carriage. He ran through the grass, beaming. Nothing had changed since the last time the family was here. Thick ivy still clung to the short wooden fence. Wildflowers still dotted the front walk. Inside, the same musty smell that to Mietek signaled the beginning of his holiday.

"Mietek, come help me with the luggage," yelled his father. Once the carriage was unloaded, the children dusted and swept their rooms. Mama cleaned the kitchen and unpacked the food basket while Papa opened the windows and stacked wood outside. It was pitch-black when the foursome retired to sit on their front porch, taking in the stillness of the lake.

The next morning, the aunts, uncles, and cousins came by to greet the Wajgenszpergs. They had arrived the day before and had already settled into their cottages. They met for a picnic lunch, spreading blankets close to the lake. The children splashed in and out of the water, returning ravenous for lunch. By late afternoon, their Wierzbnik neighbors had arrived, one by one, and Uncle Henry invited everyone over that evening for supper.

Mietek finished organizing his room and began reading the new book he got for his birthday. Like many eleven-year-olds, he was fond of adventures on the high seas. Sometimes he'd read aloud from a pirate story to scare Klara, but he couldn't bring himself to do that today, not with her bookmark sticking out from under the cover. Excited to leave for his uncle's place, he found it hard to concentrate.

“When are we going, Mama?” Mietek asked wandering into the kitchen. Sonia untied her apron, signaling she was done slicing salami and bread.

“Give me ten minutes to wash up.” She brushed her hand across his cheek.

The smoky waft of wood burning ushered in the evening. Mietek and Klara raced ahead to their uncle’s house where everyone set out their baskets of food. Aunt Hannah had arranged wildflowers in glass canning jars so that the rustic pine table looked like an enchanted forest. That’s what Klara said.

Once the grown-ups finished a beer toast, everyone lined up for dinner, scattering inside and out to eat. Mietek brought his empty plate inside when he heard his uncle Henry’s voice. “I’m worried what Hitler’s Nazi troops will do next,” he said almost in a whisper. Henry was well-traveled and spoke other languages, German among them. Everyone in the family looked up to him. “They’re using our radio bands to spread more lies, pretending we’re attacking one of their German radio stations.” Mietek listened as the grown-ups discussed how the Nazis were claiming that Poles were mistreating ethnic Germans living in Poland. “Can you imagine?” Uncle Henry said. “The German government has accused Poland of planning to break up their country. Is that what you’ve been doing in your work all this time, Isaak? Conspiring with the British and the French to break up the German empire?!”

Rumors mixed with facts, so nobody knew what might be true. Luckily, Uncle Henry and Isaac Laks both spoke German, so they could decipher more news than their neighbors. It was becoming increasingly clear to both of them that Nazi rule was a threat to all of Europe—especially the Jews.

Music drowned out the discussion. Mietek ran back outside. This was one of his favorite tunes! The radio blared Oberek Polish folk songs into the night. Out on the front porch, his aunt and uncle took each other's hands and began dancing. His cousins jumped in and Mietek grabbed a giggling Klara to join them. He broke into his best dance steps, gliding side to side, arm in the air. Stopping quickly, he jumped up—both feet in the air, losing his cap when he landed. His sister laughed and twirled. The starry night set their stage. Best of all, the children were allowed to stay up late every night.

The two weeks passed quickly. On the last day, Mietek helped his father gather the leftover wood and pack the carriage for the return trip home. Mietek moved slowly. It was always a letdown because every day here was spent filled with family, picnics, swimming, and games. Even the grown-ups had been more relaxed. But the trip home promised to be fun because they would be following Uncle Henry's carriage and stop for another picnic on the way. One more visit with cousins. One more meal under the trees. One more breath of a great time at the lake house. And one young boy who hoped their vacations would go on forever.

Summer vacation, 1939
Front row (left to right) Klara, unknown, Isaak, Sonia, Renia

CHAPTER FOUR

When trouble comes, it comes fast. Despite the news reports, despite all the rumors and the fears, the people of Wierzbnik listened to their radios in stunned disbelief. The unthinkable had happened: German troops had invaded Poland.

Typical of bullies, Hitler justified his aggression. The Germans had been "suffering" under the Treaty of Versailles. They lost land. They paid dearly through reparations. It was an economic disaster for the Germans, and on top of that, they suffered the ignominy of being blamed for the first war. "As always," Hitler said, "I sought to bring about a change by peaceful means, by offering proposals to remedy this situation which meanwhile had become unbearable." Now he was left with *no option* but to expand Germany's living space—*Lebensraum*—into Poland.

Tensions were rising across Europe. On the same day that Hitler announced his aggressions—September 1st, 1939—the town council of Wierzbnik voted to eliminate the name for their smaller Jewish community in the vain hope that folding themselves into "Starachowice" would somehow protect them. Across the country, Jews were doing what they could to "blend in."

The Wajgenszpergs and Laks gathered after dinner. Sonia served coffee and pastry, but her trembling hand missed the china cups as she poured from the pot. Mietek and Klara had been sent to their rooms, but Mietek lingered at the top of the stairs, listening as Isaac Laks explained what he had read in the German newspapers. Hitler had taken away all the Jews' rights in the German-occupied areas. Austrian and Czechoslovakian Jews had been stripped of their civil liberties, their countries annexed by Germany just a year before. Native German Jews, many of whom served their country in World War I, had been the first to suffer under Nazi discrimination.

"Take away all the Jews' rights?" asked Sonia. "How can this be?"

"You know I've been sharing incidents with your husband from the Austrian newspapers," Isaac responded. "But it's incomprehensible that Germany," he lifted his chin, "a refined country, could discriminate against their own Jews. To what end?" He ran his hand on the side of his head, messing up his straight, trimmed hair.

"What does this mean for us? I know we've talked about this Isaac, but I can't understand that we won't be allowed to run our businesses."

"That's not all," Isaac came back. "We won't be allowed to work. We won't be allowed to use public transportation. It's inconceivable!"

Sonia wrung her hands. "What about the children?" she asked, her voice cracking. "I don't want to alarm them—"

"But we have to keep them safe!" Pola cried. "What can we do?"

Isaak ran his fingers through his hair. "We have to move quickly. The cities will most likely be bombed."

Isaac agreed. "We mustn't panic. Let's gather … we must talk to the neighbors."

Their coffee grown cold, the Laks headed for the door.

“We won’t have to go to school for a whole week!” Klara squealed. Mietek paused—Papa wouldn’t even take him fishing for one day if there was school. He had a math test. What would happen if he missed it? How would he ever make up all his homework?

Papa called up the stairs, “Come on down! We’re ready to go.”

Knapsack hoisted on his back, Mietek picked up the two books he hadn’t finished reading. Klara took her favorite dolls and dragged her sack across the floor—she had packed too much, but Mietek hadn’t the heart to chastise her. Besides, Papa had stacked as much luggage as he could pile into the carriage, and it looked like they were planning to be gone far longer than just a week.

Mietek helped his little sister to her seat, watching as his neighbors rushed to get ready. The Kutners walked out their door with knapsacks strapped to their backs, ushering their small children toward the distant forest. Hunched forward, Brandla and her brother Dawid struggled to carry their overloaded backpacks. Dangling pots bumped their backs with every step.

“Papa,” Mietek whispered. “Why are so many people leaving their houses?”

“We’re not sure Starachowice will be safe if the planes fly over town,” Isaak explained. Mietek knew that the Germans had invaded, but he envisioned men in green uniforms carrying rifles. He hadn’t thought of planes.

“It will be okay, Mietek. We’ll only be at the lake house until they have gone. Then we’ll come back home. It won’t be long. You’ll see.”

Sonia left last, balancing a large pot and pan in her arms, as if there were no kitchen supplies waiting for them in the lake house. "Isaak, can you help me?" she asked, breathless, as he reached to pull her onto the carriage.

Sonia looked at their house as if to memorize the blooming Dahlias that clung to the front stairs. Who knew when they would return to their home, to the courtyard where the children played, where they sipped lemonade on summer days. The closed shutters sent a chill through her. Then Isaak snapped his wrist and cracked the reins. They were off.

But the lake house was not the refuge the family had hoped. This was early in the war when nobody knew what to expect. Everyone was trying to manage the unmanageable, to keep their families safe and hold on to the belief that life would soon be back to normal. Isaak's family was among thousands who had sought to escape danger, only to move closer to it. It all happened so fast.

After a late supper and beds hurriedly made, they awoke the next morning to hard, repeated knocking. Throwing on his undershirt, Isaak opened the door.

"I'm Walter." The skinny boy stood up straight to command some importance. "Your neighbor, Dr. Jacob Kramerz, sent me." He took off his shoulder strap to get papers from his sack.

The doctor had gone to the trouble of hiring a gentile courier to minimize the risk of being followed. This would not be good.

His eyes widened. "I've got news from town."

"Wait please," Isaak responded. "Sonia, come to the door," he yelled. He walked to the next cottage to begin the task of assembling the neighbors.

Walter waited in front of the Wajgenszperg's cottage until

everyone had gathered. He cleared his throat. "German aircraft are shooting into the forests and driving everyone out of the rural areas. The families who fled to the forests heard the shooting. When they returned to their homes, they found them untouched. Just the outskirts of our town were bombed." Lowering his head, the boy continued, "German troops have arrived in Starachowice."

The group stood motionless, only to inhale a drawn-out gasp.

"So many homes are empty. Your neighbors are afraid the troops will ask where you are. They believe it's in your best interest to return to town immediately."

Mietek squeezed his father's arm.

"Let me talk to Mama," Isaak said to his son.

He conferred with Sonia before turning to their neighbors. Mietek tried to follow what was being said. Phrases like "hunting us down" and "taking our chances" jumped out at him. Whatever was happening back home sounded dangerous. But the Germans were shooting into the forest. What could be worse than that?

So for the second time in as many days, horses were readied and carts were loaded. The group proceeded carefully, a sense of uncertainty shrouding the long trip back, an uncertainty coupled with a sickening, unthinkable fear. Halfway through the somber journey home, the travelers heard staccato shots in the distance. Mietek turned to his father. His mother pulled his sister close.

CHAPTER FIVE

Returning was a shock. After the joint invasion by Germany and the Soviet Union, Poland was split into three sectors. The central part of Poland, occupied by the Nazis, was designated as the *General-gouvernement*—the General Government. This zone of occupation was the seat of the Nazis' corrupt, immoral government in Poland. It held Starachowice in its grasp.

Soldiers were everywhere in the once proud town. The streets were clogged with military vehicles and the Germans took over the steel mill. They assigned one of their special SS units to oversee the project and began the work of converting it to a war munitions factory. It wasn't long before the plant that had employed a great many men, that had played such a critical role in the town's economy, became the focus of cheap labor. Slave labor in the case of the Jews, who had already been stripped of their civil and human rights.

Wierzbnik was now an occupied town. The Jews were robbed of their livelihood, of their ability to provide for their families. They couldn't own radios. They had to give up any and all weapons. They couldn't venture out of their houses after 6 p.m. Mietek was devastated to learn he couldn't play soccer in the evening with his friends. Not even in their own yard! In those early days of the occupation, it was this first imposed ordinance that hit hardest. The freedom to run, to play, to see friends was taken away. It was unimaginable. Mietek had played soccer as long as he could remember. Even his uncles from Warsaw and Krakow would come to see him compete. When he had scored a winning goal in the last tournament, Uncle Mendel had jumped up, promising his team new uniforms. It wasn't right, what was happening. It wasn't fair. "Yes," his father agreed. "This is not right. But you must keep these feelings to yourself. The Germans are in charge, now. They and their guns and their vicious dogs."

The Polish Army had been no match for the Germans, who outnumbered the Poles three to one. They couldn't stand up against German artillery and the first jet fighter warplanes used in combat. On September 27th, the German troops had taken Warsaw. The next day, Poland surrendered, and the country was split between the Germans and the Soviet Union. In a mere month, the Polish government was overthrown, the country captured and divided.

"What do you mean we can't go to school anymore?" Mietek pleaded. No, no, no! He couldn't dream of a life without his favorite teachers, friends and classes—how could they take that away? How would he learn? A whiz on the slide rule, he had just started an advanced math class. He was midway through a map drawing project in his geography class.

"What will I do every morning, Papa?" he pleaded.

Isaak tried to calm his son, despite feeling sickened himself. "Mama and I are figuring things out. A tutor would be the answer. We're trying to find one, but you need to be patient."

The Nazis considered the Poles "hewers of wood and drawers of water," mere instruments to carry out their bidding. New laws surfaced almost daily, adding to the chaos. Those who resisted were rounded up to be transported. The term "concentration camp" crept into the conversations of horrified Jews. Germany had been known as the land of poets and thinkers: *Das land der Dichter und Denke*. How was it that these same people had exported such a gruesome brand of brutality? They torched synagogues and mowed down innocent civilians with machine guns. Ordinary people—men, women, and children—were slaughtered as aircraft fighters sprayed villages and farms with bullets. This was how it began. Nobody could imagine where it would end.

Within two months, most of Isaak and Sonia's neighborhood was under house arrest. Mietek and Klara weren't even allowed to walk on the sidewalk when the Nazi soldiers patrolled with their foul language and fierce dogs. Sonia would only allow Mietek and Klara to walk to the Laks' house to visit with the three sisters. Otherwise, they had to be accompanied by one or both of their parents.

In November the governor-general issued a new ordinance. All Jews over the age of ten were to wear armbands on their upper right sleeve: white cloth emblazoned in blue with the six-sided Star of David. It was one of the first Jewish Star mandates of the war.

Compliance was mandatory. Punishment was severe. Get caught without an armband and you could be sent away or worse, killed. It was that simple.

Mietek ran home just making the annoying 6 p.m. curfew. He was feeling a little brighter, having spent time at the Laks' home playing cards with Renia and her sister Rosalie. They had talked about their teachers and their friends at school. They missed their classmates—Rosalie joked that she even missed her geography class—but all agreed they needed to stay positive. They had to find their way to feeling productive while living in this shell.

"Mama, I'm home," Mietek yelled.

"I know, dear, I know." She was hunched over the dining table, focused on some task.

Mietek saw his mother lift up her hand, pulling tightly—she was sewing. "What is that, Mama?" he demanded.

Her expression was guarded, sad. "Papa was going to tell you tonight." She turned away to compose herself. "You will have to wear this armband … whenever you go out. Papa and I will wear it too," she said, trying to soften the news.

"I'm not wearing that!" Mietek bristled. But he saw her swollen eyes. "I'll talk to Papa in the morning," he offered. Then he kissed her good night. Feeling defeated, he took the stairs to his room one at a time. A rarity for him.

"Papa, I don't want to wear this thing!" Mietek snapped, pulling at the star affixed to his armband the next day.

"Everyone in our neighborhood is wearing them, you'll see," he said. "All your friends have them, too."

"Not *all* of them," he blurted back, face red. Mietek thought of the children who wouldn't have to wear armbands, the ones who didn't play with him anymore, who couldn't even come to his house. "I'm sorry," Josef, his soccer teammate told him. "My papa … he won't let me." The Nazis had made it clear that non-Jews could not associate with Jews, whom they considered a different race. Neighbors who had known the family for years now looked at them with suspicion. It was happening everywhere. Non-Jews would cross the street to avoid the people who had once been their friends. They wouldn't speak to them in the market. They'd turn the other way in the paper store.

Every day, Nazi soldiers would harass and humiliate the Jews. Exposed to hateful propaganda, Hitler's followers considered Jews to be an inferior race. They were pushed randomly against walls, taunted and beaten. Their beards were cut off, their clothes torn. Sometimes the Germans unleashed their attack dogs. The assaults were vicious and constant, a hideous routine of everyday brutality. A Jew couldn't even walk on the same sidewalk as a German. Brutality was as commonplace as fear.

"I have news," Isaac Laks told them, one evening after dinner. Mietek and his family had just finished eating—a humble meal of potato soup and bread—when Laks knocked on the door. Klara went quietly to her room, but Mietek was allowed to stay. "I just heard that Hans Frank has ordered the establishment of Jewish councils," Isaac said.

Mietek knew Hans Frank as the man who had ordered the loathsome armbands.

"The Germans call them *Judenrats*," he continued, referring to the Jewish councils that were being formed to carry out the orders of the German government. "Each community has to elect its own leaders."

"Why?" Isaak asked, although he already knew the answer.

"You know why," he said, his eyes darting around the room. "The Germans will use our group to do what they want. More laws, more demands."

"Of course," Isaak said, folding his hands behind his neck. "Of course."

"We'll want people we can count on," Isaak said. "Leaders with negotiating skills … leaders with a backbone, with a strong moral compass."

Mietek recognized these qualities in his father. The community did too, and they elected him to serve on the *Judenrat* as a member of the Jewish Welfare Committee. Everyone faced hardship. Everyone was hurting. But not everyone had the same resources to deal with privation and adversity. It was up to Isaak and his fellow committee members to figure out how to help those who needed it most. Manipulating the Nazi thugs would be hard, but they had to do what they could to protect the residents of Wierzbnik.

Hard as it was for the committee members to correspond with the Nazis, it had to be done. How else to devise survival strategies for the weakest among them? Since the Nazis were demanding periodic payments from the Jews—*extortion*, Isaak called it—the committee responded by analyzing each family's wealth and assessing their share accordingly. Some affluent folks had already hidden their small valuables, the silver and jewelry they could secret away; the *Judenrat* wouldn't know about that and didn't want to. But the poor had little to hide, so they ran out of valuables sooner. That's when the *Judenrat* stepped in. One member of the council acted as treasurer, tallying the payments, while another met with the German commander or his subordinate to deliver the valuables. It was a degrading practice, but the members of the Jewish Welfare Committee did their best to treat their neighbors with dignity and fairness—two qualities that were in short supply under the German regime.

The situation was dire. The Nazi scourge had no limits. They terrorized Jewish males by randomly removing them from the streets to perform menial labor. Men were reluctant to leave their homes for fear that they would disappear because whenever the Germans wanted something done—farm labor, street cleaning, quarry work—they'd grab a group of men in the morning and drop them off late in the day or at night, whenever their labor-intensive jobs were done. It was a daily menace and the Germans didn't care who saw. Mietek once witnessed two soldiers grab his friend's father, prodding him with a stick as they led him away, his body stiff with shame.

Eventually, the president of the *Judenrat*, Sychma Mincberg, approached the German commander to explain the hardship. He had developed a cordial relationship with the man. For the sake of his people, he had to.

"With all due respect sir," Mincberg started, "their families count on these men and suddenly they are gone. Vanished into thin air. Anything you can do to help us would be appreciated."

The commander sat back behind his desk, taking it all in. He would of course use this request to his advantage. "I'll tell you what," he rubbed his chin, "we'll stop the practice if you provide a list of men available to work every day. I mean young and strong men, not your throwaways. This will be on you."

"Thank you, sir." Mincberg stood up straight. It was imperative to show respect. That was key to dealing with the Germans.

That was how the *Arbeitsamt*—the labor division—came to be formed in Wierzbnik. Isaac Laks was assigned to head the unit, with his oldest daughter Chanka working with him to establish lists of men who were fit to work. As more out-of-town Jews arrived in Starachowice, the Laks had to register and tally all the newcomers between the ages of twelve to sixty for the *Arbeitsamt*—name, age, town of origin, trade, family members, and a list of their worldly possessions. As with so many things that happened under German rule, everyone had to comply.

Mietek had finished cataloging his stamp collection. He was tired. Alone in his room, he stared out his window at the forbidden outdoors. He would give anything to be back in school, sitting behind the wooden desk next to Alex. How many math tests had he missed? How many history lessons?

But he mustn't feel sorry for himself. He had it better than most. As his father had said, "If you can't go to school, then school must come to you!" That's just what happened when they set up a classroom of sorts in the dining room with Renia's older sister acting as teacher.

"Good morning class," Chanka said, flashing a smile.

Mietek found it strange at first, having a friend for a teacher. Yet he quickly grew to appreciate her and their little make-shift arrangement.

"Mietek, Rosalie, and Renia," Chanka called. "Please sit in that corner." She pointed to the far left of the dining table. "Bring your science book and notepad to answer the questions I assigned last week from chapter four." She turned to Klara and her friend, Sara. "You two set up over here. Open your math books to page twenty."

Chanka peered over Mietek's shoulder. "What happens if you mix these two chemicals together?"

"They explode," he answered.

"Then write out the reason behind the cell contents that cause that chemical reaction." She moved onto Renia, lifting the silver candlesticks out of the way so that she could spread out her papers.

Sitting with Klara and the younger children, Chanka said, "Give me your multiplication test papers from Friday." She quickly reviewed and graded them. "Sara, you only had one error. Go over that one because we're moving onto division today."

Pencils moving, the children's heads were down, absorbed in their assignments. Chanka watched. The blue-rimmed fine china stamped with Korzec caught her eye. She loved the matching coffee carafe and demi cups stacked in the dining hutch and hoped her mother would pass it on to her. Her sisters didn't care about it as much as she did. Renia only wanted to inherit the German encyclopedia Papa brought from Austria. It stood out in the locked cabinet next to the hutch. The leather bindings and gold pages were revered by their family and friends.

"I need to go to the bathroom," Sara said.

"Go, go." Chanka looked at her watch. "Heads up," she said to Mietek's group. "Please put your pencils down." Chanka strolled over to the older group to collect their papers. It felt like school. They were learning every day.

The war effort was escalating and the Germans needed more manpower, not only for road and water improvements, but also for munitions factories. The existing rosters of able-bodied men were no longer adequate, so in May 1940, a mandate was imposed to comprise a list of all male Jews between the ages of sixteen and forty-five. Its purpose: to serve the Nazi war machine.

This latest ordinance was a huge blow, impacting dwindling resources for the Wierzbnik residents. Until this point, many Jews had been making a modest living working their crafts or businesses.

This new edict put an end to that, now that the names of most men would be on a master list for the Germans to draw on at will. The shoemaker could be taken from his shop. The tailor from his sewing machine. The tool repairman from his workbench. All would be subject to forced labor, often in the smelting factories and quarries. It was a pitiful means of existence, but their very survival would depend on it.

Germans continued to believe their government's promise that Jews would be transferred out of Poland, thereby allowing them to further expand German living space in the occupied country, and to get rid of the Jews themselves.

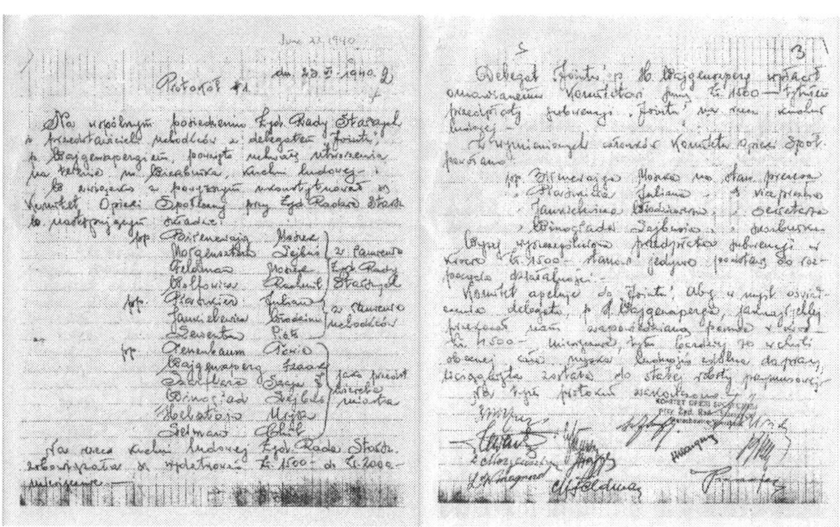

Original Minutes of ***Judenrat*** Jewish Welfare Committee Meeting

On June 23, 1940, Isaak Wajgenszperg, a delegate from the Joint Council, agreed to establish a community kitchen. The committee established food banks for those less fortunate.

June 23, 1940

Minutes of Meeting #1

During a joint meeting of the Council of Jewish Elders and the representatives of refugees, with the delegate from "Joint" Mr. Wajgenszperg, an agreement was reached to establish a Community Kitchen in Wierzbnik. In connection with the above, a Welfare Committee, affiliated with the Jewish Council of Elders, was formed. The following are its members:

Moszek Birencwajg
Lejbus Morgensztern
Moszek Feldman
Rachmil Wolfowicz
Representing the Council of Jewish Elders

Julian Praszkier
Wlodzimierz Jankielewicz
Piotr Lewentan(?)
Representing the refugees

Towie Tenenbaum
Izaak Wajgenszperg
Szaja Szarfarc
Lejbus Winograd
Urysz Helsztajn
Chil Lerman
Representing the town

The Council of Jewish Elders committed to spending 1,500-2,000 zloty per month for the Community Kitchen.

The representative from the "Joint", Mr. H. Wajgenszperg, gave the Committee the sum of 1,500 zloty as a down payment for the Community Kitchen.

The following members were appointed to the Welfare Committee:

Mr. Moszek Birencwajg	- for President
Mr. Julian Praszkier	- for Vice president
Mr. Wlodzimierz Jankielewicz	- for Secretary
Mr. Lejbus Winograd	- for Treasurer

The above mentioned received 1,500 zloty to start the enterprise.

Following Mr. H. Wajgenszperg's statement, the Committee is appealing to the "Joint" to send us the promised help in the amount of 4,500 zloty as soon as possible, now that the town's able-bodied people were rounded up for forced labor on a permanent basis.

-1-

Translated minutes of meeting, June 23rd, 1940
by Regina Gelb (Renia Laks)

CHAPTER SIX

For over a year, Mietek and his family hunkered in the relative safety of their homes. The influx of Jews from other towns and regions placed an additional burden on their community. Mietek couldn't believe how many strangers showed up in his hometown wearing the hated armbands. Day after day, he adapted to change. What choice did he have?

Then came the staggering news that they had to leave their home. The edict came down on April 12th, 1941 that the Jewish community of Wierzbnik was to relocate to a restricted ghetto in the old Jewish quarter. Three days' notice was all they were given. While Jews were being fenced-in all over Poland, the amicable relationship between the *Judenrat* and the German commander paved the way for the residents of Wierzbnik to live in an open, fenceless ghetto.

It was the evening of April 15th when the soldiers came. "*Raus! Raus!*" they said, while pounding on the family's front door. Isaak straightened his shoulders and let them in. A young soldier grasping a rifle yelled at them to vacate their home. He was little more than a boy himself, but his brute intention was clear. They had thirty minutes. The Wajgenszpergs had prepared as best they could. Isaak folded his smallest chess board, cramming it into his backpack.

Maybe Mietek could teach Klara how to play. He and Sonia strategized, gathering supplies that might help the family survive in the ghetto. The children were allowed to pack more sentimental things. Books and stamps for Mietek. A doll and art materials for Klara.

"Papa, where are they taking us?" asked Mietek, lifting his bag.

"We'll have to see, but we must always stay together," replied Isaak. Everyone had heard the stories about people going missing. Vanished. Separated from their families. No one knew where they went, or if they'd return. God only knew what happened to them. "Do you hear me, Mietek? We must always stay together. No matter what."

"Yes, Papa," Mietek replied solemnly. "Always stay together."

Klara clutched Sonia's dress folds, tears running down her cheeks. "Can I bring both my dolls, Papa? Please? I really need them."

Isaak hesitated, his face drawn. Mietek could see how his sister's request tore through his father. Like lightning, he thought.

"Of course, Klarunia," he said softly. "Just put them in your knapsack." She ran upstairs to gather her other doll; a brief moment of joy.

Mietek stayed close to his father, helping him gather the last of the supplies as the family continued the process of leaving their home. "Don't forget your best cooking pans," Isaak reminded Sonia. "Mietek, get your warmest coats. Put them on, one over the other. Then help Klara with hers."

"But Papa—two coats? They're so heavy."

"You'll need them both," his father said thickly. "Also, we will have less luggage."

Mietek was sorry to have questioned his father. He knew he must to do everything quickly and ran upstairs to don the coats and help Klara to do the same. He heard the soldiers return. Their harsh words were muffled and he couldn't make out what they said, but the menace in their voices left a chill down his spine, despite the layers of coats.

Mietek took Klara's hand and walked downstairs. Standing by the kitchen for the last time, he held his breath and closed his eyes, breathing in the lingering smell of his mother's baked bread. He exhaled slowly. Hearing footsteps, he turned to see his mother descending the stairs, head held high.

Isaak had heard about the ghettos. He was prepared. Together, he and Sonia had sorted through their silver and jewelry—anything small, anything with value.

Sonia's dragonfly brooch with ruby stone eyes. Light danced off the beveled gems when she had removed it from her jewelry box. Sonia remembered the brooch on her mother's coat lapel. She felt her mother's warmth, her loving words to be her best. Then she felt helpless, utterly helpless. She couldn't bear to think how her mother was holding up under the Nazi cruelty in Lodz. Other items were hidden. Some valuables were given to dependable Christian neighbors to hold onto. The silver cups and teaspoons, an heirloom pocket watch, and Sonia's gold necklaces. Such luxuries had no value now but to help ensure their safety. Only two gold bands were saved.

The soldiers lined up everyone in the neighborhood. *"Schnell! Schnell!"* they shouted, pushing and hitting the slower family members. Isaak steadied the agitated horses. Snapping dogs barked incessantly. Isaak hoisted his canvas bags onto the carriage, Sonia stayed next to her children. The Wajgenszpergs and their neighbors closed their doors for the last time. They believed they would return when this nightmare was over. When the Allies would finally stop the madness. The Jews of Wierzbnik walked alongside their overloaded carriages for a half hour to the newly established ghetto.

The soldiers stopped the caravan when they reached a cluster of small houses surrounding a dusty courtyard. More rules. Poles would be allowed to enter the ghetto to sell goods and some Jews would be allowed to leave the ghetto for work, but that was all. No one could leave without permission.

The two-bed apartment was nothing like their home on Pilsudskiego street. The musty smell of wood reminded Mietek of the old library that had flooded. Bare walls exposed faded dusty outlines where paintings once hung, a reminder of the looting of valuables, of personal treasures stolen. Another shocking change: The Wajgenszpergs had to share the tight flat with another family. One bedroom each. The Bermans had three boys and an elderly widowed mother living with them. Ten of them would live together, one tiny windowless kitchen serving both families.

Waiting until his mother and Klara were out of the room, Mietek set his sack on the bedroom floor. He went to help his father push the mattress to the corner to make room. "Papa," his fist clenched near his mouth, "there's no running water, no heat ... How will we survive?"

Isaak pulled Mietek to his chest. "We stay strong. We keep our heads up and help each other."

Mietek felt more responsible. They would work together, they could do this. No more privacy, just one more sacrifice.

After settling his family to sleep, Isaak collapsed onto the crowded bed, shaken and exhausted. Mietek peered at his father from the pillow. Eyes wide open, he turned to stare at the ceiling. He could hear muffled yells as others found their way through the building. His father gazed at him in the dark. No words were needed. Mietek understood—adapt.

Chores were hard, the days crowded and tight. The children missed their home but felt secure with their parents. Adjusting to change, they watched how their mother cordially shared the kitchen space, setting up later dinner times for her family so that the Bermans could eat first. Isaak left during the day for meetings and came home with a loaf of bread, eggs, or potatoes. No one questioned where he got the extra food. Favors were exchanged. A new way of life was emerging.

Chanka continued to tutor Mietek, Klara, and a small group of children. A sliver of normalcy in the crammed quarters.

"Good morning," she said cheerfully, doing what she could to keep the children's spirits up. Klara, Sara, Renee, and two other children squished side by side on the edge of her bedroom's mattress.

"Today we're reading a book by one of my favorite authors, Janusz Korczak. Who's heard about his book *Kaytek the Wizard*?"

Klara thrust her hand in the air. "Me, me. I love Kaytek!"

"Wonderful. Do you know that the author is a doctor—a children's doctor?" The children shook their heads. "But he stopped being a doctor. Who wants to guess what he does now?"

Lenny raised his hand slowly. "He writes more books?"

"Well yes, that's for sure. But now he heads up a Jewish orphanage in Warsaw. He really cares about children, don't you think?" They nodded. "Each of you will read a chapter out loud today. You'll read from this book and pass it on. Klara, you should start since you're familiar with the book. Have it to Lenny by tomorrow. When you're done reading, I want a report on the story. What you like about Kaytek, what you don't like, and what he learned at the end. Remember, try to write in small letters and use both sides of your paper. We have to be frugal with our supplies."

Later morning, Chanka worked with the older children who had asked her to help them write a play. She instructed them on scripting the play, assigning directors, producers, and actors, and gave them latitude on staging it.

Chanka's schedule was tight. After her mornings teaching, she had to help her father with the Nazis' labor list. Newcomers descended on their town daily and the tally sheets had to be updated to include them.

Renia, Chanka's younger sister, and Mietek were close in age and they spent more time together in the cramped conditions. Their families were like-minded—honoring education, loving to read, and sharing a reverence for books. But books were scarce in the ghetto.

"I'm still upset about our German encyclopedia set," Renia said while walking the courtyard with Mietek. "Do you know we had to wash our hands before touching any of the books? So much information, and so many pictures. The outside of the pages were embossed with gold." She clasped her hands over her cheeks.

"What happened to them?" asked Mietek.

"The German soldiers came to our house a few weeks after they took over." She shook her head. "Papa kept it locked in our hutch and one of the Nazis asked him to open it. I thought I was going to die. I loved those encyclopedias … the lousy soldier took them. All of them."

He thought hard. "I bet … I think …"

"Yes, Mietek. You bet … you think …" Renia joked. "What is it, my friend of few words?"

"We should try to figure out a way we could share books here. I bet we could do it. We brought books … of course, not many."

"We have some too!"

"We could borrow the books from our neighbors and—"

"They'd be afraid to lose them."

"But we could catalogue them, you know. Keep a record on each book."

Excited, Renia blurted, "People could sign in and out. That might work. We can call it our Lending Library … the R and M library." She laughed.

They shook hands. Deal.

CHAPTER SEVEN

There were no Hebrew classes in the ghetto. No synagogue. No Torah. Bar mitzvahs were forbidden. And Mietek was about to turn thirteen.

He remembered Chaim's bar mitzvah. His friend had looked proud in his Tallit, a blue striped prayer shawl, as he read from the Torah. Chanting in Hebrew, he moved the silver pointer on the page and read from the scroll. *"Ma tovu ohleh-cha, Yaacov, mishnk'notecha Yisrael,"* a prophet praising God's blessing for Israel.

The party that followed had family and guests spilling into Chaim's house and out into his yard.

"Alright everyone, gather round," the accordion player had said, readying his instrument. "Are you ready, Shlomo?" The clarinetist wet his reed. "One, two, three, four"—and music filled the rooms. The accordion stretched for chords to "Hava Nagila," and then it was time for the *horah* dance. Klara wore a new dress that Sonia had made in her favorite color, sapphire blue. She grabbed her mother's hand, eager to join the circle. "Come on, Mama. They're starting." The music picked up tempo, the clarinet went down the scale striking each staccato note. Klara's white bow bobbed up and down as she ran to keep up with the grown-ups. She wouldn't stop until the music ended. Kosher foods lined the table. Mietek's favorite potato latkes were piled high in the center. Cucumber salads and mounds of oranges and grapes were scattered on the long table.

Now it was Mietek's time, but instead of studying the Torah, instead of learning to read the scrolls and translating his assignment, he was in this Godforsaken ghetto.

But God had not forsaken them. Family and friends gathered together in their crowded home on the first Shabbat after Mietek's birthday to hold a quiet prayer service to honor him. Surrounded by his mother, father, sister, and grandparents, Mietek lit a candle to honor those who had passed. He recited a Hebrew phrase he learned before the war. *"Asher nishbati l'avraham l'yitzchak u-l'ya-a-kov." Which was sworn by me to Abraham to Isaac and to Jacob.* He chose it because it honored his grandfather and father's name. Abraham's face softened. Mietek believed it took his grandfather back to a time when his religion and rituals were a comfort, where he allowed himself to feel at peace—just for a few minutes.

"Amen."

"For you, Mietek." Abraham and Chana handed him an embroidered pouch. Not prepared for any gifts, Mietek pulled the ribbon open and took out eighteen *zloty*—the number symbolic of giving *chai*, a blessing for a long life. He reached out and hugged his grandparents, then put his head between Sonia and Isaak, gripping their shoulders. It was a coming of age celebration for a boy far older than his years.

Mietek was a man now, accountable for his actions. Looking to his father, he understood that manhood meant work and dignity, doing what he could to make things better for those around him. In those days in the ghetto, it meant putting their lending library in place. He and Renia had a plan. But first, they had to get permission.

"Well look at you," Isaak said. "That's a great idea. A terrific venture."

It felt good to earn his father's praise. "One word of caution though, set up your table out of the guards' sight. Just a safeguard."

"Have you two considered what you'll do if it rains?" Sonia asked.

"We have," Mietek lifted his chin. "We'll close for rainy days, but we'll stay open an extra two hours on the first dry day."

"You've thought of everything!" Sonia pecked his cheek.

Mietek ran to Renia's home. Their crowded quarters were loud this evening. The Laks' roommates' young sons were chasing each other screeching not to get caught. Renia came to the door and broke into a wide smile. "Hello partner," she said.

Mietek put *War and Peace* and *The Adventures of Tom Sawyer* into his cart. Renia added *Robin Hood* and *Alice in Wonderland.* They knocked on their first door.

"Good morning, Mrs. Glickman. How are you today?" Mietek said.

"Hello you two. What do you have there?" she asked, pointing to the wagon.

"We're starting a lending library," Renia said. "And we wonder … well, we wonder—"

Mietek jumped in. "We wondered if you had some books you'd be willing to share."

Renia opened the notebook. "We would take good care of them. Look—we're going to keep a log so we'd be sure to return them to you after others have had a chance to borrow them."

"How can I refuse!" Mrs. Glickman said. "Let me get my copy of *Robinson Crusoe*. That's a favorite. My name is written on the inside cover."

Renia recorded *Mrs. Glickman*: *Robinson Crusoe by Daniel Defoe*. Mietek placed a card inside the cover with a space for a name, a signature line, and two dates—the day the book was borrowed and the day it needed to be returned. Carefully, he placed it in the wagon.

The two friends spent the morning going to adjacent homes collecting books. Soon the wagon was piled high with copies of children's fairy tales, mathematic textbooks, woodcraft magazines, cookbooks, and historical novels—precious volumes brought from people's homes. Almost everyone contributed. Mietek and Renia meticulously catalogued the volumes and set them on a table in the courtyard.

Mrs. Guterman was first to browse the makeshift library. She signed out the Tolstoy book for a week. Mr. Kaplan was thrilled to pick up a copy of *Ulysses*. The younger children loved spending time picking out their own. Klara hung around too, offering to help them select their reading material. "Over here," she said to little Leah as she led her by the hand to where *Alice in Wonderland* was kept. "You'll love this one. It's about Alice and cats and rabbits and there's magic too." Leah nodded and asked Klara to help her sign out the book.

Word of mouth brought a steady stream of patrons, so the would-be librarians found it best to set regular hours: nine in the morning until noon.

Sonia was proud of her boy. "Mietek, such good things you are doing. You've brought happiness to our neighbors when they needed it the most."

"You know what else?" Papa continued. "You organized. You took action. You made something out of nothing. Good for you. Good for you both."

Mietek felt gratified that families had something to do other than chores, something other than worry to occupy their minds.

In the meantime, Chanka helped her preteen students write and direct their own plays, assigning scriptwriters, directors, and actors for each performance. Hanna Tencer took over as director. She had a knack for it, clearly communicating to her actors where to stand and what to convey to the audience. Mietek portrayed a judge who had to rule on the fate of a girl who had adopted a homeless child but mistreated her. Mietek took his role of magistrate seriously, debating the evidence produced by the defending and prosecuting attorneys. "My verdict: the girl will be monitored and ordered to check in with the court. At that time, I will determine if this woman is fit to raise this homeless child." The play was a rousing success.

Back row, third from left, Mietek as the judge in play

But outside the world of the imagination, things grew worse. Spring came, and with it news that residents of all European ghettos were forbidden to leave, other than to work in the forced labor groups. This decree put additional pressure on the Jews, who no longer had the opportunity to barter outside the ghetto walls. Now they'd have to invent new ways to care for themselves.

Food was scarce because the Nazis controlled distribution of all the food. The ration coupons they supplied provided meager amounts of bread, potatoes, sugar, cabbage, and beets. Rations for Jews were based on about eight hundred calories a day, a starvation diet not enough to sustain anyone. Non-Jewish Poles received about twice that amount. Jews couldn't get meat, fish or poultry, or vegetables unless they had the means to barter on the black market, the free market. The Wajgenszpergs didn't suffer as much as some of the poorer families because they had brought goods to barter, but the less affluent members of the ghetto had little to trade and suffered more.

Mietek didn't like to be at the mercy of the ghetto system. He needed to be more creative. "Mama, I have an idea, but I need your help. Do you think you could use the ration coupons to get ingredients to bake cakes and pies? Yours are the best. Everyone else thinks so too."

Smitten with her son's inventive notion, she replied, "I can try dear, but what do you have in mind?"

"Well, if you make pies and cakes, I think we could trade up, get better food and perhaps other things we need."

Sonia didn't have to think long. "Another wonderful idea. I'll do it." The Nazi guards didn't care what happened inside the ghetto perimeter, as long as it didn't affect them. Mietek's efforts were paying off. He built up a customer following. His neighbors in the ghetto got comfortable; they trusted him. His wider base supported bartering more household items as well as the pies, finding that even belts had great value among the poor. His optimism grew, he had purpose. He was helping support his family like his father, like a man.

While most people were confined to the ghetto, a lucky few were permitted to leave each day to work. Craftsmen were fortunate. Anyone who could provide labor directly to the Germans—tailors and shoemakers, bakers, butchers, and the dentist—might obtain a permit to venture beyond the perimeter of the ghetto. Here, too, Mietek saw an opportunity. He found a "job" accompanying a disabled man who had a license to deliver seltzer water outside the ghetto. Mietek was given a small commission to push the old man's wagon, and every time he sold a bottle of seltzer, he'd receive a few *groszies*. Mietek also bartered for food outside the ghetto walls, smuggling it back in under his clothes.

Once again, Mietek worked the situation to his advantage. He knew that the guards had assumed that the boy who attended to the cripple—that's what he was called—also had a permit to venture beyond the gates. At thirteen, his youth gave him an advantage. So did his appearance. With his soft features and short cut hair, he didn't fit the Nazis' template of the *typical Jew*, so once outside the ghetto, he was allowed to pass relatively unnoticed. He'd do what he could to score food—bread, butter, and potatoes on a good day. Until the afternoon when a German soldier thought he was too young to hold a permit.

"HALT!" the guard shouted. He cocked his rifle, aiming the barrel at Mietek's head. Mietek froze, heart pounding. His hands

were clammy, his head was swimming. Sweat pearled on his forehead as he tried to breathe. He'd been caught.

"I'll shoot you now or we'll hang you!" barked the soldier.

Miraculously, Isaak's brother, Henry, witnessed the confrontation.

"He's just a boy, sir," he said in German. "Let us take care of his unruly behavior." The soldier hesitated, then lowered his rifle. Henry saw his opportunity. "Let me offer you a fine new pair of leather boots," he said in a calming voice. "Just to make up for the lad's poor manners."

The soldier understood the thinly veiled bribe. "If I ever see this filthy Jew cross over the line again," he pointed to the cobblestone curb, "I'll kill him on the spot."

"We understand sir," replied Henry.

"You'll have those boots to me in two days. Size eleven."

Henry nodded, walking backward, dragging Mietek by the arm. He had owned a shoe factory while working with Isaak in the lumber industry before the war. He would make the boots.

Mietek returned home, shaken. Isaak and Sonia had understood the risk Mietek had been taking, but he had downplayed the frequency of leaving the ghetto, telling his parents that he was merely helping a disabled man when he wasn't feeling well. Putting food on the table was worthy of danger … but not his life.

"Do you understand, Mietek?" asked Isaak, voice tight. "You were almost killed. God!" He glanced at his wife and daughter and then back at his son. "You have to live by their rules—all of us do."

Sonia spoke, lips pressed. "No more risks, darling," she added sympathetically. "You've been very brave." She picked up the corner of her apron to wipe a tear. "Thanks to you, we've had more food on the table." Sonia straightened her shoulders. "Now we'll put our heads together, you'll see."

"They'll take out the whole family if one of us slips up now," added Isaak for assurance. He grabbed his son's head and hugged him close.

CHAPTER EIGHT

Suffering in Starachowice escalated. An attack on German administration staff would alter the town's history once again. Some believed the members of a Polish underground movement committed the act. Others thought it revenge by frustrated Poles. Regardless, the men responsible were not caught, which prompted Walther Becker, the head of Security Police, to take action. Following Sunday mass, a group of Poles were surrounded by soldiers upon leaving their church. A few men, women, and one child were singled out for persecution. These poor innocents were led to makeshift gallows, where a group of young Jews were waiting. These Jews, also handpicked by the Germans, were forced to tie a rope around the Catholics' necks, then kick the stools out from underneath them. The innocent victims hung in the town square until the following day, a grim reminder that the Germans were not to be interfered with.

Isaak and Isaac Laks huddled together over his chess board. "What do you make of this horrendous act in the square?"

Isaac shook his head. "Just be happy you and your family weren't there. I heard from our tailor—he also works for the Nazis—well, he told me that they forced people to watch. These poor Poles were just coming out of church. Can you imagine?"

“God, so cruel. The SS, those beasts seem to be even worse lately” Isaak moved his bishop, as if concentrating on the game. “Does Pola know?”

“Word got around fast, but I don’t think she wants to believe it. I stay quiet about it, you know, the children.”

Isaak nodded. “It’s been harder this summer. It’s like everyone is losing their minds.”

By August 1941, living conditions in the ghetto had worsened. Following orders from Berlin, the German troops had become more hostile. They shot to kill any Jew who didn’t follow commands. Those who were caught trying to smuggle in food were executed on the spot.

Isaak now worked at the steel mill factory in Starachowice, thanks to his father. He didn’t know how he secured the position but understood that his father had worked closely with community leaders and had most likely called in a favor. A Jew who had work, who was important to the Nazi war effort, had better chances of survival. Isaak was assigned to inspect bombshells, a good job at the time. After two months, Mietek was recruited to work in the factory as well. At thirteen, he operated cranes, moving ammunition parts as directed by the foremen.

Mietek survived by watching and listening to his father. They labored hard together, sharing the burden of work. Mietek saw that delays had consequences—a beating, or worse, punishment meted out on someone close to you. With little time to make decisions, Mietek learned to assess situations quickly. He learned to pay attention to detail and grew to understand how precise work sustained you. Loyal friendships were critical, he learned. Family was everything.

Isaak was in charge of a large group of Jews. As supervisor, it was his job to follow orders and keep his men working, but at least he could use his position to keep them safe, improving their opportunities for less strenuous work whenever he could. Yet as much as Isaak took on the responsibility of watching over his friends and colleagues, he kept himself safe in order to protect Mietek. It was a hard balance, but in turn, their friends safeguarded them. That was a lesson Mietek would never forget.

Father and son walked the hour and a half to the factory early each morning. They put in ten-to-eleven-hour days, then walked another hour and a half back to their home in the ghetto. Mietek and Isaak were treated poorly by the Germans who didn't supply them with food, despite the length of their shifts. Thank God for the good Polish people who strolled by the factory, leaving sandwiches on benches as they nodded to the workers. Small mercies. That's what kept them going. That and their home life. As compromised as it was, the family took great comfort in their staying together.

"Dinner is ready," Sonia called after Isaak and Mietek returned home one evening. "I could only make lentil soup." She wiped her brow with the stained apron. "No meat or potatoes anywhere." Her husband and son were exhausted. Their weight loss was troubling. How could they keep working long hours and walk miles every day when there wasn't enough food to keep them going? Sonia did what she could, but the Germans confiscated food from the farmers and the ration coupons were worthless.

Isaak placed his hands on his wife's shoulders. "My love, you've done a great job. No one puts a meal together with so little." He rubbed her shoulders, feeling her bony frame. He hated what these past years had done to her, to his family.

It wasn't long before Sonia was assigned a factory job stacking bricks onto carts for the loading crew to haul away to dry. It was grueling work and every morning she awoke with a back aching from her tasks the day before. But every morning, after tying a red kerchief at the nape of her neck, she would tiptoe into ten-year-old Klara's room to check that her daughter was still asleep. Sonia was grateful to have the frail Mrs. Berman hobbling around their apartment in the morning, even though she napped most of the afternoon. "I'll see you later my sunshine," she would say as she kissed the top of her daughter's head and hurried out the door. It was five a.m.

CHAPTER NINE

Rumors spread quickly. Through illegal radios set up by Jewish rebel groups, the people of Wierzbnik learned that the Nazis were eliminating all ghettos. Isaak and Sonia knew this was not good news. They were accustomed to working in factory labor locations, but they did it while living together. Not their real home, but a home nonetheless. Again they heard that Jews would be transported to camps: labor camps, death camps, concentration camps. Isaak thought it could be true, others didn't believe it.

It was clear that the Germans felt invincible. They had invaded Norway, Denmark, France, Belgium, Luxembourg, the Netherlands, Yugoslavia, and Greece. Heinrich Himmler kept advancing racism and anti-Semitism through Western Europe. Hitler was proud.

"How could this be?" asked Isaak when he heard from one of his former *Judenrat* council members. "Was the world asleep?" Isaak had resigned from the council because it was becoming impossible to deal with the Germans who pressured them for more money—money no one had. But he continued to aid the poor and new arrivals.

Jews from nearby towns continued to swarm into Starachowice. Work opportunities were given to healthy males. Desperate after their ghettos were liquidated, they tried to secure work permits in the armaments' factories. Corruption was rampant. Securing a position at the weapons and munitions factories became the best calculated risk for staying in town. For survival, really. People bartered for permits, many giving up the last of their valuables. Wealthy Jews strived to preserve their families by giving up jewelry or furs they'd hidden, anything to find their young children a home with Christian families. It was a huge risk. Many of these attempts failed, and the children, once found, were shot. But the Nazis would not consider children and the elderly for jobs. What else could they do?

The takeover of the Starachowice steel and munition factories had turned out to be a Godsend for strong healthy Jews. German manufacturer Göring was the first to establish a holding company to take control of factories throughout Poland. The company assigned its subsidiary, Braunschweig Steelworks, to operate the Starachowice factories. Highly regarded for their precision manufactured products, the company established satellite work camps, or *Arbeitslagers*, near the factories to house non-residents with coveted work permits. Their prominent role in supporting the war effort made them invaluable to the Germans.

Isaak was consumed with worry to keep his family safe. He called on his friend, Isaac Laks. "Is there any way I can obtain a work permit for Klara?" he implored. "I've tried. I've lied about her age. Are there any permits for simpler tasks that a young child can do?" He paced in Isaac's apartment.

"They're almost impossible to get hold of. She's so young. There are so many desperate families—you know I'll do what I can." He put his hand on Isaak's shoulder.

So it was that in the fall of 1942, Heinrich Himmler, the man in charge of the Final Solution, set about closing the ghettos. This "resettlement" imposed another drastic change for Jewish labor conditions as Jews not fit for work were to be driven out of the ghetto while those who were deemed essential to the war production effort would live in isolated camps. What's more, these workers would become the *property* of the SS and as such would no longer receive pay for their labor. With the closing of the ghettos, they would become slaves to the Nazi regime.

Tensions were running high, however, as no one knew who would be honored on the day of *The Selection*. Mietek, now fourteen, was closer to the prime work age of sixteen years. Children under twelve did not go to work. Eleven-year-old Klara was at tremendous risk.

Stress consumed them all. Isaak developed a desperate plan, mapping out an escape route with his close friends. The surrounding areas were wide open, so getting to the woods was life threatening. Those attempting escape were shot. The risk was unimaginable, but so was the alternative. He had to keep his children safe. Time was running out. He and the others made plans to disappear the night before the ghetto closing, which they believed to be October 29th.

As former Wierzbnik Jews tried frantically to save their family members, Uncle Henry came by and broke the terrible news. The Nazis had surprised everyone—they were on their way, two days before the rumored closing date. Isaak sank his head into his hands—he couldn't escape. How could he save his family?

CHAPTER TEN

Early in the morning of October 27th, 1942, a chill settled over Wierzbnik. Dew beaded on the rooftops as menacing crows banded together to surround the town. It was the SS in their gray-green uniforms, double lightning bolts affixed to their collars. Selection Day had come.

"Everyone out! Leave now!" The first orders came from the Nazi-appointed Jewish Police. "Anyone who does not comply will be shot!"

Isaak shuddered. To hear such words in their own language—and from one of their own. The local police had been ordered to carry out the initial roundup, thus paving the way for the SS who followed closely. The clout of jackboots echoed through the stairwells. Then came the sound of fists on doors.

Sonia wept quietly. She wiped her tears and handed Mietek her embroidered handkerchief, kissing him on the cheek.

"Get out now!" The police pounded on their door. *"Zglosic sie na Rynek!"* Report to the market square.

Sonia prayed. "I come to You today, bowing in my heart, asking for protection from evil." She rocked Klara in her arms. The children remained quiet.

"It is time, my family," Isaak said. Mietek reached out for

Klara's hand. Together the family made their way through the crowd, their feet moving cautiously on the slick cobblestones. Soldiers in their steel gray helmets were waiting for them in the market square, rifles cocked, ready for the slightest transgression.

The SS troops assigned to Wierzbnik specialized in ghetto closings. Having performed these evacuations in other towns with a gruesome efficiency, they had brought their ruthless system to Wierzbnik. Before many Jews had even left their houses, the SS soldiers beat the slow-moving elderly and the infirm. The weakest residents were shot immediately, some in their beds, many in front of their families.

People stumbled about, pushed and prodded by the SS. Rifle butts cracked skulls. Leather boots kicked ribs. Piercing screams, shouts, and shots rang through the ghetto. The scene was utter chaos. Frantic, everyone listened to the unmerciful orders and witnessed the beating and shooting of their own people.

"SCHNELL, SCHNELL!"

Walther Becker, the German commander who had been assigned to Wierzbnik, carried his pistol. That was standard issue. But today he held a whip with metal balls at the ends. He had always worked with the *Judenrat* in a businesslike manner. He wasn't trusted, of course—what Jew would trust a Nazi officer? He was greedy—but he had treated them with something that resembled humanity. Now he was a crazed animal, running back and forth in the market square, slapping his whip left and right. Was he drunk? Were his savage orders beyond his comprehension?

An elderly couple arrived, arm in arm, dressed in their finest. Becker raised his pistol and shot them dead.

The SS, accompanied by their dogs, ordered everyone to line up in rows of five. Families tried to stay together. Soldiers continued to pull the frail, elderly, and slower-moving Jews out of line and shot them. Panic escalated. Fear raced through the crowd like lightning. Isaak, Mietek, Sonia, and Klara stood tightly together. Isaak and Sonia tried in vain to hide their fear from their children. Whips cracked left and right. The odor of gunshot residue wafted through the air.

The Laks family was in the factory working the overnight shift. All but Pola who hovered over Renia three rows in front of them. Sonia barely had time to understand what was happening when she saw Pola pulled out of line, forcing her to leave Renia behind. "I'm going with you!" yelled Renia. Pola was adamant. "No, absolutely no!" She didn't resist the soldier for fear her daughter would be hurt. Tears streamed down Renia's cheeks. She understood that her mother's arthritis deemed her unfit for the workforce. The Wajgenszpergs stood helpless behind her, having to bear the memory of this heart-wrenching scene.

Isaak held his breath, heart pounding, uncertain of their fate. Oh, merciful God, that Mietek and Klara could somehow be considered strong, skilled workers.

When the roundup was complete, the Wierzbnik families crowded the market square like cattle herded for slaughter. Bodies lay everywhere; the cobblestones puddled in crimson red. When the SS ordered *"RUHIG!"* a defenseless hush fell over the square. The selection process was about to begin.

First up: separating the men from the women. Screams pierced the silence as mothers begged to stay with their boys, with their husbands. *"Nie, nie, prosze!"* They sent the men with work cards to one side of the market square.

Sonia pulled Mietek close and grabbed Isaak's hand, her eyes on fire.

Isaak held her shoulders, steadying her. "We have to go. They'll kill us if we don't. Stay with Klara. We'll find you when this is over." Isaak stroked the top of Klara's head. He stepped forward, as ordered. Mietek followed his lead.

"No Papa!" cried Klara. "Don't leave us!" Sonia kneeled swiftly to quiet her daughter, fearing the soldiers would beat her.

Isaak and Mietek were forced to stand a few rows back. Isaak tugged at Mietek's elbow gesturing to look down. He nudged a brick toward his son. "Stand on this" he said in a hushed tone. "Tell anyone who asks that you're fifteen." Mietek stood still, hardly daring to inhale. "Do you hear me, Mietek?" his father implored. "Fifteen."

Mietek was light-headed, terrified, sick. "Stand tall and strong," Isaak whispered. He was having difficulty breathing.

A whip lashed across an elderly man's back. He screeched in pain. A soldier loosened his grip on his snapping dog's leash. The dog, leaping at a confused man, bit deep into his calf. Shrieking reverberated across the square. The man fell and was shot. The Nazis pushed and pulled people out of line as they selected who would stay to work. Those who had a work card and didn't step forward immediately were beaten with clubs and whips. Barking dogs strained at their leashes. More shouting. More tears. More gunshots.

Mietek searched frantically for his mother and sister. He saw them briefly and nearly stepped off his brick, aching to be with them, to protect them. He recalled his father's words when they left their home on Pilsudskiego Street. "We stay together. Always." Now this. Mietek watched as soldiers wrenched Klara from her mother, shoving Sonia into the line of women with work permits.

Klara screamed, *"Matka! Matka!"*

Sonia tried to resist. When digging in her heels didn't work, she let her body go limp, but the soldiers merely pulled her by the arms and dragged her away. Sonia was wild with fear. Eyes ablaze, her hair matted to her forehead, she couldn't control her rapid, spurting heartbeat. She forced her mind to focus on her daughter, on what to do to help her, to save her. She tried to speak, but no words came. It was as if her body wanted to shut down. How could it be that her baby would be taken away? Klara. Klarunia. Her child.

She pointed to her daughter. *"Proszę. Proszę,"* she begged. "I must be with my daughter, my child." Sonia would not let Klara be sent away alone. "Please, in the name of God. I beg you." If she couldn't save her, she wouldn't leave her.

"Quiet," the guard said. "*Genug!* That's enough."

"*Geh*," he said. "Go!"

It was efficiency, not humanity, that reunited Sonia with her daughter. A strategy calculated to keep the deportation process calmer and more efficient. The Germans knew better than to separate panic-stricken women from their children. Sonia and Klara were together in the same line as Pola Laks. It was the group that would go to the train station. That's where they'd board the cattle cars headed to Treblinka.

We didn't get to say goodbye.

These were the words that ran through Mietek's mind as he caught a glimpse of his mother moving away from him, her chestnut brown hair pulled back in a knot. *Don't go ... don't leave me.* Tears welled in his eyes, but he couldn't cry. He couldn't show weakness. He couldn't scream. The Nazis shot anyone making a scene. He pulled his mother's handkerchief out of his pocket and inhaled her floral scent. His heart ached. His body was numb. He couldn't comprehend what had just happened. At fourteen, his life has been altered forever.

Isaak could scarcely breathe. He looked down on the bricks, closing his eyes. He must do everything in his power to protect his son against these vicious beasts. He knew full well that the cold precision of these acts was meant to create havoc, to catch everyone off guard. This SS squadron had calculated human responses to weed out all but those fit to serve their German masters. Isaak had long ago decided that survival would come at any cost. But whose survival? His wife and daughter were gone, perhaps forever. He looked over at his beloved son, doing what he could to maintain composure in the face of unassailable cruelty. The boy had to survive.

Mietek stood straight and tall on the brick as the Germans continued to evaluate their captives. A few seconds was all it took for the Nazis to determine strength, capability, and endurance. They were ruthless. Any visible signs of weakness—a damaged eye, a mouth swollen by toothache—could render a man worthless to the Nazi machine.

"Name and age!" barked the SS soldier, gripping his clipboard as he pointed to Mietek.

"Mieczyslaw Wajgenszperg, fifteen," he responded hoping his voice wouldn't crack. This small lie felt like a powerful act of defiance. Mietek kept his chin up, willed his hands to stop trembling. Isaak looked straight ahead. Sweat outlined his forehead. The two of them waited, suspended in time.

The soldier checked his clipboard. "You," he pointed to the man to his left. "Name!" Mietek took a breath.

The soldier had moved on.

CHAPTER ELEVEN

CONNECTICUT

I remember the first time I saw a photo of Klara, her little hands pinching a bunch of freshly picked flowers at their stems. Her light brown hair is streaked with golden strands, just like mine. But it was another photo of my dad sitting on the edge of a bed that gave me pause. He might have been eleven, maybe twelve. Peering at the pages of an open book in his hands, his expression is serious, but there's a serenity too. His face shows the beginning of a smile and seems to contain understanding. He's looking down at his book, but he's aware of his sister, happy she's there. Klara is reclining on the bed, listening. Her head is propped up with her hand and her eyes are looking straight at the camera—straight at me. Her little face is both curious and wise.

There's something intriguing and self-contained about this priceless picture. Klara's white, round-collared blouse buttoned to her neck, she seems peaceful as she listens to her brother read. Her soft features spoke to me the first time I saw this photograph—and every time since. Her delicate mouth and rounded cheeks exude sweetness, health. I saw the resemblance of a garden statue of an angelic girl, clasping a bundle of wheat shoots. Dad purchased that—it reminded him of Klara. But despite their different positions, the shadows cast on the wall behind them were almost identical. I felt I was there, listening to my father read, taking in his telling of story. There's something lovely and captivating about this precious picture.

People said I looked like my father—did I look like Klara too? My mother would bring her up in conversation, how young and bright she was. She knew a little, probably from their early years when Dad opened up to her, the first person he could trust with his heart. Why was I claustrophobic? Why did I carry an unanswered sadness like an invisible piece of baggage around with me? I always related these questions to Klara, the young girl who has always been a part of my life.

At eleven, I would go to school where I'd learn math and study history. I'd see my friends and at recess I would join them in a pickup game of baseball. Then I'd go home and, after dinner with my parents, I'd practice my flute for a half hour. After picking out an outfit for school the next day, I'd go to my room and settle in my safe, warm bed. Opening my journal, I'd write about my day. Who I played with, what I needed to work on, what teachers I liked. But when Klara was eleven, she was murdered. I guess that's why, when I turned eleven, I would have flashes of her gripping her mother's hand, stepping off the train at Treblinka, walking to her death. That was something I couldn't comprehend, and yet it was always as if I kept a space for her somewhere deep inside. My father thought of her always, but he carried her memory in a very different way.

Mietek reading to Klara

Klara, 1930s

The Nazis continued their selection in the Starachowice town square, forcing those with work cards to march to one of two destinations: Tartak, a lumber camp located just across the railroad tracks from the market square, or Strzelnica, a munitions factory on the northeast border of Starachowice.

The march through the Kamienna River Valley—four miles uphill—was a terrible hardship for the five hundred men and women sent to Strzelnica. The unusually warm October weather added to their misery, since each person had donned several layers for The Selection. Worn clothing covered tired bodies as terrified Jews were forced to march to their slave labor camp. German and Ukrainian guards fired shots into the air to quicken the pace while their dogs nipped at the captive's heels. Two men fell behind. They were shot dead.

Isaak and Mietek were assigned to Strzelnica, a six-barrack camp that had been hastily erected. Their group—the second to leave the market square—proceeded without incident because the Ukrainian guard took a bribe from a shoemaker. Killing prisoners wasn't a useful way to secure labor, the shoemaker told him. If no one gets shot, he promised to make the guard a pair of ski boots. As was so often the case, commerce ruled over ideology. Self-interest ruled over all.

If Mietek's time in the ghetto had taught him anything, it was to be aware of his surroundings. Be still. Evaluate. Don't make eye contact. He stood in his father's shadow, not daring to breathe. When his group arrived at their barracks, Mietek tried to look strong. He and his father had to stand for hours to be processed. Yet it was all he could do to convey his weary body to an overcrowded bunk stuffed with thin layers of straw. He was in shock. So was Isaak. Together they clung to a shard of hope that they would see Sonia and Klara again.

The commander in charge of the *Werkschutz*—the work guards—was a man known only as Meyer. Ralf Alois Althoff—who went by the name of Willi Althoff—served as the manager in charge of factory security. Althoff gave the newly arrived prisoners their first order: surrender your valuables. Refuse and you will be shot. Hide your valuables, and you will be shot. Lie about your valuables and you will be shot. Isaak's coat had delicate strands of gold jewelry sewn into the seams. It was a calculated risk. He knew what would happen to him if he was found out, but he also knew that such valuables had kept his family alive and fed until now. He was counting on the notion that his extra clothes would be of no value to the Germans.

The SS established the same sort of hierarchy in the slave camps as they had in the ghetto. The Germans directed daily operations and used prisoners to maintain order among themselves. Jews who had prior relationships with the Germans were put in charge of camp police (*Lagerpolizei*) and assigned to the camp council (*Lagerrat.*) And because the Germans were more comfortable with those they knew, the first person to be appointed was a former *Judenrat* messenger. This man, and others like him, had carried out orders for their captors, including selecting which Jews were to be beaten by the guards. Members of the *Lagerrat*, a council similar to the *Judenrat*, had access to extra food and clothes so could, at times, bestow small mercies on their fellow internees.

Life was hard in the ghetto.

It was even harder in the labor camp.

Mietek and his father rose between four and five each morning to stand in line for their meager rations of weak coffee and a single piece of dry bread. Then they had to line up for roll call, sometimes for hours. At the end of each twelve-hour workday they would receive another piece of bread and watered-down soup. Foul-smelling turnip broth was the worst. Mietek had trouble keeping the disgusting concoction down despite his extraordinary hunger.

The Jews had become used to deprivation during their time in the ghetto, but this was the worst yet. Everyone was bone thin. So many people were sick. The Nazis had become masterful in their low-calorie distributions. Following the invasion of the Soviet Union, they had created a "hunger plan" to guarantee the slow starvation of the occupied population. Now they fed the Jews four hundred calories a day or fewer.

Keeping Mietek alive was Isaak's only goal. "Here son, eat this." He ripped his bread in two. "I'm working on enticing that young Ukrainian guard, Petro. We should have a little extra to eat if he's willing to trade." He bartered sparingly: a spoon or necklace could be counted on for extra bread or potatoes.

Ties to the Polish community had been a definite advantage to the Starachowice Jews.

Before moving to the ghetto, Isaak and Sonia had left some items for safekeeping with their Polish neighbors. Now an underground system for bribing guards allowed Isaak and a few other prisoners to leave camp to retrieve their valuables. Isaak would wait for one of the approachable Ukrainian guards to come on duty, then he'd sneak out under cover of night to pick up his belongings. The guard knew that he would receive one of Isaak's salvaged treasures upon his return. Isaak always returned. He understood that Mietek would be killed if he didn't.

Father and son were assigned to the shell assembly site, on the steel smelting production line. "Steady, don't rush it," said Isaak watching his son perform a herculean act for a young boy. Sweat poured down Mietek's face as he carried red hot steel pallets on huge tongs to the furnace. There were many such intolerable jobs. The unbearable heat made it essential for the men to rotate positions every two hours. Isaak set up precise assembly rounds giving each prisoner specific, timed tasks in the smelting process. No one could leave until production was complete.

Mietek, like his father, had a talent for engineering. He had an innate ability to look at a machine, understand how it functioned and, perhaps more importantly, why it had malfunctioned. He and Isaak soon understood how the smelting machines worked and how to repair them. That made them stand out to the German factory guards—they needed workers that kept production moving.

Showers were infrequent at the labor camp, but on one windy winter's day, Mietek was assigned to march with a group to wash. "I'm leaving, Papa." He wanted to be sure his father knew where he was going. "I get to wash off the filth and grime for a day—but it's freezing out." He had become accustomed to living with dirt, but standing naked in line outdoors meant shivering in the frigid air. The shower itself was cold water only, and afterwards the guards forced Mietek and the others to run until they dried. The chill was so deep inside his body it took him hours to warm up.

Isaak, Mietek, and the men lying next to them settled in that evening after their guard bellowed, "Lights out." Mietek tossed and turned to find a sleeping position in his cramped bunk, trying to get his body temperature up.

"This can't go on forever," Isaak said, a prayer as much as a statement. "The work, the filth is unbearable."

"I can't believe it's gone on this long," whispered Moshe, their bunkmate. "They're getting away with murder. Literally, murder."

"We must have hope," Isaak responded, mindful, as always, to be optimistic in front of Mietek. "We must always have hope—it's our ultimate weapon." He rolled on his back, staring at the boards above him.

"Yes, Isaak," Moshe continued. "The Germans have made so many enemies, surely they'll be attacked at some point."

It was hope that kept them going through the long, grueling days and the harsh, anxious nights. Hope that the world would intervene, and they would be saved.

Less than two months after the Selection Day, a dreadful illness spread through the labor camps: high fevers, severe muscle aches, and weakness. "Papa," whispered Mietek after waking up, "I can't move. My head's on fire. Everything hurts." Isaak stared into his son's bloodshot eyes. He had to think fast. There was a barrack set aside for the infirm, but Isaak didn't trust it. There was little value in the life of a sick Jew.

Soon the prisoners were able to put a name to the disease: typhus. Their exhaustion and immune systems had been weakened by the work in the smelting plant. That, coupled with crowded, filthy conditions, made them vulnerable to the disease. Unable to wash and launder clothes, the prisoners were riddled with lice that hastened the epidemic. Many died as the illness spread. This gave the Germans more reason to humiliate their prisoners. Even though it was the filthy conditions the Germans imposed that made them sick.

The situation grew dire. Tired of losing the workers and piling up more sick Jews, Althoff went to the barrack where the ill were kept and pulled out his pistol, systematically shooting the sick, one by one. Isaak's intuition proved to be true. When others stricken with typhus learned about the methodical murder, they stopped going to the designated barrack and relied on family or friends to shelter them and keep them alive. Some were propped up during work while others performed their duties for them.

All the prisoners had been exposed. It was just some lucky immunity that kept everyone from contracting the disease. The healthy hid the sick, nursing them as best they could, though if they were caught, Althoff eliminated the healthy caretakers along with their patients. He decided to run the prisoners down the stairs to determine who couldn't keep up or run in a straight line. Those who failed the test were shot.

Althoff was a sadist, the worst kind of human being.

Mietek struggled under the disease. His head pulsed when his fever spiked. His muscles ached and his body went limp. He couldn't stand up straight. Delirium made his head spin. Isaak applied cool rags to his head every night and as often as he could in the daytime. He monitored Mietek's fever. He and his friends, Josef Tauber and Murray Gutterman, covered for Mietek and hid him when opportunity arose. In the midst of these dark times, Mietek found comfort being near his father. Isaak's love gave the boy reason to recuperate. It also reminded him of his mother's tender care. Isaak and their friends kept him safe for eleven days. By the grace of God, he recovered. Just in time.

Mietek recovered before the Nazis ordered another roundup of Jews for slaughter. The transport would take an unknown number of prisoners to the nearby Bugaj Forest, located directly behind the camp in December 1942. When the selected prisoners arrived at their destination, the men were lined up on one side of a ditch, the women on the other. They were ordered to move to the edge of the mass grave and shot.

CHAPTER TWELVE

EARLY 1943

Isaak collapsed in late February. Forty years old, worn down by hard physical labor and poor nutrition, his body was ravaged by typhus. Mietek and Murray picked him off the floor and placed him on the dirty straw bed. Isaak opened his eyes and jerked to get up—a conditioned reaction. Was he late for roll call? He flopped back down, too dizzy to stand. His blood pressure was dangerously low. His headache and fever made him weak. Mietek gathered rags and soaked them in the snow outside their barrack, comforting his father with cool cloths on his forehead. Isaak pointed to the bucket in the corner used for nighttime relief. Mietek fetched it just in time for him to vomit. Murray helped Mietek roll Isaak further back in the bunk in an attempt to hide him amid the matted straw. Thank God Althoff was off duty.

Isaak was unconscious for most of the day. Mietek and their friends had to report to work, but they did what they could, taking turns to cool the rags and hydrating Isaak with small sips of water. His abdominal pain kept him from eating. The next day, his blood pressure returned to normal. He forced himself out of the bunk, vomiting into the bucket. Muscle pain radiated through him. His backache made him slouch, so Josef and Mietek got under his arms to hold him up. They had to hide his symptoms from Althoff. Isaak forced his mind to focus, to do what he could to control the fever and the tremors overtaking his body. His friends stayed by his side. In a few days, he began to recover, but he had lost more weight and had a lingering cough.

Isaak's weakened condition made him a target for transport. Despite all efforts to blend in, to appear strong and healthy, he was seized on March 3rd. Mietek's heart raced as his father was loaded onto the truck. Wracked with fear, he watched as the convoy left the camp, knowing that no one had survived the transport in December. He felt helpless, lost. His mind flashed to his mother and Klara, waiting in line for the last time. He couldn't keep the memory at bay.

That night he prayed. It was all he could do.

"Baruch ata Adonai Eloheinu, melekh ha'olam po'ke'ah ivrim."

Blessed are you, Lord our God, King of the universe, who restores the eyes of the blind.

Then a miracle. His father's voice woke him from his fitful sleep. How could this be? Nobody returned from the transport trucks.

"Even I can't believe it Mietek," he whispered. "A woman caused a scene, refusing to get off the truck. She just kept screaming." Isaak shook his head. "She kept the guards busy, this one small woman, so I seized the chance to escape, to steal back to the camp—to be with you."

Mietek sat up in disbelief.

His father had escaped death.

Meyer died of typhus on March 22nd, 1943. Althoff mysteriously and suddenly disappeared. Meanwhile, the General Government district officials continued eliminating the ghettos that didn't support the war effort. Faced with a labor shortage, factory management retained the trained workforce in Starachowice. It was at this point that the disposable German slave labor policy changed and the prisoners' situation improved. For one thing, prisoners were allowed to recuperate from illness or injury before returning to work. They were still overworked and underfed, but they were no longer routinely shot. Small mercies.

But the improved conditions weren't enough to keep Strzelnica open; it was shuttered in the summer of 1943 because of the extremely unsanitary conditions. Some of the strongest prisoners had been ordered to build new bunks in the established nearby satellite labor camp situated a couple miles from the munitions factory. Overlooking the Kamienna River Valley, Majowka served as a brick and munitions factory. Mietek and Isaak, along with the rest of the prisoners, were marched and prodded once again to the new site. They were joined by an influx of prisoners from distant camps.

The sweet scent of wood greeted Mietek in Majowka, thanks to the newly erected bunks. The sleeping quarters were still stacked unmercifully close, but fresh straw was a luxury. The stench of dried perspiration, factory oils, and steel dust didn't linger here, at least not yet. Mietek rushed in with his father to secure their place, making certain they stayed together.

Conditions at the Majowka camp were better than at Strzelnica. Kurt Baumgarten, the factory manager, wasn't sadistic like Althoff.

In fact, he made use of the camp *Lagerrat* and *Lagerpolizei* to keep order and sustain production. He even met with Jewish leaders and listened to their concerns. Baumgarten understood that healthy prisoners were productive prisoners, so heartier meals were served. Soup was cooked with potatoes, not just leftover peels. Steamed cabbage replaced spoiled, rotten turnips. Thick dark slices of bread, sometimes buttered, were a coveted improvement. Father and son slowly regained some strength, although Mietek's weight continued to drop from the grueling work and small rations. Isaak bartered for extra food with his diminishing stash of valuables, taking advantage of the black market, always doing what he could for his son.

Despite his more benign treatment of the prisoners, Baumgarten eagerly took bribes. The Jewish council fed his corruption, trading confiscated valuables to improve their own living conditions. A watch, a ring, a gold necklace were treasured pieces. Bribery and the black market continued to be a way of life. One side stole from the other and traded their goods. Food and favors were in highest demand. It was a vicious cycle. Mietek had learned the art of the black market from his father and their trusted friends. It was how they survived.

Soon after their arrival at Majowka, a man by the name of Walter Kolditz became the head of *Werkschutz*—operations security. He worked to keep the camp clean and free of typhus. But despite the new construction, the place still lacked adequate sanitation or proper facilities for washing clothes. Lice and bedbugs appeared once again; the environment was ripe for disease.

Mietek and his father marched to and from work in all sorts of weather, surrounded by machine-gun-toting guards. These guards counted the prisoners throughout the day: at early morning roll call, during the two-mile march to the factory, upon arrival at the factory, and at the end of the day upon their return to Majowka. Mietek hated the constant attendance checks, the grip of apprehension as they confirmed no one had escaped. Standing to be counted, sometimes for hours, made the long workday more agonizing. Work was necessary, but the roll calls broke your back.

Uprisings in other labor camps in late 1943 drew SS Chief Himmler's attention. Outraged, he gathered his SS troops from all over Poland's General Government district and ordered a massacre. Forty-two thousand Jewish laborers were murdered in the Lublin camps over the course of two days. Eighteen thousand were shot on "Bloody Wednesday," November 3rd, in the Majdanek camp. Himmler's message was clear: Uprisings would not be tolerated. He and his troops were in power.

On November 8th, the Majowka camp came under siege.

"I'm up, Papa," said Mietek shaking off the cold. As usual, he scrambled to get out of the bunk, racing ahead of the others to relieve himself at the open-hole latrine. Then he heard the commands over the loudspeaker: "All prisoners must leave the barracks. Report outside immediately!" It was too early for roll call. Another selection.

Isaak felt a surge of panic. He had barely survived the last one. "Follow me outside," he said to Mietek. "But stay directly behind me." When he saw the machine guns trained on them, Mietek's heart raced. He lined up with his father. They tried to stand in the back rows whenever they could; Isaak felt they'd draw less attention there. Father and son looked straight ahead as guards singled out the elderly men and women, the weak and the very young.

"Think of something else, anything," whispered Isaak when shrieking women resisted being separated from their children.

Mietek swallowed hard. "I'm trying."

Father and son were passed over the first round. Despite his weight loss, Mietek's muscular physique and youth kept him eligible for the work force. Legs weakening, he once again flashed back to the last moment he saw his mother and sister. He wanted to cry out—to rage, to rebel. But he kept silent. Keeping his feelings in check was automatic now.

The commanders separated out a group of about one hundred sixty people, loading them onto trucks. In the meantime, Kolditz went to the sick barracks and ordered everyone out of their beds. Those unable to rise were shot, a nightmare revisited. Kolditz's killings began a new period. But it didn't last long. He was soon dismissed, to the relief of the prisoners. The rumor was that he had clashed with Baumgarten.

Clothes belonging to the prisoners who had left in the selection were soon returned to the camp. Survivors grabbed what they could. Shoes were like gold. They deteriorated from miles of walking and the harsh weather work conditions. Even if they weren't the right size, they could be bartered. Wearing the shirts and trousers of their compatriots, the survivors were left to wonder when it would be their turn, who might wear their clothes.

CHAPTER THIRTEEN

An unusual calm spread over the Majowka camp at the start of 1944. The prisoners' routines, although harsh, were predictable. Long work days, lengthy walks, and roll calls were a given. Inadequate food rations, scratchy crowded bunks, and dirty toilet holes were the order each day. But the killings had stopped.

Mietek hated the lack of privacy. There was no place for solitude, no time to reset his mind. His father felt the same. Everyone did. No space to hide, to think, to grieve. No door to close. What did get them through was having each other, and of course, friends from their hometown. Familiar faces made all the difference. Someone cared that you were alive.

The guards and administrators became lax. Mietek and Isaak allowed themselves to recuperate from the daily feelings of terror. They were grateful to wake each morning merely to get ready for their long work days while fighting off starvation. Unfortunately, this period was short-lived. In April, a group of more than 150 prisoners from the Majdanek concentration camp in Lublin arrived in Starachowice. These men were strong and, in a number of cases, articulate and well-educated. Many had worked in a special camp providing skilled labor for the SS before their transfer to Majdanek.

Tall, muscular, and with a crook in his nose, Piotr, one of the Lubliners, reached his hand out to Isaak.

"*Dzien dobry*, I'm Piotr. I've heard you were a fair man. It's a pleasure to meet under these crazy circumstances."

Isaak graciously responded. "Same here. Welcome to our town, our camp. It's a shame you have to see it now. This used to be a wonderful community." He released their grip. "How were things when you left Lublin?"

Piotr stroked his head. "It's a mess, like the rest of the country. The Red Army is moving into central Poland, pushing the Germans out. We could have been retained at the Majdanek hell hole. Or worse, the gas chamber in Treblinka, but thank God it's been closed. Working for SS, we heard stories I won't repeat."

Isaak went white. He had heard rumors that the Selection Day transport headed to Treblinka—with his family. He was sickened.

As the days wore on, the Lubliners came to understand how the Majowka camp worked. They were surprised to see that the Jewish elite had kept their families with them—and appalled by their own harsh welcome. Emboldened by the special privileges they enjoyed under Baumgarten, camp leaders forced the newcomers to give up their possessions and relegated them to a lower station with harsher conditions. The new arrivals were hostile toward the Jewish authorities and resolved that they were not going to accept lower-grade food rations or work privileges. Who did this leadership think they were?

Isaak sensed danger. He heard it in the voices of the Lubliners who huddled outside the barracks to discuss their new reality.

"We've survived many labor camps, but never, I mean never, were we treated with such disrespect by other Jews," said one.

"We have no ties to this community," said another.

A small group of Lubliners hatched a plot to escape. Plans laid out, they rose in the middle of the night, waiting for the guard to relieve himself. They slipped outside, army crawling between the searchlights pooling the grounds. The men scuttled under the barbed wire fence where they'd dug a shallow trench, then leapt over another. Running toward the woods, they heard shots ring out. Sirens wailed. Screams of *"Halt"* and pops of gunfire filled the night air. Two of the men kept running, not looking back. The rest were shot dead.

Everyone waited for the aftermath. The German and Ukrainian guards scoured every barrack, looking for the culprits among the prisoners. "If you are with the group planning an escape, we will shoot every one of you. It doesn't matter that you're not involved, you will be shot. So maybe you'll kill these others yourselves," the beady-eyed soldier threatened. "You can save us time."

Always looking to improve the German war machine, the Nazis felt that the prisoners' long march from Majowka wasted precious hours that could have been used for factory work. In response, they ordered some of the Lubliner prisoners to build a new camp barracks adjacent to the munitions factory. The prisoners arrived in the new barracks in early July, just before Mietek's birthday. He would be sixteen on July 11th.

Isaak was determined to celebrate his son. The boy was mature beyond his years, and Isaak was proud that he had gained inner strength without losing his compassion for others. Mietek skillfully anticipated changes. He could read others and assess their characters; he had acquired keen survival skills. Isaak bartered for a sweet cake, an after-dinner surprise. That evening, father and son found a private moment to hug hard. They understood what was missing. Even in moments of joy, things would never be the same again. Just knowing was too much to bear. There was no Sonia. There was no Klara. Neither would ever speak of their loss aloud.

Rumors about gas chambers and the advance of Soviet troops had everyone on edge. Up to that point the prisoners knew the Germans valued their labor toward the war effort. But if the Russians crossed into Poland, the Nazis would most likely send everyone to an extermination camp or kill them outright.

Amid all the rumors, Mietek and Isaak's work assignment changed. They were moved from the production line at the factory and given the job of disassembling the massive machinery. It seemed an ominous sign.

"Do you think the factory will close?" asked Murray, slowly sipping his soup ration.

Isaak looked up from his meager bowl. "It looks like it. Why else would they reassign us to take the munition machines apart?"

Mietek asked the obvious question, "Does that mean we'll be sent to one of the camps we keep hearing about?"

They remained silent. No one wanted to state the obvious. Would an extermination camp be next?

Mietek and his father huddled with friends to gauge their options. The new camp had two watchtowers and was surrounded by a double wall. The inner section consisted of barbed wire, the outer of wooden plank fencing, a construction that made it almost impossible to escape. Some of the prisoners had made secret plans to buy weapons from the Ukrainian guards for a future uprising and possible escape. It was tempting, but neither Mietek nor Isaak would risk losing each other. When the Germans identified those they thought might try to escape, they shot them and beat anyone connected to their work group. Father and son knew they had made the right decision. As the Starachowice camp began preparations for evacuation, Mietek and Isaak heard shots one night after the first group of men tried to flee. The number of attempted escapes surged, but most prisoners were quickly caught and shot.

Mietek and Isaak spent their last day in their hometown on July 28th, 1944. Mietek tried to recall the Wierzbnik he grew up in, not the ghetto or the camps he and his father endured. Just a moment of normalcy—watching his mother cook potato soup, his sister listening to him read, his friends picking him up for a soccer game. He yearned for just one moment. Almost two years after Selection Day, the Starachowice slave-labor camp was officially closed.

Mietek and Isaak lined up with the others to board the transport. Over one hundred people were wedged tightly in each car. Crushed next to his father, Mietek couldn't sit or move. Men gasped for air as the cars sweltered under the blazing July sun—the only ventilation strained through the small cracks in the boards. Soaked in sweat, starved and thirsty, Mietek wretched from the stink from lack of sanitation. Weakened passengers collapsed, giving in to the tormenting conditions. Many suffocated to death.

And because war has a way of meting out its own rough justice, the members of the *Lagerpolizei* who fulfilled Nazi orders without compassion were targeted on their overheated car and killed. Riding in the first transport car, twenty of the *Lagerrat* council were also besieged. This group of elders that had taken good care of themselves and their families, that had stolen from the out-of-towners, paid dearly for their abuse. They, too, died at the hands of their fellow prisoners.

Isaak and Mietek fell out of the crowded train cars as the guards opened the door, stumbling and struggling to stand. They gulped in massive lungsful of air, nauseous from the stench of corpses. Overwhelmed with their insufferable conditions, they paid little attention to their destination. They had traveled some 140 miles, a journey that took thirty-six hours, without realizing where the transport was headed.

Auschwitz.

Mietek took deep breaths until the stink began to dissipate. He peered down the tracks, unable to ignore the red brick building that straddled the rails, looking oddly like a gigantic bird that just landed. A tower with a pyramid-shaped roof sat atop the open entrance with two sets of tracks merging under the arch, resembling a monstrous, open jaw awaiting its prey.

They had reached Birkenau, Auschwitz II, where the Nazis processed new arrivals. It served as the killing center for the camp. Because it was the largest of the concentration camps, it had been divided into three sectors: Auschwitz I, the main camp; Auschwitz II, Birkenau; and Auschwitz III, known as Monowitz.

Mietek forgot to breathe.

CHAPTER FOURTEEN

Everything was gray. The buildings, the roads, the air. The prisoners' and their striped apparel, Nazi uniforms, all gray. Flecks of ash drifted as far as the eye could see. Emaciated prisoners in their oversized tops and pants were the first to approach the new arrivals. They waited for their order to stack suitcases to haul away, just as they'd done time and time again. There were none on this transport.

Mietek was struck by the prisoners' bony faces, drenched in sallow complexions. Their shoulders hunched over. Withered bodies shuffled everywhere. Protruding eyes reflected a deep, dark sorrow, worn down by misery.

Their transport was on a newly constructed rail line that led directly to the gas chamber. The usual selection process determining who would go to the gas chamber or who would be sent to Dr. Mengele's medical experiment location or labor group was not performed that day. Perhaps because it was a Sunday, perhaps because the new rail wasn't aligned with orders, but it didn't matter. This extraordinary stroke of luck saved most of them, especially the children, who had, miraculously, survived to this point.

Almost immediately, everyone from the transport was forced into lines. The guards led Isaak and Mietek's group to a building where they were ordered to undress and hand over any personal items. Every piece of clothing, their socks and shoes, any small personal keepsake left on their bodies after bartering, was confiscated. Everything. Lined up in rows of five, the naked men were pointed to a table. Barbers shaved heads in quick succession, then shaved their entire bodies. Each person was disinfected with a sharp-smelling chlorine compound that stung against their bare skin. It was an assembly line. Impersonal. Mechanical. Eerily efficient.

Once the men had been disinfected, they were driven to the showers. Mietek's heart pounded when they were turned on. He had heard the horror stories. But why bother to disinfect them, shave them, spend any time on them? To his relief, it was water that came out, not gas. Once clean, he and his father received gray-striped uniforms, wooden clogs, and tin bowls, which they protected fiercely. It was to be their only utensil for food.

The last step was registration and branding. Everyone filled out a card with personal information that would be filed by the camp's administration. According to the July 30th, 1944 Auschwitz registration lists, 1,298 men and 409 women arrived on the transport from Starachowice.

Isaak nodded to Mietek, leaning to whisper in his ear, "This camp is eerie. We don't know if there are groups here that kill, steal, and practice other rituals, so staying together will be our best chance to survive. Write down our name beginning with a G—Gajgenszperg. We should be able to stay close to Murray Gutterman and our other friends whose last names begin with a G." Mietek stayed close to Isaak, hoping that they might be placed together in this numbering system.

Auschwitz, because it was huge, was the only camp where

the Nazis tattooed prisoners. The authorities used this numbering system to brand their captives. It facilitated identification of the overwhelming numbers while they worked, and at time of death. This number was also sewed onto their prison clothes.

Mietek winced when it was his turn, as the man used a feather-like pen to scratch each number on the inside of his left forearm: A-19104. He would wear this number, inked into his skin, for the rest of his life.

Names were meaningless at Auschwitz.

After branding, Mietek and Isaak were marched to their new quarters, which were in a quarantine zone. Once settled into barracks, they noticed one significant change from their labor camps in Starachowice: no lice. It was a strange trade-off—the shaving of their hair and bodies, the disinfection, the forced shower, the donning of a required uniform and the total loss of their personal identity, in exchange for an existence free of vermin.

They had about ten days to adjust and absorb Auschwitz's inhumane conditions. Breaking in their prisoners, guards began roll call in the middle of the night. *"Raus, raus!"* they commanded. Everyone had to stand. *"Wir singen."* The man with a bullhorn began singing, *"Deutschland über alles,"* and everyone had to join in the national hymn, Germany Over All. Then they'd have to jump up and down, as if exercising, whatever floated their captor's fancy. Isaak guided Mietek through the horrific changes in their new surroundings, trying any way he could to protect his son.

Black smoke from the crematoria wafted through the air—an ever-present reminder that death loomed over the camp. The quarantine regimen began every morning with shouted orders to line up outside and exercise for hours. Anyone who was slow or fell out of place was beaten. Exhausted after the drills, the men had to stand in place and repeat German phrases, over and over again. Later in the day, the men returned to their barracks, which were already overcrowded and filthy.

Mietek and his father were housed next to an encampment of Romany gypsies during the quarantine. In the evening, Mietek would approach the wire fence. "I'm Mietek," he nodded, looking at a young man about his age. "You?"

"Manfri," replied the dark haired boy with coal black eyes.

"How long have you been here?"

"A long time. About a year, but it feels like forever." The boys communicated in broken German. They met at the fence after dinner the next evening. Manfri lived with his family and cousins here. Mietek had a pang of jealousy. A whole family. Manfri thought there were about three thousand of his people enslaved here. He looked forward to seeing his friend, a break from the inhumane routines.

But on the night of August 2nd, 1944, screams erupted from the Roma camp. Mietek heard the familiar shifting gears of trucks. More shrieks roared through the thin walls. He couldn't sleep, even after all the commotion ended.

Lining up for roll call the next morning, Mietek looked past his neighbor's fence. No one was in sight, not one living soul. He was gripped with a recurring feeling of loss. The stink from the chimneys nauseated him. Fresh ashes rained down.

CHAPTER FIFTEEN

Grief was a luxury the camps didn't afford. Mietek had no time to recover from the loss of his friend. Following another long roll call on another sweltering morning, the prisoners received news that they were to be dispersed throughout several subcamps. There were more than forty subcamps outlying Auschwitz. Most used slave labor to operate their industrial plants. A few were dedicated to farming.

"You will leave tomorrow. You will be marched out in groups starting at dawn," the SS officer bellowed. "You're dismissed, dirty pigs."

Isaak waited until they were inside the barracks. He motioned for Mietek to sit down. "Son, we have to prepare for the worst. They may send us to different camps." This was no time to coddle him.

Mietek had thought the same thing.

"You are sixteen. You are strong, smart, and resourceful. Despite everything you've been forced to do, forced to give up, you've grown to be a remarkable and compassionate human being. Don't lose that." He pressed his lips. "I couldn't be prouder of you, Mietek. I don't know that I could have been as brave as you."

Mietek stuttered. He tried to hide his fear. His father had been the best example to him in the worst circumstances imaginable. Because of Isaak, Mietek had become a strong, honorable man.

Because of Isaak, he had survived. Now it was his turn to give his father solace, to let him see the person he had become. "If this happens, I'm prepared Papa … because of you." He clamped his hand over his father's, squeezing tight. "I couldn't have made it through. I never take your love and sacrifices for granted." He hesitated. "It gives me the will to live."

Isaak clasped his son's head, pulling it to his chest.

"Keep your head up. Don't make eye contact. Work every minute of the day," Isaak whispered in his ear. "I'm always with you. So is … your mother and our Klarunia." There. He had said it. He had to, it might be the last time.

The following day, the sun rose over the vast expanse of Auschwitz. Thick, hazy rays blanketed the camps on this humid August morning. Mietek and Isaak held onto each other's arms, squeezing tight, before lining up outside. The roll call began. But this time their tattooed number was followed by a camp name. Father and son held their breath, waiting. Like a blur, the numbers and assignments were blasted by a high-pitched Nazi guard yelling into his megaphone. Next to him stood a man with a clipboard. Other officers, primped and polished, paced back and forth in tall shiny boots, waiting for the drill to end.

"A-19104," shouted the guard, "Monowitz." Mietek was selected to work at the satellite factory three miles away. He looked up, waiting to hear his father's number to be called. *Monowitz*, he repeated to himself. *Monowitz*. Father and son both craved a miracle. It didn't come. Isaak was assigned to another satellite subcamp. Mietek couldn't even make out the name. His legs buckled. Isaak grabbed his son's elbow and held him up. For five long years they had survived. All of it. Every humiliation. Every horror.

Every brush with death. And now this. They would be torn apart.

Isaak closed his eyes, breathing deeply. He thought about his son. They drew strength from each other's resolve. He was part of him. Mietek gave him a reason to push through each grueling day, to keep him safe.

Anxiety overcame Mietek. A dread of loss. Losing the only man he admired, who always knew what to do, who always reminded him that he was a worthy person. The only man he loved. Memories flooded his thoughts: he saw his father looking affectionately at his mother, his father holding Klara's hand tugging her doll, his father screaming "Kick the ball Mietek," with his uncles cheering next to him. All that gone. His eyes welled up. Weakness wasn't allowed. Tears could get you killed. He could not say goodbye. Please God. He just couldn't.

"Monowitz group, line up," came the next order. Isaak brushed Mietek's hand, a goodbye gesture. His only relief was that some of his hometown friends were with him, along with Emil, a young Polish prisoner whom he had recently befriended. As the roll call wound down, Mietek kept looking toward Isaak, who had been ushered into another line. He wanted to go to him. He wanted his father. He wanted all of this to be over, this terrible nightmare, but it was all he could do to stand tall, like his father.

The prison orchestra began to play a piece of quick tempo music. Jewish musicians had a place at Auschwitz, and the Germans' love of music kept the instrumentalists alive. The newly formed prisoner groups were ordered to march; Mietek to the Monowitz-Buna camp, and Isaak to another subcamp. He watched Mietek step to the music that drowned out the camp's eerie silence. His eyes moistened. His son disappeared.

CHAPTER SIXTEEN

The Monowitz camp—also known as *Buna Lager*—was clean and organized, as had been rumored. This IG-Farben plant supplied precision parts for rubber production and liquid fuels, making a significant contribution to the war effort. Management here expected an efficient and well-maintained work environment. Kapo Drucker, the camp head of Commando 1, seemed more businessman than tyrant. Monowitz was almost like the public sector, except that this factory used slave labor. That said, once trained, the prisoners were considered more valuable and less likely to be exterminated. Work conditions were hard, but work was Mietek's salvation.

Mietek's first job at Buna was loading and unloading boxes while maintaining a list of supplies. Sometime later, he was assigned to a munitions floor to work with deadly *electro magazin* (electric currents). With steady hands, he learned to navigate around the currents, in the process becoming a valuable asset to the factory. He missed his father, but having received word that Isaak had been housed close by—in the next camp, in fact—Mietek felt some hope. Hope was everything.

Mietek heeded his father's advice and listened carefully to the experienced captives. Huddling together with other prisoners was important, he had learned. Survival depended on it. Having friends or family in the same unit helped the men stay optimistic and gave them strength to endure cruel and humiliating treatment. Those without family nurtured friendships, keeping an eye on one another and sharing intelligence and rations when they could.

Mietek had been in the camp for seventeen days when the U.S. Army Air Force bombed the I.G. Farben factories. The camp went into lockdown as the thundering bombing continued for twenty-eight minutes. Mietek heard the bombs whistling by before they dropped. They didn't hit the camp directly, though. Were they trying to destroy the supply route to the factory? One plane flew so low, he could see that it was American. A glimmer of hope. A positive sign. The Americans knew about the camps. They were engaged in the war.

After the bombing stopped, Mietek and Emil were transferred to tent number two. A second bombing ravished the camp a short time later when, on September 13th, an air raid bombed Monowitz for thirteen minutes. Mietek and most of his group were then moved to block eleven, along with one of their kapos, Pipel, a political prisoner who treated the men with compassion. He followed the strict Nazi orders but elected to refrain from the usual beatings and impulsive behavior other kapos adopted.

Things calmed down and Mietek went about his day—the excruciating routine of too much work on too little food. Then, inexplicably, he felt an agonizing sensation spirit through his head. Mietek couldn't account for the sudden pain, but he remembered it the next day when Emil came to the door of their barracks with a familiar figure standing behind him. Mietek instantly recognized the fair-skinned boy from his hometown.

"Pinchas," he cried out, "what are you doing here? How's the second-best soccer player?" he teased as he stood up.

Pinchas smiled softly. Mietek had been around enough tragedy to know that this couldn't be good. Emil asked their bunkmates to give them a moment alone.

"Sit down, Mietek," directed Emil. "Pinchas has come with a message for you."

The quiet room felt eerie, as if someone was listening in. Mietek tensed up. Eyes wide, he stared at his old friend.

"I'm so sorry," said Pinchas, face grim. "I got word yesterday." He stopped, running his hand on the side of his bald head, trying to find the right words.

No, thought Mietek. *Don't.*

"Your father … Isaak," he finally spurted out. "Shot. Killed."

Mietek sat without moving. No words came. He almost lost consciousness as sudden pain shot through his chest. His heart actually hurt. Silence. He couldn't breathe. His body rocked forward and back. The blood rush to his ears blotted out everything outside his own thoughts. No dear God. Shot. Killed. No. NO. He stopped rocking. Eyes red, tears washed his cheeks. Years of anguish flooded out. He couldn't go on.

CHAPTER SEVENTEEN

Mietek's losses took residence in his soul. Everyone he loved had been murdered. He knew he had to keep working, no matter how he felt. Years of conditioning helped him to endure and survive the slave labor camps. But his father's death haunted him every minute, every day. Thank God for his friends. He would never had made it through if not for his friends.

By December, the Nazis had dismantled the gas chambers after Himmler ordered a halt to the exterminations. Evidence of the mass murders was to be eliminated. Though the killings had ended, the prisoners continued to struggle. A great many died. Overworked, slowly starving, harassed and beaten, they succumbed to Nazi deprivations and physical abuse. Regular beatings to improve productivity didn't have the intended results. Starving men received barely enough rations to keep them alive. The Jews of the camps lived on the edge of death and hope.

Prisoners continued to work slower than the German construction workers at the plant. Mietek, in good shape when he arrived at Monowitz, persevered because the food rations had been better in the Starachowice factory and he had some reserves to draw on. His work ethic and productivity were more developed than many of his colleagues too, and his prior camp experience helped him navigate

Auschwitz. He and his group bartered for extra food rations where they could, but they were still malnourished. He was reassigned to the planing division, where he smoothed and leveled factory parts. Twelve-hour workdays took their toll. He grew weaker.

Everything was an order. Even bathing. The Kapo regularly ordered the prisoners to wash in order to keep the camp clean. The men would take off their clothes in the barracks and go down to the shower area wearing only shoes—as they had in Starachowice. Once showered, the men received a tiny towel that didn't dry them completely, so they ran back to shelter, the freezing winter air biting into their naked flesh.

On December 18th, Mietek hadn't finished buttoning his shirt when another attack on Monowitz had everyone running for cover. The U.S. bombers damaged the pump and compressors at the I.G. plants. The Russians had advanced into Poland. Everything was changing. The Nazis were shaken and couldn't eliminate evidence of the atrocities at the camp fast enough. Access to food became more daunting.

The meager food rations had weakened Mietek. He woke up one morning feeling lightheaded. The Nazis would not tolerate excuses, he knew, as he rushed to line up for the 4 a.m. roll call. Shivering, he struggled to maintain his balance. Reaching the factory, he stood at his station. He kept his hands steady, applying pressure to the planing tool, but by the afternoon, his arms felt numb.

Nino, the foreman, noticed the change. Mietek was one of the most consistent and reliable workers; nevertheless, any hold up in production mandated a beating. Nino walked up behind Mietek and raised his wooden club. Mietek turned around in time to see Nino smashing his forehead. Blood spewed from his head and spattered on the factory cement floor. Mietek reeled, and because he fell to the floor, Nino struck him again.

Emil, working close by, asked for permission. "Sir, may I help?" Nino nodded. He took a rag from his pocket and held it to Mietek's forehead, pressing the flap of skin in place. But the bleeding wouldn't stop and he was losing consciousness. A guard was called to remove Mietek because the blood was making such a mess. Emil was ordered to keep on working. The guard took him to the sick barracks.

The doctor tended to Mietek's wound and kept him in the infirmary to recover. Grateful for the reprieve from work, for the chance to recuperate, for the time to mourn his father, Mietek nevertheless missed his friends. They provided hope for each other. Here at the infirmary, he had to build up the gloomy prisoner naysayers and keep his own spirits alive. No one talked about the reality of life here, no one. No one spoke of lost family. It would unravel their emotions, make them weak. He pictured his father's face, heard his words: "Hope. You have to have hope."

On December 26th, another heavy airstrike targeted the I.G. plant. Mietek's bed shook when the whistling bombs streaked past the infirmary before exploding. He was afraid the next bomb would hit his work site. He feared for his friends, but was grateful for the attacks. They all were. Even though prisoners had been killed in prior attacks, the raids were finally making an impact. He could only hope it would cripple Nazi efforts.

Weakened from the head wound, Mietek needed time to recover, but as soon as two weeks were up, he was forced to return to work. Nino wanted him back; he was a good worker. This was the mixed blessing of being proficient at his job.

In late December, the German factory officials held a meeting regarding work performance. An internal study at the production plant concluded that the low prisoner productivity rate was a result of the lack of food for the prisoners. Reluctantly, the officials ordered a small increase in rations. They would not give up the war effort. Not yet, anyway.

CHAPTER EIGHTEEN

JANUARY 1945

Mietek woke early, startled by a thunderous boom. The sound reverberated through the barracks, shaking the ground like an earthquake. Emil woke next to him with a jolt. Another Russian cannon exploded louder than the first. Mietek forced himself to recall the date. January 17th. He had survived in the camp for almost six months. It was his dream to be free before his seventeenth birthday in July.

"The Allies and Russians are coming closer, Emil," Mietek said. "They're eliminating troops in their way." They forced themselves to stand, moving in place to try to warm their bodies as they stood at attention, an automatic gesture by now. The familiar gnawing pangs of hunger ached in Mietek's belly. A short, stout guard made his brisk entry, yelling at them to stand up straight. After the usual head count, the guards ordered the prisoners to move to the mess hall. Mietek smelled the watered-down coffee. He recollected mornings watching his mother pour boiling water over the coffee grounds at home. He recalled his mother, father, and sister every morning. It gave him comfort and helped him stay strong. With his family in mind, he could make it through another day. In his heart, he would keep them alive.

The guards assigned clean-up duties; everyone was grateful for the indoor work. By suppertime, Mietek sensed a change as the guards rushed around the camp instead of hovering over them.

Darkness soon cast its shadow over Auschwitz. The cold, dry day brought a freezing night. Everyone had settled in their barracks when suddenly the guards yelled for the men to get out and line up again.

The prisoners fell into line behind a tall, thin SS officer. He was dressed in uniform with his stiff-peaked cap and long gray winter coat, belted at the middle. He stood, legs apart, accentuating his black leather boots. Holding his wooden club in his gloved hand, he delivered the orders.

"We are evacuating all of you at Buna camp. Everyone will be assigned to a marching unit. You will proceed with that group tonight. If you are too weak to walk, you must stay behind. Other prisoners will follow from nearby subcamps." He couldn't have been more stern. He couldn't have been more clear. "We are moving fast, so you must return to your barracks for supplies and further orders."

The men were pushed to move to their barracks quickly, taken aback at seeing supply tables set up for them. One by one, they moved to the first table and took a hard loaf of bread. They were told this had to last them for days. At the next table, they were handed a gray wool blanket. This alone had to keep them alive in the frigid temperatures along with their undershirt, long johns, and gray denim uniforms.

Mietek and Emil stayed close together, agreeing to share any extra food rations and watch out for each other, as they'd done in the past. They returned to their barracks and dressed, paying special attention to their shoes.

"Watch this." Mietek waved to Emil. With precision, he folded and sheared strips of newspaper he'd taken from the cement bags at the factory. "Wrap the paper around your foot, layer by layer," he demonstrated. As if he'd done this before, Mietek bit off a piece of string with his teeth and tied it around his foot, placing the knot near the inside sole. Sliding his foot into the wooden clog, he instructed, "Check that it's tight enough so you don't fall out, but not too constricting." Satisfied he'd got it right, Mietek added more strips of paper, binding his clog. Breaking off three pieces of string, Mietek tied the paper at the toe, middle, and heel of the wooden shoe. "What do you think?" He peered up at Emil, handing him the shredded paper.

Nodding, Emil let him know he liked it. "You've made cement bag socks," he said. "And we have God awful wooden shoes—with traction. It's brilliant."

The boys worked carefully to prepare their shoes for trekking in ice and snow. Mietek had "repossessed" enough paper to take care of his friend. He wiped off factory dust from the remaining bags and handed half to Emil.

"Stuff them close to your body—anything to insulate us," he explained, cramming bigger sheets under his shirt. "We have to keep warm."

Emil followed every step. It gave him an ounce of comfort that they might have a chance in the freezing cold. It was rumored to be one of the coldest winters on record.

The sick, elderly, and young were to remain. Some of the prisoners in the main camp were told they could stay or move with the guards to reach the German border and be transported to other camps.

Panic set in with the prisoners staying behind. After recuperating in the infirmary with a foot injury, Elie Wiesel, a Hungarian Jew, frantically requested to get out of the infirmary after hearing about the evacuation plan. He had to make sure he was out in time to join his father at Monowitz. The same age as Mietek, Elie also worked in the Buna plant, although he had been fortunate enough to stay with his father.

The young man next to Elie's bed, still convalescing from an infected wound, shared his fears. Would he and the others be murdered because they could no longer work? And if they weren't shot, would they starve or die from hypothermia?

Elie tried to console him as he prepared to leave the infirmary. The allies were on their way, he told him. You had to have faith; they'd all come this far.

Nightfall stole the last glimmer of light. An artic chill descended on the frozen grounds of Auschwitz. The guards ordered, "Everyone out!" Mietek and Emil grabbed their meager supplies and followed them outside.

Once the Auschwitz evacuation was complete, the reality of moving in the dark night set in. Mietek, Emil, and the other prisoners began a four-day march in brutal subzero temperatures. They stomped the frozen snow with every step, holding tight to their blankets. A cracking sound made them jump. As Mietek turned around, he saw an inmate bleeding from his head. A few minutes later, there was another pop. They soon passed the corpse lying in the snow.

As on other marches, the guards shot prisoners who tripped or fell. No one who stumbled was given a chance to right himself, to pick himself up and continue. As the survivors marched on, these killings became so routine that the prisoners looked straight ahead, immune to the clap of gunshots, navigating as if by nature around the dead bodies. On the second day, as they continued west, their unit was told they were going to a subcamp of Auschwitz named Gleiwitz II. The buildings there had originally housed chemical factories. No one knew what might be there now.

Mietek's fingertips had turned a deep red. They felt numb, as did parts of his face. Frostbite had set in. Fearing they would end up like others who had frozen to death, he and Emil huddled with at least two other men each night in order to conserve body heat. They were all starving but would only take small bits of their bread in hopes that they could make it last.

They arrived in Gleiwitz on January 21st, outlasting four days and nights of bitter cold. Mietek could barely move, but as he stood before the historic building that was to be his residence, he had to believe a miracle had kept him alive. His father was watching over him, he was sure of it. *You got me this far Papa, I won't let you down*. He heard his father's plea to never give up. Never.

Mietek dragged himself inside. Surveying for a landing spot, he moved to the far corner and collapsed on the floor. Breathing heavily, he rolled on his back, staring up at the ceiling. Every part of his body ached. He feared losing toes to frostbite, as he felt them thaw. Close behind, Emil shuffled over to him, allowing his buckling legs to give out next to his friend.

Other inmates from different subcamps lay in clusters, thankful to be alive. Within the hour, they had all received some coffee, bread, and small bits of sausage. The rations came too late for some. They died where they lay, one by one, gaunt eyes open. The rations barely sustained the remaining survivors.

Approximately three thousand prisoners died during the thirty-mile route to Gleiwitz. More than sixty thousand prisoners took part in the death marches from nearby subcamps; over fifteen thousand died.

Of course, many more would die on the trains that headed to Dachau, Buchenwald, Bergen-Belsen, or Mauthausen. In the end, only a fraction of these boys and weary men would survive.

CHAPTER NINETEEN

Dark storm clouds loomed overhead, blocking any chance of sunshine. Mietek heard the familiar clank of wheels approaching as the SS guards ordered everyone to move up to the tracks. The locomotive arrived and the men were jammed into the uncovered cars, packed so tight that they were forced to stand. The brutal cold was torture to the already weak prisoners. Some exposed men shivered violently. Teeth rattling, heads pulsing, they lost control of their bodily functions. Moaning stopped, their bodies went limp. They died upright, pressed against the others. Frozen. The stench of body fluids, vomit, and death dissipated gradually, petrified by the deep freeze under a black starless sky. A ghostlike silence pervaded the train car.

Those who endured took uniforms and shoes off the dead. Maybe the layers would increase their odds of survival. Naked corpses froze. Mietek and Emil squeezed close together, each taking solace in the other's company, in the remnant warmth of the other's body. Standing near one of the stiffened men slumped on the floor, Mietek ended the trip sitting on this frozen body. Mentally numb, physically immobile, he strained to concentrate. He had promised himself that he would memorize dates and places but, being disorientated, he lost track of time. And then the train stopped with a sudden jerk. The guards dropped the plank and ordered the men to throw out their dead. Mietek, Emil, and ten other teenage boys were ushered out. The train pulled away, leaving them behind in a strange little camp on the side of a mountain.

A gray-haired man greeted the boys, a burly lumberman whose name was Johann. The Russians, Americans, and their allies had squeezed the Germans' resources, making them desperate for manpower. This necessitated the appointment of local farmers to oversee the prisoners' work on the tree farm.

The surroundings felt familiar; Mietek was reminded of his father's forestry business. Staggering up a steep incline, he envisioned tiers of the Starachowice forests zigzagging up the Holy Cross Mountains. Overcome by a pang of homesickness, he savored the smell of the wood-burning smoke wafting from the chimney. As his group entered the expansive log cabin, the locals greeted them warmly. Their look of horror when they saw the condition of the emaciated boys evoked a strange solace in the young prisoners. Compassion was foreign to them. A mature woman with a brown braid twisted in a bun hurried out of the kitchen.

"Britta," she called to the young girl working on her needlepoint seated in front of the fire, "round up some warm meals for our guests. There's plenty of soup left in the kettle." Her eyes examined the boys. "And tell Hans to fetch some clothes for tonight." She straightened her wool skirt, then rolled down her sleeves.

The main house was clean and heated by wood stoves. An oversized fireplace glowed in the center of the room. Heaped with wood, the fire crackled and hissed under the sound of the roaring flames. The woman introduced herself: *"Meine name ist Hilda."* She wiped her hands on her oversized apron. "Please sit down by the fire." Warmth penetrated the boys' frail bodies. Mietek was comforted by the yellow glow coming from the fireplace. Emil closed his eyes, trying to remember the last time he hadn't felt cold. The boys' reverie was interrupted when a skinny youth with suspenders holding up his sagging pants came over with bundles of clean clothes. "Please give me your dirty clothes and I will return them to you, washed, in the morning." Mietek wondered if he was dreaming.

Once bathed and changed into clean shirts and pants, the boys received a home-cooked meal prepared by neighboring farmers. Slowly, they dunked slices of dark bread into the hearty potato and vegetable soup. Their emaciated bodies struggled to digest their meals. Soon the exhausted boys fell asleep in comfortable bunks with clean blankets. The kindness of the villagers filled the boys' emotional reserves. They began to think they might survive.

The next morning, Mietek and Emil sat down to warm bowls of oatmeal, sweetened by a touch of honey. They exchanged glances. This was how it felt to be cared for. They recalled their parents, their childhood routines. They remembered being happy. Thick wool shirts were passed out before the group was sent outside. Johann guided them up the mountain and instructed them how to put trees on their shoulders and carry them downhill to loading stations. The elderly guards were patient and didn't push. They spoke with kindness. There were no early roll calls here. No one to assault the boys if they fell behind. Mietek, Emil, and the rest of their group repeated this exercise for days, gaining strength from good food and warm lodgings, from being treated like human beings.

And then it was over.

At the end of the week Johann delivered the news that a transport would arrive for them in the evening. Their work was done.

"Here," said one of the guards from the village. "Bread. My Marta made it. Hide it under your shirt." A second guard gave them a brick of cheese. A third gave them some landjäger sausage links. Johann made sure they had long johns and clean clothes before they walked down to the railroad tracks. Together they waited for the train.

"We will never forget what you did for us here," Mietek said. "Thank you, thank your friends. You have been so kind," he said in his best German. Johann smiled and nodded, his eyes showing concern. *"Sei gut, jünger Mann. Möge Gott mit dir gehen."* Be well young man. May God be with you. And Mietek felt a little less alone.

It was nightfall when snow began to cover the mountainside. The moon cast a magical glow, reflecting off thick snowflakes. The countryside was quiet and peaceful for a short time before the boys heard the drone of the engines growing louder by the second. A blast of the steam engine and the train stopped. Nazi guards stepped off, shouting to the boys to board the open car. No one knew where they were headed next, but for the moment, they were alive and fed. Despite all they had suffered, they had evidence that there was still kindness in the world. These farmers were Germans, and they cared. Mietek felt a glimmer of dignity. He was a person with value here. He remained positive. There was life to look forward to. There was hope.

Soldiers yelling, sticks hitting slow prisoners. Mietek and Emil were prodded into the compound. They had arrived at Buchenwald, one of the first concentration camps, and one of the largest forced labor camps in Germany. Buchenwald was less orderly than the Buna plant, and with a wretched population. The men and women here were dirty and exhausted. Walking skeletons, thought Mietek. Once settled in their grimy bunks—an all-too-familiar undertaking—Mietek and Emil huddled with two men, asking about the routines, what they should and shouldn't do, and who to avoid.

Georg, a political prisoner from Austria and veteran of the camp, was most informative. "These monsters gave me a viral infection, then injected me with vaccines to test their theories. Hundreds of humans died every month in their research center. I became violently ill but recovered. They sent me back to work, to continue my twelve-hour labor shifts." He leaned forward. "What's really ironic—the great German literary writer, Goethe, lived in the nearby city of Weimar." Shaking his head, he said, "It just doesn't make sense." Georg was weary but articulate and spoke the Nazis' native language. Most likely the reason he survived this far. Mietek and Emil quickly assessed the survival patterns that prevailed in the camp, a skill they learned from years of deprivation. Morning roll call was sloppy, a sign that the Nazis knew their days were numbered and were preparing for the worst. "You will line up here," the guard called out. "You are to march. At ten kilometers you will reach the great city of Weimar where you will be put to work. Now move!"

The boys had heard rumors that the infamous city of Weimar had been heavily bombed. This could be a fortunate assignment. If they were charged to clean up the debris on the street and sidewalks, they could sneak into vacated cellars and scavenge for necessities. Families stored much of their food, especially potatoes, in the cool dark basements. It was the best way to preserve their provisions. The boys were counting on it.

The cleanup began. Cement walls lay broken and strewn everywhere, covered with thick particle dust. The boys had to clear the cement chunks from the streets so that German tanks and armored trucks could gain road access. One by one, the boys took the opportunity to enter basements, many exposed from the bombing, to forage for scraps. “Emil,” whispered Mietek, “here.” He pointed to broken glass smeared with raspberry jam. The boys set to it, licking the larger pieces of the jars, being careful to avoid the sharp edges. Tiny rations of sweet preserves, a great find.

By evening, the guards marched the young men ten kilometers back to the barracks, a routine repeated for many days. Food became scarce. As the devastated remains of the city were picked through, the young prisoners worried that they would end up starving like the others at Buchenwald. No one spoke of it aloud, though. To do so would be to admit the proximity of death.

As they marched back to camp one evening, Emil turned to Mietek. “I need a bite of your bread from this morning. I’m getting dizzy again.” This was not an unusual request; the boys had long ago agreed to share their food. Mietek reached for the miserable ration he had been given that morning. It was gone. He looked at Emil and shook his head. “It’s not here. Someone must have stolen it from me!”

Exhausted and famished, Emil said, “You ate it, didn’t you?”

“Of course not!” Mietek stared at him horrified. “I can’t believe you would even think it.” All this time, they had trusted each other implicitly. Honor was one of the only things they had left. Emil’s accusation was a hard blow. Mietek was hurt. But more than that, he was worried for his friend. Overcome with emotion and fatigue, Mietek did something he had never done before. Not ever. He bumped into a man on his work team and pilfered a piece of bread. He was deeply ashamed. But this was for Emil. He had to help his friend.

Emil avoided eye contact as he ingested the ragged crust. He trusted Mietek. Of course he did. How could he have incited his friend to such desperate measures.

Hardly audible, he leaned over and whispered, "I'm ashamed, Mietek. I am sorry." Mietek placed his hand on Emil's shoulder. "What's happened to us? We can't let those animals change who we are." Emil apologized again for doubting Mietek's loyalty. Relieved, Mietek nodded. He understood. They only had each other.

Mietek and Emil felt the bonds of their friendship as they walked into the camp that evening. The humiliation of their actions that afternoon had brought them closer. When they were ordered to prepare for another transport, they maintained their pact to stick together. Two friends among five thousand. The Nazi guards were rushing, visibly overwhelmed because they needed to evacuate as many prisoners as possible. The American forces were approaching Buchenwald.

"Schnell, schnell!" they ordered. *"Im Laufschritt, marsch!"*

Mietek and the others marched to the railroad tracks without any provisions. But as they were being loaded onto the open transport cars, a Nazi guard pulled Emil out of line, pointing him to another train. When Emil hesitated, trying to stay with his friend, the guard struck him in the head with the butt of his rifle. He had no choice but to move. Horrified, Mietek called out, "Emil!" Pushed from behind, Emil turned his head toward Mietek, blood soaking his collar.

Mietek's car pushed forward. Within minutes, Emil's silhouette disappeared. The boys had held each other up, body and soul, for more than two months. Now Emil was gone. The only person he cared about. Gone.

Racing ahead of the advancing Americans troops, the trains took a tortuous route from Thuringia through Saxony, to Czechoslovakia. While the cars sped through a train depot in Czechoslovakia, people standing on the second level of the terminus threw sandwiches and other food into the fleeing cars. Mietek lunged for a sandwich, clutching it tight. The food meant everything to the starving boy, and he would always remember the kindness of the people who, having seen the transport trains pass through their war-torn country, did what they could to help.

For three weeks, Mietek had to help throw dead bodies off his train. They had come full circle. After reentering Germany, exhausted and starved prisoners died daily. Almost half of those who boarded didn't make it. The death train entered Bavaria. More men succumbed to the deprivations forced on them. There was no time to stop to unload their bodies. Only eight hundred sixteen emaciated prisoners survived. Mietek was one of them.

CHAPTER TWENTY

APRIL 1945

The majestic Alps cradled the thousand-year-old town of Dachau, Germany. The narrow cobblestone streets were meticulously maintained, as were the homes that bounded them. Dachau's eighteenth-century castle sat high on a hill overlooking the landscape, providing a magnificent view of Münich, Bavaria's capital, located only ten miles away.

It was late April. Empty window boxes sat dormant, waiting for warm weather to breathe life back into the sleeping plants. People shopping along the streets still dressed in heavy coats on this unusually cold spring day. On the east side of town, a screeching train whistle alerted the camp guards that a transport was arriving. The SS troop in charge of Dachau was not pleased. They were racing to evacuate prisoners from the camp. The weakened Nazi party wanted to destroy all evidence of concentration camps as the Allied forces approached, so why increase the number of prisoners?

Mietek felt the train come to a halt. Delirious and starving, he forced himself to stay conscious. Weighing less than ninety pounds, he was a shell of a boy at sixteen. Two Nazi soldiers unlocked the boxcar doors and ordered everyone out. It was around noon on

April 27th.

"Raus, schnell," they shouted. "Get out, fast." Several corpses fell to the ground. Many had lost the will to go on. The soldiers continued shooting men who were too weak or ill to get up. The few men, women, and children who survived the trip were close to death. They gazed at the familiar insignia over the front gate: *Arbeit Macht Frei.*

Work Will Set You Free.

Staggering, Mietek watched as five skeletal men from his transport collapsed and died in front of him. Then four more. He had to veer around them. Knees buckling, he dropped, crawling on his hands and knees, still moving forward. The eager SS just wanted to clear out the cars. They'd been held up for hours overseeing the camp's evacuation, putting them behind schedule to vacate the prisoners who had been living in the camp.

Dachau was overcrowded with disease-ridden prisoners. Mietek doubled over near the grimy crate they called a bed, nauseated from the smell of rotting corpses, intermingled with the odors of vomit and excrement from those who couldn't make it to the overcrowded latrine. Gaunt, many were unable to stand. An additional two hundred people who had survived transport died that day.

Everyone talked in muted tones. No one had the energy to be loud. The barracks housed thousands, crammed with four or more men in each stacked wooden-crate-like casket. There wasn't enough room for the sick, the dying, the dead, and the incoming prisoners of war from the last transport.

That night, Mietek lay next to a Dutch Catholic priest. Breathing heavily, and laboring to speak, the ailing priest whispered in his ear, "If you survive this and get food, eat small amounts, and slowly, or you'll die. Bless you, son." Later the priest woke him, gasping for air. Mietek gently set his arm on his shoulder. The priest died before dawn.

On April 29th, two days after arriving at Dachau, the megaphones blared, "Everyone out of the barracks!" The command was repeated over and over. Mietek had learned that orders such as these were designed to trick the prisoners so they could be herded outside for slaughter. But this announcement was in English. What did that mean? Mietek spoke several languages, but he knew very little English. The other prisoners, representing nearly forty nationalities, struggled with English as well. Was this another deception designed to trick them into disobedience?

A few men walked outside hesitantly, unable to look up because their eyes were sensitive to daylight. Barely living, too weak to stay upright, more folded up and died. Mietek made his way slowly outside, trying to stay concealed behind a group of other prisoners. He expected to see the usual Nazi guards. He didn't recognize these green uniforms.

And then a murmur spread through the ranks of the prisoners.

Amerikanisch. Amerykańsi.

Americans.

PART TWO

CHAPTER TWENTY-ONE

Dachau was the only camp my father would talk about. Even then, he didn't say much. He told me how he arrived, a shadow of a man weighing less than ninety pounds. He told me about his state of delirium, about the indifference of others. When he described his barrack, he told me only about the dying priest. As I lay in bed, warm under my lofty down comforter, I pictured my father unable to turn in the tight crate amid dirty straw, hearing only the wheezing priest. I hated imagining the starving men, my father close to death.

I wondered how they went on. Their bodies frail, their minds in a state of foggy delirium, beyond exhaustion. Did they think about the people they lost and loved? I'm sure my father did. His mother. His father. His sister. But he couldn't talk about that. Few could. With his liberation from Dachau, the unthinkable cruelties may have come to an end, but—how could he live past that?

My father wasn't bitter. He believed that the perpetrators of war were of two factions: the soldiers who were forced to serve and follow commands, and those who took a debauched pleasure in dehumanizing Jews, subjecting them to unwarranted tortures. He knew all too well the power of fear. Of course, there was a reason to fear. If you went against the Nazi command, your family could disappear. They could be punished or murdered. But my father still believed in the good in people. He believed in humanity and did what he could to live his father's dream and keep hope alive.

Knowing this helped me cope with what happened to him. I've always been in awe of my father, of the way that he could overcome his adversity, his young life's nightmare, and differentiate good from evil. I'm eternally grateful he passed that belief onto me.

When I told my father that my husband and I were going to Germany on business and planned to tour Dachau in April 2000, he surprised me with maps and materials for our visit. He became animated when talking about the camp and offered suggestions on getting there. I was stunned. I assumed he'd clam up, just like he did when we brought up his family or his life during the war. It would be one year later when I'd fully understand why this one camp, the last one outside of Münich, would be different. It wasn't just the fact of his liberation that made him refer to April 29th as his "other" birthday. It was how he, completely alone, would restart his life—how and with whom.

The Forty-Second Rainbow Division, along with the Forty-Fifth Infantry Division, crossed the Danube River, seized the camp, and freed thirty-two thousand people. Before entering the gates of the Dachau camp, Lieutenant Colonel Felix Sparks, commander of the 45th Infantry Division, spotted a string of about forty railway cars lined up outside the camp. Emaciated human corpses lay haphazardly in the cars, many spilling out onto the ground. Cement structures by the entrance turned out to be coal-fired crematoriums; they too were piled with naked, wasted bodies. Looking over the prison yard, Colonel Sparks saw hundreds of dead inmates lying where they had fallen in the last decomposition. The stench of death was overpowering.

Dante's *Inferno* paled in comparison to the real hell of Dachau.

Standing behind the colonel, Ben Cooper canvassed the grounds inside the Dachau gate. The combat medic with the U.S. Army's 45th Infantry stood in disbelief. "They're skin and bones—they're human beings … some can't even walk they're so weak." He couldn't comprehend the scene in front of him.

The troops were blindsided by the horror. Disease, starvation, conditions like no one had ever seen or could imagine. These demoralized prisoners of war needed medical help. They needed food. They needed a miracle. Mietek reeled. Death hovered at his doorstep. The final transport had starved and dehydrated his body. But they hadn't taken his instinct for survival. His father had not suffered and protected him for all those years just for him to die now, when help was at hand. He had to have hope. Now that the Americans were here, he could believe again. For the first time since leaving the little mountain camp, he could let his guard down.

What should have been a glorious celebration found many survivors too weak to rejoice. Some smiled faintly and those who could waved their arms to show their gratitude. There were no words. A solemn aura engulfed the Dachau concentration camp. Mietek watched and listened as the Americans rounded up the Nazis. The men who had inflicted such pain, who had been the architects of such terror, found themselves facing down the barrel of a gun. Once again, shots rang out. Mietek knew instinctively that the Americans were killing the German guards and he didn't care. There was no mercy here.

CHAPTER TWENTY-TWO

2003

"So the United States Army had arrived to liberate the camp, Martin." Bryan searched for words, flipping his notebook to the next page. "I can't begin to imagine. How did you deal with being a free man?"

"At that time, I was just coming back to the reality of life. I needed time." Dad sipped his afternoon coffee.

I had to catch my breath after hearing these horrific details for the first time in my life. I couldn't contemplate what he had survived. How broken he must have been.

Then he turned to me. "There was no choice; you just had to get by to exist. You don't think about your conditions, because it doesn't help," he responded. "Remember, my daughter, you brought me a little plaque for our beach house: *You Can't Direct the Wind, but You Can Adjust the Sails?"*

I sensed we were all holding our breath. Well, I knew I was. When you love someone so deeply, you live their painful truth.

Then Dad added, "Like today, when we see what goes on in this world, in other countries, the last one was Monrovia. It's becoming a part of what happened (the Holocaust), because it's still happening. That should be a lesson, to have people prevent these things in the future."

"You've got that right, Martin," said Bryan. We never seem to learn." Bryan looked to Ed and me—could Martin continue?

"Dad, are you alright? Can you go on?" asked Ed.

"The war is over." He sighed with a nod. "What happened next was somewhat of a miracle."

Among the first U.S. troops to arrive at dusk were the men of the 3512th Quartermaster Truck Company. Under the command of newly appointed Lieutenant John Withers, the Company had carried supplies to the men on the front lines, administering food and other necessities, but not engaging in combat themselves. Now they were bringing aid to the survivors of Dachau.

The starving Germans watched the army supply trucks roll through the countryside. It was a large shipment, even by American standards. The lieutenant scratched his head, bewildered. Fifty truckloads of powdered milk, bread, canned foods, and other provisions, including massive first aid supplies, arrived.

While his men entered the camp with the much-needed rations, Lieutenant Withers remained outside. Officers were not allowed into the camp until the army had assessed the former prisoners' health status for diseases. The soldiers had never entered a concentration camp before. They had no idea what to expect, no sense of what happened inside the electrified fence. Wheeling in stacked boxes of canned goods, bread, and milk, the first soldier stopped short. Eyes wide, his jaw dropped. He threw out both arms, a reflex reaction to halt his men.

Everyone stopped, a momentary freeze—their senses shut down—they were in shock. Naked, stacked skeletal bodies lay heaped up against the doorway to the barracks. Discarded human corpses thrown haphazardly onto massive piles. It was like a horror movie, but it was real, and the troop could never unsee the barbaric scene. Emaciated men dressed in blue-and-gray-striped garb meandered the grounds in listless circles. Chaos. Too many sick, dying men needed medical attention. Cleanup of rotting bodies and body waste was underway. Diseased former prisoners needed to be isolated, but where? Clothes, blankets, bedding were nonexistent. Sickened at what they saw—shrunken, dying prisoners, and the grim horror of abandoned corpses left exposed among the living—they had to pull themselves together. They had to overcome the vile smells. There would be time to process the horror later. For now they had a job to do, so they hastened to bring supplies into the camp, tripping over each other, wanting to feed the starving survivors.

The 3512th Quartermaster Truck Company was African American, segregated from their white compatriots thanks to the Jim Crow laws. At home, they attended black schools, ate at separate restaurants, and had to use different bathrooms. These men could fight for their country—could lay down their lives for their country—but they were still not afforded the same civil rights as white servicemen. The men of the 3512th Quartermaster Truck Company came mostly from the Deep South of Georgia and Alabama, where they had witnessed the indignities of racial segregation. They had lived it at home, and now they lived it overseas.

The weary soldiers returned to their base late that night. They had no desire to eat. Playing games or watching old movies were staples each evening. Not this night. No one would pick up a horseshoe or set up a screen and folding chairs. No one would gather for an evening beer and share stories from home about crazy cousins or weddings gone bad. There would be none of that. The lieutenant and his men went to bed quietly, awash in disbelief that such a place could exist. They had fallen into a deep hole of sheer darkness and exposed an unutterable hatred of other human beings.

Mietek received his first ration of food. Faint from starvation, his eyes were hungry, but he remembered the priest's warning. He slowly spooned the broth and ate miniscule crumbs of bread, waiting for each morsel to move through his body before attempting another bite. He did the same with water; small sips, very slowly. That evening, several others succumbed to death after eating. Their weak bodies, unable to digest food, surrendered.

Within a few days, Mietek and the other survivors were disinfected and evacuated from Dachau. Climbing onto an army truck, they were driven through the countryside past barren open fields. Bombs had destroyed much of the city of Münich and its surrounding areas. Heaps of piled rubble scattered the roadside. Cows, sheep, dogs, and homeless animals wandered the grassless fields. The ashen landscape was a bleak sea of faded brown.

Sitting amid strangers in the back of the truck, Mietek held onto his cap. He'd been caged in for so long, he didn't mind taking a long ride. He wanted to see the scenery, even the battle-weary remnants of this town. A set of barracks, lined in a row, came into view. This compound stood out against the postwar chaotic landscape.

He thought it appeared orderly. A short distance later, their truck slowed down, driving through a gate entering a former Nazi SS compound (SS Kaserne) in Freiman, outside of Münich. Former military compounds were now referred to as "displaced persons," or "DP" camps. These temporary homes for former inmates of the Nazi concentration camps were established all over Germany, Austria, and Italy. Segregated from the public and Allied troops, survivors were confined to monitor the spread of disease. The Kaserne was clean. The SS had always made sure of that.

Mietek stood in a long line. American soldiers sat behind long tables, ready to assign everyone a bunk. When it was finally his turn, a redheaded soldier asked for his name and country of origin.

"Mieczyslaw Wajgenszperg, Poland," he responded, just like in the camps. He was tired now and wanted to find his bunk and rest. A Polish interpreter walked back and forth behind the tables, explaining English orders.

"You're in barrack number eight, bunk two. The seated man reached down and pulled up a small case. "This is for you." Handing Mietek the beige case, the interpreter continued. "These are your personal items. Take good care of them because we have a shortage of clothes, especially underwear. The redheaded soldier lifted the cover exposing a pair of socks, underwear, and tee shirts. In awe, Mietek accepted his small suitcase. Something of his own after having nothing for so long. Less than nothing, in fact. A precious gift, these simple items were all he had.

Mid-morning, three days later, Mietek slowly walked outside, mindful of his frail body. He still couldn't keep much food down, despite his small portions. His stomach pains had subsided—for now. He needed to breathe fresh air and take in his surroundings, but he felt bitterly the absence of all he had lost. His father was dead. Emil had disappeared. His group of Auschwitz friends were probably dead as well. Mietek felt utterly alone. There had always been a reason to hope when he had family or close friends in the camps. Having that one close person who believed in you made all the difference. Mietek knew his parents' love was the foundation for his survival. His ordinary childhood was filled with extraordinary love—until the Nazis destroyed it. The numbness he had harbored so long was still present. He just couldn't feel anything. But he wanted to.

Looking up at the blue, cloudless sky, Mietek noticed a patch of yellow wildflowers scattered across a hill. He wanted to appreciate nature as his family always had. He remembered quiet evenings at their summer cottage, the sun setting behind towering trees, while the filtering light danced across the lake. That life seemed like forever ago.

Returning to the Kaserne, Mietek looked for his small suitcase. It wasn't under his cot. On his knees, he searched under the cots next to his, he searched everywhere. "Who has it?" he cried out. "Who has my suitcase?" It was gone! He froze, shocked—one small thing and it had been stolen. They had suffered so much together, these people. They had been through the same things. How could they do it? How could anyone steal his only possession? Rage pulsed through his chest.

ENOUGH!

He had been a slave for six years, told what to do, when to sleep, when to eat. Every move was ordered and watched. Still, he was not free. He heard the call for lunch at the mess hall. No more. No more. He wanted to be in charge of his own destiny.

His face tight, he looked up.

Papa ... it's time, I have to set myself free.

He vowed to find another way. Nowhere to go. No money. No one to trust. Mietek lifted his head and peered out the window to the fields beyond the camp.

Rising slowly, he stood and walked out for the last time.

He was done with camp life. Done.

CHAPTER TWENTY-THREE

It wasn't until I became an adult that I grasped the reality of my father's history. Even then, it took years to face the unsettling details of his losses. Slowly, I came to understand the nature of extremism, how human beings could be driven by fear and hatred to abandon not just goodness, but their very humanity. How else could the Nazis and others like them assume license to terrorize and kill other humans?

We talk of anti-Semitism and of Hitler's determination to exterminate the Jews. I hate that word—"exterminate"—and all that it represents. As if the Jews were vermin, pests to be killed off, a contaminant to be eradicated. The truth is, Hitler and his henchmen were determined to *murder* the Jews—all the Jews. He made this clear when he addressed the Reichstag on January 30th, 1939, and called for "the destruction of the Jewish race in Europe." And yet, devastating as Hitler's language is—and the reality it represents—we seldom use the word "racist" to describe the Nazis and their murderous rampage. It seems easier, somehow, to focus on the madman behind the policies rather than the political and social forces that brought him to power. Make no mistake about it: racism was the soil in which Nazi ideology was planted.

The Nazis believed the Aryan race, an ancient Nordic Caucasian race, to be superior. Because they considered the German people to be part of the Nordic race, they considered all others, specifically Slavs (a category which included the Jews), to be inferior. This abhorrent philosophy was based on a theory established by racial theorists who were given voice in the 1920s. Hans F.K. Günther, for example, wrote a book called *Racial Science of the German People* in which he dissected his theory. Jews, he believed, were racially mixed, their origins a blend of Near Eastern, Asian, Nordic, and Negro. It was the theory that made the Jews "a race of second order." And it was the theory that Adolf Hitler heard when he attended one of Günther's lectures in 1932. That's the mindset that ignited the racist flame that murdered six million people.

Imagine then, how these African American soldiers felt when they walked through the camp gates. Bob Bender, a Buchenwald survivor, remembers the "black soldiers of the U.S. Third Army, tall and strong, crying like babies, carrying the emaciated bodies of the liberated prisoners" (Holocaust Chronicle 606). Accustomed to racial intolerance, to being regarded as inferior, the African American soldiers were devastated by what they had seen. Starvation and torture, slow death sentences for people. Innocent people.

Leon Bass of the 183rd Combat Engineer Battalion of the U.S. Third Army saw the bodies of Buchenwald survivors. He wrote, "I came into that camp an angry black soldier. Angry at my country and justifiably so. Angry because they were treating me as though I was not good enough. But [that day] I came to the realization that human suffering is not relegated to me and mine. I now knew that human suffering could touch us all... [What I saw] in Buchenwald was the face of evil … it was racism" (Holocaust Chronicle 606).

Mietek had walked out of the SS Kaserne and hadn't looked back. He tipped his face toward the heavens and let the wind brush his cheeks. A slight chill ushered in impending rain. He breathed in nature's scent, the smell of damp earth ready for planting. He was feeling something—a memory before the war, those wonderful days in Poland when spring summoned its lush greenery, its promise of sprouting flowers and vegetables, its perennial magic. He remembered life.

Everything seemed dreamlike now. Not just the liberation of the camp, but the years that had preceded it. The grueling, horrifying years in which he was debased in a way he never would have thought possible. It meant so much to be able to breathe fresh air, to wear clean clothes. He needed to believe he was in control of his destiny, uncertain as it was. So he was willing to transition one more time, to one more place, if only to get away from camp life. Was it wrong to look for opportunity, to believe in other possibilities? It was these questions—and Mietek's fortitude in even being able to ask them—that differentiated him from those who couldn't look forward, who might never believe it possible to move past the trauma and horrors of war.

Like victims everywhere, Mietek was haunted not just by an endless loop of atrocities, but by his very survival. Yet somehow, he allowed himself to feel a sliver of optimism, a brief glimpse of hope. He would always be troubled by the question of why he lived while so many died. The question of *why* would follow him everywhere. But he had to persevere, to endure. Mietek felt a tremendous responsibility to carry on for those he had lost. He couldn't let them down. He had been given another chance at life and he had to take it. What that life would look like, he had no idea. But he did know one thing. He was determined to carry on the legacy of his family. He owed it to them, to their memory.

Walking slowly, dizzy at times, Mietek's mind focused on what he'd do next. Hunger still wrenched him as his body adjusted to the slow intake of food. He headed toward the forest behind the DP camp, but soon he was ready to rest. Carefully seating himself on a fallen tree, he pulled out a piece of bread and began taking tiny bites. The birds chirruped, as if they were communicating with each other. The sound soothed him, made him feel a little less alone. He got up and followed the meandering trail that became a dirt road ahead. He left the forest and headed south, stopping often. He felt tired, thirsty, and weak. What would he do when it got dark? Where would he stop? His head hurt, his stomach cramped. He was depleted. But he kept walking.

CHAPTER TWENTY-FOUR

In the distance, Mietek spotted a military camp, the same one they'd driven by on the way to the DP camp. A massive stone building, arched at the entrance, appeared to be their headquarters. Wooden buildings lined the right side of the long driveway. Barracks, he assumed. Familiar mounds of rubble sat at the corner of the fenced compound. Walking closer, Mietek could make out the sign near the gate: Flak Kaserne. He felt nervous as he neared the complex of the former German quarter. Thoughts of Nazis prompted a real and visceral fear. Then he heard the soft sound of voices.

Two black soldiers were working outside, washing pots and pans. The men were singing while they worked, their deep round voices carrying gospel tunes beyond their quarters. Mietek had never heard this sort of music before, and he certainly couldn't make out the English words, but it had been a very long time since he had heard heartfelt singing. He flashed to the bands back at Auschwitz. Forced marching tunes to help control the prisoners as they walked to and from the factories. This was different. These were the voices of free men.

Mietek slowed, taking in the music. He wanted to follow the song and to trust his intuition. He was drawn to these tall, muscular men. Human beings who lifted their hearts in song. They were singing in harmony now, one voice rising as the other fell. He felt a glint of hope. Picking up his pace, Mietek reached the Flak Kaserne fence. He raised his arm, waving to get their attention. The two soldiers stopped washing pots. They stopped singing. Mietek couldn't speak English. Moving his hands to show the men that he could work, he pantomimed that he was willing to wash the heavy pots.

Mietek had no way of knowing that he had come upon some of the soldiers who had entered Dachau right after liberation. He had no way of knowing they had been segregated from the white population all their lives, before they entered the military—and after. But the men understood that they were looking at a camp survivor. He was wide-eyed, slight, weighing less than one hundred pounds. And so young. Yet here he was willing to barter work, to pay his way. The soldiers looked at each other. They knew the rule: no association with former prisoners of war. Diseases were running rampant in the camps and U.S. troops didn't know how these survivors would cope on the outside. But they also remembered their first impression of Dachau and felt the boy's pain. How could they forget the stink of rotting flesh and the desperate sunken eyes staring from hollow faces. The men didn't talk about what they saw, even among themselves. Some things were just too horrifying for words. But they understood prejudice. They understood that this boy was damaged and in pain. They knew with the compassion of decent men that the person standing before them needed their help.

Who would they be if they turned him away?

Mietek stood perfectly still, just as he'd done during roll calls. Except this time he made eye contact; this time he didn't want to be invisible. He watched as the two men talked to each other, their hands gesturing in question. Mietek couldn't understand what they were saying, but when they nodded their heads and smiled, he sensed his fate was about to change. They had decided to break the rule and help him. Motioning to Mietek to enter the gate, the soldiers beckoned him to sit, then gave him a glass of water with a buttered biscuit. An unfamiliar emotion flooded Mietek's senses. Jarred by their kindness to care for him, he felt a glimmer of sentiment, one experienced by receiving an act of generosity. The soldiers stared as he slowly sipped water and nibbled on a quarter of the biscuit. Mietek closed his eyes, bowing his head to thank them.

He stood, ready, pointing at the stove. One soldier handed him a small pot, showing him the dishwashing routine. He went straight to his appointed task, working diligently. They wouldn't let him clean the largest pots or lift heavy barrels of food. It felt strange to work for people who were considerate, but he was willing to do these tasks, any tasks, despite his weakened state. Peeling back layers of numbness, he felt some relief. His first day out of the DP camp, he had felt a tinge of spring nostalgia and now, compassion. Too early to hope. He knew better.

The men were compassionate and encouraging. They smiled a lot. Thc tallest soldier went to the kitchen and brought out a bowl filled with steaming soup and packets of crackers. Patting the park bench, he pointed to Mietek to sit down. The soldiers would eat later with the rest of their platoon. Right now, they would keep him company.

They couldn't believe this boy, bright-eyed but weak, had emerged from the ungodly place at Dachau. Watching him dip his crackers in the hearty chicken noodle soup, the soldiers felt a sense of satisfaction. Pointing to the kitchen's back entrance, then to his soup bowl, the men offered him a second helping. But Mietek declined. He had to.

After working in the kitchen for a few hours, the men were eager to feed Mietek again. They offered him supper and encouraged him to sit. They served a small, wurst-like sausage, and he tried to repeat their name for it—"hot dog." Mietek blinked his eyes and nodded to thank them. The men sat with him as they ate. No other soldiers from the troop had come into the kitchen, so their secret was safe. Following cleanup, they checked to see if it was clear outside the back door so Mietek could sneak out. He stood behind this lanky man, waiting for orders. The soldier signaled him through. Waving goodbye, the soldiers hesitated, hoping he would be safe. They locked up and headed to their barracks for the night.

Mietek felt something he hadn't experienced in a very long time: a sense of accomplishment. He had earned his meals and could tell that the Americans were pleased with his work. He had survived that first day on his own. Now he needed to get through the night. But Mietek wasn't afraid. He had lived through six years of cruelty, loss, and the terrible unknown. Every decision meant life or death. Nothing could compare. He let his positive day guide him forward.

Peering through the fence at the world beyond, Mietek realized how safe he felt inside the compound. No, he wouldn't leave. He would sleep here. The crescent moon cast a soft light over the darkened army campgrounds. Mietek looked up at the starlit sky. Alone, for the first time in years, he was free. What did that really mean? He didn't even have a place to lay down, he didn't have a home, and no one gave orders on what to do next. Post-supper stomach cramps plagued him. He was paying for a few bites of his "hot dog," but it was worth it. Exhausted, his body craved sleep.

He just had to figure out a way to make it on his own. Feeling secure here in the army compound was unusual. When was the last time he could let his guard down? He couldn't remember. Looking around the campgrounds, Mietek spotted a wooden picnic table, conveniently situated behind a tree. He walked up to it, then climbed onto the table. Wearing only his shirt, pants, and cap, he curled up, crossing his arms to warm himself. The starry night set a stage, the tree frogs croaked back and forth, as if answering each other. He fell asleep in minutes.

CHAPTER TWENTY-FIVE

Mietek woke up startled. It had been dark when he climbed up on the wooden table, but now, at daybreak, he was able to see where he had slept the night before. Deep green trees surrounded the compound, their foliage contrasting with the dusty gray mounds of rubble. A few loose boards clung to doorways of the army base entrances, but most of the compound remained intact.

He fell asleep alone, but he had company now. The same two soldiers were standing a few feet away, once again taking in the site of this raggedy dressed teenager who seemed to have found his way back. Three other men were with them—cooks as it turned out.

Once again, Mietek took up his pantomime to show that he was ready to work. Once again the men offered him food. They directed him to the latrine first and motioned him to return to eat breakfast. The smell of fried potatoes and eggs cooking on the griddle reminded Mietek of breakfast at home. He loved fried eggs, especially when he dipped his buttered bread into the runny yolks. It had been so long since he'd had such a meal—he was thrilled to accept their invitation. He sat at the table and sensed warmth among these men. It felt good.

"What's your name, boy?" the bushy eye-browed soldier asked. He spoke with a heavy Southern accent, but Mietek understood the name part, and responded in Polish, “Mieczyslaw Wajgenszperg.”

These men were from South Carolina, Alabama, and Georgia, south of the Dixie line. And while they had spent the last few months in Europe, they still found the Slavic names almost impossible to pronounce. There was no point in even trying. The soldiers looked at each other—chuckling a little over the hard sounds of the *z's*, *y's*, and *j's* they had just heard—before turning their attention back to this skin and bones boy. He was barely five feet six, there was only one thing they could call him.

“Your new name is ‘Pee-Wee,’” they said, pointing at him. He raised his eyebrows, gestured to the man who named him, flipping his right hand, palm up in his direction.

“My name is Dave,” he said. “I’m sure glad to meet you, Pee-Wee.”

Mietek pointed at himself and repeated, “Peevee.”

After breakfast, Mietek, now Pee-Wee, repeated his kitchen duties from the day before. He was meticulous about his work. Never allowed to make a mistake—the Nazis had seen to that—he scrubbed, washed and dried the pots, pans, and cooking utensils, lining them neatly on the work counter. He heard the soldiers talking outside, using his new name. Mietek was annoyed with himself for becoming exhausted after only two hours of work. He tried to cover his fatigue, but the man named Dave had come in and made him sit.

Dave noted Pee-Wee’s sallow complexion, his bony body moving carefully. He brought him a mug of coffee, humming a gospel tune—“I’m so hungry, I want me something to eat. I’mmm so hungry, I want me something to eeeat … I’m so thirsty, I want me something to drink.” Cutting potatoes, Dave kept singing, bobbing his head to the rhythm. He wanted to comfort the boy. He thought about his own family back home. His younger brothers and his nephews. Things could be tough for a young black man in Alabama, but this … Dave was unable to comprehend what this kid had lived through. And to be here on his own, apparently with no family or nobody to care for him. It was unthinkable. And yet, here he was. Dave decided to talk to his group.

They set up lunch again in the back of the mess hall, inviting Pee-Wee to sit with them.

"What y'all think?" asked Dave, looking at each of his comrades. "Can't be putting this boy out on the streets." He shook his head. "You see where he slept? Outside. What we gonna do?"

The bushy-eyebrowed soldier named Jim cut in. "God—I want to help him too—but how can we do that? We could get into big trouble here boys!"

"Could he just come by every day to eat … you know, we'll sneak him in and feed him," replied the tallest guy in the group, trying desperately to find a compromise and keep the troop out of trouble.

Suddenly they were quiet. Mietek became concerned. Would they let him work the rest of the day? Was he too weak for them to bother? He couldn't think about that, he'd get back to work and hope it was enough.

Breaking the silence, Dave said out loud what the others were thinking. "We gotta take care of him. He works hard and can't hardly stand. He got no one. The men shook their heads. They understood.

"But what are we gonna do with him when the lieutenant comes back?" asked the other soldier. "We got orders not to mix with them. We can't hire him. It's against the rules."

"Do we have the authority to do any of this?" asked the head cook.

"We'll hide him when the lieutenant or officers come round," said the tall, burly soldier.

Their heads down, the soldiers shook them back and forth.

"He's homeless," Jim said. "Doesn't want to go back to a camp again. He's got no family, nobody to take care of him." He looked up, squinting.

"I'm in," blurted Dave.

Jim sat up. "Me too."

The others caved like dominoes. They would hide Pee-Wee when the officers were close by. They would feed him and get him back on his feet. They would show this kid that people cared. The soldiers of 3512 Company knew all about the sharp edges of racism. They had experienced it all their lives and now they had heard reports of Jews being killed in camps like the one they had marched into just days before. Some said the numbers were in the millions. It was unfathomable. But here in front of them was one boy, one Jewish boy. They could help him. They could make a difference. Their families would be proud of them, they were certain of that. And it was the right thing to do.

That night, they took off their aprons, locked the mess hall, and led Mietek to an empty barracks. Their comrade, Izzy, had suffered chronic gastrointestinal pain and had been honorably discharged to be treated back home in the States. Pee-Wee could stay in Izzy's quarters. Mietek stood at the doorway, stunned. The room was clean and tidy, with a bed, a bureau, and a locker. It had windows. Dave nudged him forward and opened the bureau drawer. Underwear, fatigues, and socks were neatly folded. He pointed to the black leather army boots on the floor, then to Mietek's feet. The soldiers said, "Good night Pee-Wee."

Hand over his heart, he responded, "Gut night."

Mietek slept in a bed with a mattress, clean sheets, and a blanket. He was in his own room, with his own bureau—with drawers. With tee shirts, shorts, fatigues, and leather boots to wear the next day. He was overwhelmed and grateful. Grateful for the compassion of these men, grateful to be clean, and grateful—beyond grateful—to be treated with respect. He had forgotten how that felt. These burly black men didn't even care that he was a Jew.

He woke the next morning, wondering if it had all been a dream.

CHAPTER TWENTY-SIX

Mietek was getting used to the Americans. They were so friendly to him, so kind. He really couldn't believe his good fortune. He worked hard, but this KP duty was nothing compared to what he had endured. Ready to be ripped from wherever he stayed, with no notice, with no belongings, he was reluctant to get comfortable. By this time in his young life, distress was imbedded in his psyche, as was the knowledge that nothing was permanent. Not even family. But he couldn't help himself, it would be wonderful to stay here. Actually, it would be a miracle.

It was on his fourth day with the soldiers when he saw another young survivor approach. Mietek put down the pot he had been scrubbing and moved forward a little in order to see the boy gazing at him through the fence.

"Hello," said the stranger, raising his voice to be heard. Mietek wiped his wet hands on his dish towel, walking toward the chain-link fence. It had only been a few days, but Mietek was happy to hear Polish spoken.

"H—hello."

"I'm Shlomo," the boy said. "Shlomo Joskowicz." His eyes darted to the right, then down to the ground. "I came from the DP camp."

"Ah. I came from there too."

“And now you work here?”

“Well, for the time being. My name is Mietek,” he said, palming his hand on the fence.

Shlomo returned the adapted handshake. Then he came straight to the point. “I don’t want to go back,” he said. “We may not be prisoners anymore…” He searched for his words. “And we may have food and a cot to sleep in … but it’s still a camp. We’re still a segregated group. I’m not even sure they know what to do with us.”

“I know,” Mietek said. “It’s not natural.”

“I want to stay out here,” Shlomo continued. “I want to get away from the crowds.” His eyes met Mietek’s. “Can you help me get work?”

“Do you have family?” It was the only question Mietek could think to ask. In the end, it was the only one that mattered.

“No,” responded Shlomo. “They were all killed in the war.” He said this matter-of-factly, as if it almost didn’t hurt anymore. But Mietek knew better.

The two boys faced each other, sizing each other up. They were used to on-the-spot evaluations. In fact, they had come to depend on them. Mietek hesitated. After the theft of his suitcase he experienced a loss of faith in his fellow survivors. But he couldn’t let that betrayal change who he was. He thought of his father, how he had praised Mietek’s character, especially his kindness toward others. But he also knew the pain that everyone in the camps had experienced. Shlomo had an honest face and looked close to his age. Mietek could read the sadness in his smile. He was taller, lankier than himself. He was also soft spoken, just like him. Had the years of being silenced taken a toll on their youth? They talked a little more. They were both orphaned, both born in Poland. They shared the misery of the concentration camps. Mietek knew they could share this, too.

He raised his finger at Shlomo, signaling him to wait. He was walking steadier now, feeling a bit stronger. Mietek hesitated at the rear kitchen door, finding the right words. Dave winked at him as he stirred the stew kettle. He nodded for him to come in. Servers dashed around the kitchen, yelling to get this and that. The clattering of utensils and dishes being stacked reminded Mietek that it was nearing lunchtime. Another man carried an oversized stainless soup pot to the serving table. Hesitantly, Mietek interrupted. He had become especially trusting of Dave, the man who was there the first day he arrived. He waved to follow him out back. Dave gestured to two of his men to follow.

Mietek approached Shlomo. He pointed to him, again signing with imaginary pots for more work. The soldiers looked at Shlomo—another sweet face, bony, with a distinctive half grin. They had the same reaction to his plight as they had for Pee-Wee. How could they turn him away? Dropping his head, Dave cupped his hands over his eyes, struggling with yet another life decision. He looked up at his men, waiting for their reaction. Jim smirked, the rest nodded their heads in approval. Dave turned to Pee-Wee and the other lad.

"What's your name, boy?"

Just like Mietek, he understood the word—name. "Nazywam sie Shlomo Joskowicz." Dave looked to Jim, both shook their heads, no way. "Here we go again. What's a good name that begins with an S?" asked Dave.

Jim's first impression was biblical. "How about Salomon? We're about to embark on a religious experience here." He smirked. "The only thing missing is the desert."

No one protested. They decided to take another risk. Jim pointed to Shlomo, then to the gate. "Welcome Salomon. Welcome."

CHAPTER TWENTY-SEVEN

Lieutenant John Withers had just returned from leave in London when he was appointed commander of the 3512 Company. At twenty-eight, he was an ambitious, educated man whose first trip out of the country had brought him to Europe, to serve in the U.S. Army.

No matter how much you learn at officer's school, managing an entire troop would be a challenge, he thought. His rank of second lieutenant had placed him in charge of a black unit. Despite the army's singular mission, blacks and whites continued to be segregated in the service.

Born in Greensboro, North Carolina, Lieutenant Withers had fought hard to break through the racist constraints holding him back. He had received his undergraduate degree at North Carolina Agricultural and Technical College, and from there went on to Wisconsin where he graduated with his master's degree. For a long time he had wanted to earn his PhD and begin a new life outside the South. Now, with the passing of the Servicemen's Readjustment Act of 1944—otherwise known as the GI Bill—his dream was coming into focus.

Withers wanted the opportunity that President Roosevelt had provided—college tuition and living expenses for World War II veterans. All he had to do was keep focused, follow orders, and maintain a clean military record.

Pee-Wee and Salomon heard the signal—a crisp, quick whistle. They dropped their potato peelers, wiped their hands, and ran to the mess closet. Wedged tight in the space behind life-sized flour sacks, they stood still. An inspections officer was nearby. Most likely he would be a white officer. The Quartermaster Corps had the advantage of a generous budget. Their transport trucks had to be maintained and reliable. Their mission to supply food, clothes, and supplies was critical during combat. But now, it was critical to manage the needs of their army medical units and an enormous population of former prisoners of war. Inspections to check truck maintenance and management of supplies were routine. The boys held their breaths. They knew when and how to be invisible. An hour later, another whistle signaled they could come out. The inspections officer had moved on to the next camp. Then it was back to work for the two stowaways.

Pee-Wee and Salomon learned their tasks quickly, among them, loading trucks for deliveries to other army compounds. They neatly stacked boxes of army uniforms and boots. Flour and sugar sacks were carefully arranged so as not to tear the burlap bags. They lined the truck with boxes of canned vegetables, fruits, and coffee canisters, separating them by category. Extra tarps were folded and piled up in the back to protect supplies in the rain.

Jim came out to check the delivery status. "I gotta say, this truck was never this clean or orderly. Well done you two." He gave them a quick hand salute.

Pee-Wee and Salomon looked to each other and nodded—job well done. They beamed. The praise felt good. On short deliveries, the men took the boys along. They knew what every box contained and where it was placed in the truck bed. They'd pass the inventory to the men, expediting the process. Pee-Wee and Salomon felt useful and part of the team whenever they were asked to join the drivers.

However, the soldiers knew they would be punished if found to have nonauthorized men working for them. Not wanting to put their troop in jeopardy, they picked their spots carefully. If found out and reported, it could land them in an administrative hearing to determine their fate. The last thing they wanted was an dishonorable discharge.

Jim and two other soldiers from their troop waved to Pee-Wee and Salomon to climb into the truck bed, dropping the panel. They hoisted up to the cab and drove toward their next delivery outside of Münich. They approached an American checkpoint—routine stops to check their papers—and drove through without a hitch. The boys relaxed as the truck continued to their destination. They lay back, hands behind their heads, enjoying the smell of fresh air and the movement of the wheels as the vehicle drove through the countryside. Until, that is, the truck came to an unexpected halt. They heard voices. Official voices. Without hesitation, they unfolded the tarps, curled into the fetal position, and covered every inch of themselves. They were safely hidden when the back panel was whisked open and Jim and the driver climbed on board.

"What's in those boxes, boy?" Asked a man with a deep, round voice.

"Jim turned and sat on the tarp covering the boys, just like a seat. "Those are coffee canisters, and these three are boxes of powdered milk." The other quartermaster did the same, sitting on the adjacent tarp, pointing and identifying their supplies.

The boys didn't flinch. Not a word, breathing shallow to diminish any movement.

"Open up that box." Raised to be extra polite to white folks, Jim automatically responded, "Yes sir." He got up and pulled back the tape on a box of canned fruits.

At last, the throaty voice commanded, "We're done here." Jim and Jake jumped off the truck, pulling down the panel. With one last salute, they climbed in the truck and put it in gear, pulling away from the surprise inspection area.

Out of range, they whistled, sending the clear message to their boys.

"Can you believe it?" said Jake after he stopped sweating. "These boys disappeared, as if in thin air!"

"Ingenious," Jim said. "Just ingenious."

Settling in at his desk, reading the daily camp report, Lieutenant Withers prepared his itinerary. But he was worried. He'd heard a rumor that morning from another officer. The details were scarce, all he knew was that two refugees were being hidden in his complex. He didn't know any more than that. But the rumor was troubling enough. A knock at the door raised him from his thoughts.

"Come in."

Lieutenant Barboza saluted him.

"At ease, Lieutenant," John ordered as he indicated to him to sit. "Thank you for coming on such short notice." He put his pen down. "I'm concerned."

Barboza tensed, arching his back.

"So I hear we have two male refugees hiding on our base. Is this true?" he said taking a deep breath.

Lieutenant Barboza cleared his throat. "Well sir, …"

"A simple yes or no, lieutenant. Is it true?"

"Yes, sir."

Lieutenant Withers stared at him. "Who let them in? Who's responsible for this?"

Barboza folded his hands on his lap, leaning into the lieutenant, making eye contact. "They are two Dachau survivors, sir, staying on base with your men."

"That's against army policy and the men know it!"

Trying to remain steady, Barboza said, "Yes, sir."

John tamped down a flash of anger. He needed loyalty and obedience from the troops under his command. He had to maintain their unit's spotless reputation. There was too much at stake, for all of them. These former prisoners of war were clearly taking advantage of the men and putting them all at risk. He understood that they had lived through desperate conditions, but the survivors were hardened prisoners. Who knew what they were capable of? Who knew what diseases and infestation they were suffering from?

"Why, Sergeant?" John asked abruptly. "Why did the men do this?" He could tell from the sergeant's downcast eyes that he'd been siding with his comrades.

"I believe they care about these two refugees, sir. They would like to keep them."

"What do you mean, 'keep them'? These are desperate men who have lived through God knows what." His eyes widened. "We have the integrity of the unit to think of. The safety of the men … we're here to do a job for heaven's sake! We're not missionaries—we're army soldiers. Do you understand?" Exasperated, he lowered his voice, "We have to think with our heads, not our hearts."

"I understand sir. But if you saw them, you might—"

But before he could finish, Withers interrupted, "They're two white Jewish men amid a black troop!"

Withers knew he had to return them to their DP camps.

"Bring them to my office," he ordered.

Barboza stood, saluted the lieutenant. "Yes sir! I'll have one of my men bring them to you right away."

Sentiment was the last thing the army had room for. Withers knew that he had to lead, to set an example for his men. He had to adhere to rules and regulations. That was what was going through his mind when the refugees arrived at his door. The lieutenant had been signing documents when they arrived. He kept his focus until, task completed, he put down his pen and looked up. His shoulders sank when the boys in front of him offered tentative smiles. This was not going to be easy. Withers had expected men, not these … these kids. They were so very young. Despite all they had been through, something about them suggested hope. They had suffered unimaginable atrocities and yet they could still offer up a smile. There was nothing hardened about either of them. The boys' plight struck a chord of compassion, of shared experience. Withers understood the pain of discrimination.

His men had taken a huge gamble in sheltering these boys. They had let their hearts guide them. Withers understood that. Admired it, even. But he took his role as officer seriously. It was Wither's job to ensure the safety and security of his men, to make sure that those under his command adhered to the military code of conduct. The lieutenant also had to heed the call of his rank to inspire and motivate his men, earn their trust, and bring them together. He felt compelled to keep in mind their unique characters and the nature of their beliefs, their very own moral code. Surely their experiences counted for something. He didn't want to jeopardize everything, but he didn't want to let his men down. And he didn't want to let these boys down.

Mietek's knees quivered as he stood before the commander. For six long years he could take nothing for granted—not the next day, not even his next breath. But everything had changed when he stumbled on the American soldiers. Now he had food, warmth, and companionship. How could he go back to the DP camp where he'd be nothing but a lost face in a crowd of strangers? He felt the pain of his compatriots, but he couldn't bear to be returned to that deep well of human suffering, to stand shoulder to shoulder with men and women whose faces reflected grave sadness and struggled with open wounds. He wanted to be with these newfound friends who sang, who laughed, who supported each other. Men who chose kindness and optimism over prejudice. An optimism unique to a free country. Unique to America. He inhaled and held his breath.

His life hung on this man's goodwill.

Who knows what it was that might tip the scales in favor of these two boys. Withers had always followed the rules, even if, as a black serviceman, the rule book was not written with him in mind. This was in the 1940s, some twenty years before the Civil Rights Act, when few whites could claim friendship with a black man. His family had struggled. His father had to work as the janitor at the high school. His mother was a seamstress, avoiding the usual role of black domestic servant. There were no whites in his neighborhood, nor the streets surrounding it. Not until he got an education. The lieutenant was committed to justice and perhaps, in view of everything he had witnessed, he knew all too well the sting of injustice. Was this a rule worth breaking?

"All right soldier," Lieutenant Withers declared. "We'll keep them!" He surprised himself. "You may return the men to their barracks."

Pee-Wee and Salomon let out a deep breath. They brought their right hands to their forehead and saluted the lieutenant. No words were necessary.

CHAPTER TWENTY-EIGHT

Withers understood the magnitude of the responsibility he had taken on. If he wanted to keep these boys safe, he had to keep them healthy as well. Unfortunately, it was clear to everyone that they were anything but healthy. So he called on his friend, an American army doctor Jacob Friedman. Withers brought Friedman into his confidence, explaining his decision to harbor Pee-Wee and Salomon. The doctor respected Withers' decision. Of course he would do what he could to help.

The rail-thin bodies of his new patients appalled Dr. Friedman. They had been prisoners to a white nationalist regime, starved and tortured just because they were Jews, like he was. Their sores, a reminder of skin worn paper thin, desperate to heal, stood out on their backs and buttocks. He cupped his stethoscope end until it was warm, gently placing it on Pee-Wee's chest, listening to his breathing. Pee-Wee's lungs were clear, a good sign. Salomon was the same. Youth, he thought, thank God they're so young. After looking in their mouths, he pointed at their stomachs. Pee-Wee rocked back and forth, hands over his stomach. Friedman knew immediately what was wrong. Rehabbing from a state of starvation induces nausea, stomach cramps, and vomiting. Salomon pointed to his mouth. No surprise thought Friedman, they couldn't keep many of their meals down. That's why they continued to grow weaker. The lieutenant was concerned that the boys might lose more weight from their already painfully thin frames.

"What have these boys been eating, John?" the doctor asked.

"Same thing as us, pretty much. Pork, beef, sausages, potatoes—hash browns, bacon and eggs for breakfast. The kitchen staff cooks Southern style, just like they did at home in the States. They love to fry everything. In case you haven't noticed, we don't have a short order cook on hand."

"Well, get one. The boys can't eat these rich, fried foods. Their digestive systems are still too weak to handle that," Friedman reported. He dug into his bag and took out a pad of paper and pencil. He sat down and wrote up diet guidelines. "Start with sips of water," he said as he wrote. "And juice, clear chicken or beef broth, crackers, toast. Once the nausea clears, introduce oatmeal, eggs, steamed rice, bananas and other fruits, beans and peas." He glanced at the lieutenant. "Wait on steaks, pork, and sweets." Withers took the paper and tucked it into his shirt pocket.

The cooks felt guilty when they learned that they had been feeding the boys foods dangerous to their health, but how were they to know? After all, everyone in the company had grown up eating fried fish and chicken, pork chops, and fried okra—even the greens were loaded with fatty pieces of ham hock or salt pork. From now on the cooks would prepare a diet of boiled potatoes, vegetables, and lightly sautéed meats. The troop rose to the occasion, watching the boys carefully each time they introduced another food.

The cramping stopped. The nausea dissipated. Pee-Wee and Salomon's' skin color brightened, and their hollow faces started to fill out. And because they could stand for longer periods of time, they worked longer hours in the kitchen where they now were able to lift the immense pots for cleaning. Proving their health, they insisted on proving their worth, too.

The boys may have been adept at hiding themselves when the need arose, nevertheless, the soldiers wanted to make sure they knew how to fit in. That meant learning English. Already they had picked up phrases: *Good morning and evening, how can I help? How are you? Please and thank.* But they seemed to understand far more than they could verbalize. Already speaking a fair amount of German, the boys had a knack for picking up foreign languages.

After lunch, Dave signaled to Pee-Wee and Salomon to follow him outside. Walking out of the mess hall, he pointed at their delivery vehicle. Running his hand down its side he annunciated the word drawing TRUCK on the dusty door, sounding out every letter. They pointed to the wheels. Dave drew WHEELS on the side of the truck, calling each letter out loud. Hungry to learn, the boys gratefully obliged, repeating each word, each letter, asking for more.

"You boys ready to make this truck sparkle?" asked Dave spraying a pretend water hose?

"Yea," they yelled enthusiastically. Working with water hoses outside the kitchen would be fun. Dave got rags and hoses set, showing them the detail for cleaning routines. After two weeks, the boys were slowly growing stronger. After a month, they had a little fat around their middle, typical of starved persons who have access to food. It's the body's way of resetting. Pee-Wee and Salomon gained weight, they gained energy, they gained some confidence.

Dave called out, “Hey y’all, great job on the truck! It’s sparkling. Now get those wheels whistle clean.”

“Yes sir, Dave sir!” the boys yelled back.

Left to right: Salomon, Dave, and Pee-Wee

CHAPTER TWENTY-NINE

Mietek and Pee-Wee weren't the only ones learning new skills. Many of the men in the 3512 Company had only a third-grade education, having dropped out of school to work on family farms. That meant they strained to read and write. The lieutenant helped them prepare letters to their families at home and, in some cases, read the letters that arrived. A patient teacher, he also mentored Pee-Wee and Salomon when he found the time. He tutored them in English until the two Polish boys acquired a Southern slang, laced with a few swear words from the troop. The lieutenant would read to them some evenings around the campfires. Pee-Wee and Salomon had always loved stories, tales from the ancient Greeks, such as Helen of Troy. Pee-Wee especially had loved books by the Russian author Leo Tolstoy. Now they listened to classic stories about Robert Jordan, the American soldier blowing up bridges in the Spanish Civil War, and Ernest Hemingway's *For Whom the Bell Tolls*, which enthralled the boys.

Withers marveled that the youngsters never admitted to illness or weakness. Had he thought about it, he might have considered that their stoicism was a result of their prisoner-of-war experiences, that it was crucial to their survival in the concentration camps. Exhibiting emotions or physical strain—sadness, weakness, illness, disability—would get you beaten, maimed or shot. It was the hardier of the prisoners who got work because they made life easy on the guards.

Pee-Wee and Salomon shared an incredible spirit and a vision for a new and better future. They never complained, nor did they speak to anyone about what had happened to them during the war. Nevertheless, their hearts lay heavy with the burden of their suffering, and they prayed each night to those they had lost. Mietek in particular liked to *talk* with his mother and father, and his dear Klara. "Every day I feel your presence. And every day that feeling motivates me—to build a future. A future in your memory," he would tell them. "I still read to you Klara," and that's when he would choke. "You are not forgotten nor will you ever be. Not as long as I have a breath in my body."

Shoulders back, Mietek checked the mirror over his bureau, adjusting his army cap. The khaki uniform boosted his moral and he never took his clean, pressed fatigues for granted. Clasping the shiny buckle at his waist, he was ready to line up for Reveille. Mietek felt proud. Standing with his comrades, listening to the trumpet call, *saluting the American flag*.

Pee-Wee also cherished the day's transition to "Taps," bugled each evening by a soldier standing next to the American flag as it waved in the breeze. The music stirred him, reminding him of the sharp contrast between the call to respect and the harsh roll calls of his recent past. He listened for the birds' and frogs' melody right after the bugle call. It was the perfect concert to end each day and he choked up every time. That's when he would remember. In his mind, "Taps" was a memorial to his father, his mother, and little sister. He believed it to be a tribute to them.

Most evenings the men sat outside inhaling the aroma of burning wood, captivated by the campfire glow. Everyone joined in singing songs and playing games. Horseshoes was one of their favorites and every time Pee-Wee heard the clack of the horseshoe against the metal pole he burst into a wide grin. No wonder, he was good at it.

"No fair, you didn't win," called Dave from the sidelines. "You stepped over the line, I saw it!" He kept egging him on, then did the same to Salomon.

Later, they'd sit in the barracks and ask about the United States.

"This is my home in Georgia." Dave pointed to the picture of his modest shingled home set on a field. "See over here, that's my three brothers. I miss 'em." The others explained that their houses were simple, some looking like shacks, but if you worked hard in the United States, you had the opportunity to buy a big house. In fact, you could move around the country if things didn't work out. Talking this way, the boys could imagine other possibilities, other futures.

Often on these campfire twilights, the troop would gather and break into song. Mietek loved gospel music. It elevated his spirit and made him believe in something beyond the moment. His body moved with the captivating, throbbing beat when the men sang. It would always remind him of its lure the first day he discovered the army base.

But it was movie nights that Pee-Wee loved most of all. He spent these magical evenings with his eyes glued to the screen while inhaling handfuls of freshly popped popcorn—a new delicacy.

Mietek had never seen an American movie before; he had only heard about them as a young boy. Now here he was, watching the likes of *All Quiet on the Western Front* with a troop of American soldiers. He sat rapt as he watched a young German boy—Paul Bäumer—move from giddy patriotism to the sad realization that he'd been duped by the rousing speeches of his teacher to enlist in World War I. The main character had lived with his parents and sister in a lovely German village. He was happy at school, close with his friends. War changed all that. Pee-Wee couldn't take his eyes off the screen as Paul Bäumer moved from disillusionment to despair shattered by the brutal experience of combat.

Mietek wrestled with feelings of loss the night he saw that movie. The wartime movie triggered the worst: why did he survive? Klara interrupted his dreams. Her innocence, her unconditional love for him. She should be here, writing in her journal, the one his mother bought to pen her fairy tales. He tossed and turned. Sweat beaded on his forehead. *Why? Why?*

Streams of morning sunlight woke him, ending his restless night. Relief. Hard to shake his feelings, hard to put them aside one more time.

One Friday evening, a few weeks after the showing of *All Quiet on the Western Front*, Lieutenant Barboza ordered his favorite western, *Stagecoach*. John Wayne, the Ringo Kid, managed the ever-threatening Apache attacks. Barboza wanted it to start after the men had a chance to unwind and enjoy a few beers. Salomon left for Bamberg. He had met a girl.

Mietek took a walk to decompress. A cool breeze marshaled out the humid day. It felt refreshing. He never took alone time for granted. He could walk freely, he had time to think. It had taken months for him to wake up and see beyond the torturous existence he lived with his father and then alone. To have time to think was a luxury. He stayed within the compound—that was habit—and it was safe.

Hearing the loudspeaker call, "*Stagecoach* in a half hour," he circled back.

"Hello Pee-Wee, come have a seat." It was Lieutenant Withers, having his own solemn moment outside his room. *The Great Gatsby* lay at his feet.

"Thank you, sir." That afternoon, the lieutenant had noticed him working on the supply truck. The engine was making noise, and Pee-Wee found the problem, fixed it, and was wiping grease off his hands.

"Nice job Pee-Wee," the lieutenant complimented him. It made him feel good. It meant the world to have John Withers notice his work and accomplishments. "You look good, kid. Your color is healthy."

"I feel good, thank you, sir." He sat. "How do you like this book?" asked Mietek.

"Someday you should read it. It's a bit about the promise of the American dream. With a twist." He smirked.

"So how hard do you think it would be to get to America?" he asked.

"You're bright and resourceful Pee-Wee, you can figure this out. As far as I know, you would need a sponsor. That might take some time." He carefully considered his next words. "You just turned seventeen. What do you think you'll do when our tour ends? You know, son, that day will come."

Mietek stumbled over his immediate future. "Salomon and I are going to look for a place to live and try to find work, that much I know." He didn't like thinking about it. But he was a realist.

"I'll bet my last dollar that you'll find your way to the U.S. I've watched you this year, working with others, analyzing solutions to just about any problem. Let's just say I'd hire you in a minute. You have abilities far beyond your years. And Pee-Wee, you're a very smart young man."

Gratitude overcame Mietek. John Withers' words ignited a flash of hope. Hope for a future. This reminded him of his own father. If the lieutenant believed in him, he could too.

Then the lieutenant confirmed his conviction. "When you come to the United States Pee-Wee, come visit me."

That night, moved by his friend Dave's description of his home in the States, moved by John Withers' encouragement to live there, Pee-Wee made another decision—he would move to the United States one day. He would make a fresh start; he would begin a new life.

CHAPTER THIRTY

The boys had been with the 3512 Company for several months when the troop moved out, first to Münich on August 10th, then to Würzburg on the 31st. They went to Wildflecken in October and Burramffemburg in December. When the troops relocated, the boys traveled with them, hiding when circumstances dictated.

"Alright boys, time to pack up again," instructed Lieutenant Derry before moving to the next town. "We've got orders for more supply deliveries. Who's in?"

"We are sir!" replied Pee-Wee and Salomon, accenting each word. They took pride in their painstaking packing process. Neatly folding blankets, towels, then bundling extras: toothpaste, soap, shampoos, razors. Once they finished the personal parceling, they'd stack food supplies, compressing boxes so they'd use every inch of the truck beds. Anything to make it easier on their troop. Their soldiers. And the men were grateful for the help. They never had to ask twice. After their convoy rambled to their next destination, Pee-Wee and Salomon were first to retrieve the supplies and set up the rooms.

Withers and the soldiers of the 3512 Quartermaster Truck Company broke the rules for seven months until General Eisenhower lifted the ban, allowing the American military to hire local people.

The order alleviated the heavy burden of secrecy that had weighed on Lieutenant Withers and his troop. Pee-Wee and Salomon didn't have to hide anymore. Diseases that ravaged the bodies of former prisoners of war were now contained. Any typhus, tuberculosis, scarlet fever, and other victim illnesses had been quarantined and in most cases rehabilitated. The DP camps were still figuring out where to send people who couldn't return to their countries. They came from all over Europe, Russia, and Asia. But the postwar threats were under control now. The Americans could hire low-cost labor to help them out. The locals were desperate for work.

In January 1946, the unit was reassigned to the 3511 Quartermaster Truck Company based in the Bavarian city of Bamberg. Having lived among the German people for a year, Pee-Wee noticed that those from the rural areas, most surrounded by farms, were less judgmental, more down to earth than those who lived in the larger cities. It made sense. Country folk hadn't been exposed to the heavy anti-Semitic propaganda that polluted the hearts and minds of those who lived in the cities. People in urban centers such as Berlin, Hamburg, and Münich witnessed firsthand the fear induced by Nazi soldiers. Citizens who failed to report the whereabouts of Jews were severely punished. Anyone associated with Jews disappeared—as did their families—transported to concentration camps or simply shot where they stood. Cities lived through the heaviest Allied bombings and suffered food shortages as well. The Germans feared for their lives, for their homes and families. An individual citizen may not have been anti-Semitic, but the law was.

Pee-Wee and Salomon stayed with the soldiers, their friends. On April 5th, 1946, the company received orders to travel to the nearby town of Staffelstein, Germany, about a hundred miles northwest of Münich. Following common practice after the war, the American unit commandeered the Grüner Baum Inn to set up their camp in this small village. The soldiers had the right to take over German citizens' homes to accommodate their troop. The family could stay but had to give up a great deal of living space, including bordering properties.

A picture-perfect Bavarian home that had been unscathed by wartime bombing, the Grüner Baum Inn was surrounded by farms and fields. Mietek loved it, and not just because he and Salomon had their own rooms in the adjoining guest house. The rural setting near farmland, the rows of corn and beans, the scent of manure, all brought him back to his childhood, his homeland.

The Green Tree Inn (that was the English translation) had a rich history that traced back to 1784. Tall windows draped in velvet curtains brought out the warmth of the mahogany paneled walls. Intricately carved high-back chairs adorned long dining tables. The guest house meals had gained an exceptional reputation in Staffelstein and beyond. The Brütting family had purchased the home a century ago. Grandson Karl Brütting and his wife Gattin Babette took over for his father in 1919. The couple and their three children were decent and honest. Like many of their neighbors in the villages nearby, they kept to themselves and tried to make a living running their own small business. Anything to stay off the Nazi radar.

Relieved to be waking up from the nightmare that was the war, the family was nevertheless fearful of Allied soldiers taking over their beloved home and business. Well aware how Americans felt toward the Germans for their role in this genocide, they worried that the troops would destroy their property and belongings as a way to give them a taste of their own brutality. But Withers and his men treated the owners well, and in return for use of the space, shared their food and supplies. Lieutenant Withers was a man of true class who kept his word—and his soldiers respectful. It was rare to see a black person in this part of the world, but that didn't matter to the Brüttings, who grew fond of the lieutenant and began to trust the men.

Pee-Wee and Salomon came in very helpful. Because they spoke German, the boys could barter for meats and vegetables with village residents. Fresh pork, chicken, or a goose were luxuries, but the boys were adept at dealing fairly to get what their troop wanted. Dressed in army fatigues, they worked alongside the other soldiers, still hosing down the trucks and camp gear and performing KP duty.

One morning, the soldiers noticed that food was missing from the basement storage area. Dave, the cook, asked Pee-Wee to stand guard at night to catch the thief. Pee-Wee, armed with a rifle, sat on a stool in the damp basement. He waited in the dark for hours, dozing on and off. Suddenly, he heard a noise. Someone was breaking in through the half window. Trying to move slowly and quietly, Pee-Wee held his breath. Heart pounding, he aimed his rifle and waited until the moonlight struck the form of a young man.

"Stop or I'll shoot!" he ordered sternly in German.

The man stopped dead, raising his hands in the air.

"What are you doing here?" Pee-Wee demanded.

The young man pleaded, "Don't shoot! Please don't shoot!" He saw by his dress that the man was a farmer. Then Pee-Wee recognized him. He worked in the kitchen for the troop during the day. "My family is starving," he said. "We have little food. I'm sorry."

"Where do you live?" asked Pee-Wee.

"I live in the farmhouse four houses up, on the right."

He thought quickly. "I'll make you a deal," he said. "I'll let you go, but you have to make sure no goods are stolen from here. If any food or supplies go missing, I'll report you." But Pee-Wee understood the farmer's desperation and let him take the potatoes he came for.

It was a fair deal. The young man would keep an eye on the house. Any missing goods were now the farmer's responsibility. Other than that burden, he didn't suffer any punishment. Pee-Wee understood both hunger and fairness.

CHAPTER THIRTY-ONE

Mietek knew well the hurt of loss and leaving. First, his liberty had been taken away. Then his home. His mother and beloved sister came next. Then his father. The last year had been a glorious respite from the terrors that had preceded it. Mietek was safe now. He had friends. New skills. A new language to reflect his new life. But he dreaded the day he'd have to leave his American family behind.

It was the spring of 1946, and Lieutenant Withers was encouraging the boys to explore further afield. Pee-Wee and Salomon ventured as far as Bamberg, the town next to Staffelstein. Salomon, especially, spent a lot of time there. He was falling for Pola, his girlfriend. Pee-Wee was pleased for his friend and tried to follow the lieutenant's "orders" to spread his wings, but more often than not he stayed close to home, spending time with Withers, Dave, Jim, and the others.

He knew he had been fully integrated by the troop the day Jim showed him how to play baseball.

"I think it's about time, little buddy. Here you are bunking with us all and you still don't know how to play our best game. It's downright un-American."

Pee-Wee was thrilled with talk like this. It made him feel like he belonged. And so, with the Bavarian Forest as backdrop, Pee-Wee learned how to swing a bat and run the bases. That's when he really shined. All those years of soccer had made him quick on his feet. "Wow, Pee-Wee," Jim shouted. "You are one fine player. You run like the wind! I wish we had you for our last game."

But the lieutenant wasn't giving up. "Come on, you two," he said. "Find somewhere nice in Bamberg," he told the boys. "I'm getting you a list of places available to rent. You have the right to an apartment based on your past." No further explanation was needed. As refugees and former prisoners of war, Pee-Wee and Salomon had first pick of accommodations. The Germans had to make room. They weren't thrilled about it, but a new reality had spread all over cities and towns in the country, and they had no choice.

Mietek wasn't keen about moving to Bamberg. Home was the Grüner Baum Inn where he had his friends and his routine. Each morning started with a big breakfast, after which he'd perform his assigned chores in the kitchen. Then on alternating days, he would barter with the locals. The farmers would give him chickens and fresh eggs in exchange for army rations of flour and sugar.

Spring had arrived in Staffelstein, and with it, a sense of positivity. Red, white, and purple tulips dotted the front of the inn. Daffodils broke ground, soon to show off their buttery faces. The earth came to life. Farmers were plowing fields again, readying their barns. Merchants opened shops, the butcher hung slabs of beef inside his window. It felt familiar and good. Mietek shared meals with his adopted family, joking and sometimes swearing with them. It was home—his first home in over six years. Leaving here made his stomach turn. Dave, Jim, and the lieutenant would go back to the States. He couldn't imagine starting over without them. And he didn't want to.

Dave pushed harder, wanting to be sure the boys would be settled. "You don't want to hang around these barracks today, do you? There's a music fest in Bamberg, go enjoy it." He waved toward the road. "Of course, you could always stay here and help clean the latrines," he said with a smirk.

Pee-Wee held up his hand in mock protest. "Okay, okay, I'll go. I'll get Salomon. We'll be back when you've emptied your bucket."

The boys found their first apartment at 91 Siechen Strasse in Bamberg. Situated on the second floor over a bakery and bookstore, the three-room apartment was half of the shopkeeper's home. Withers continued to guide them. He gave each boy a watch and promised supplies they could use for barter when they moved out on their own. At seventeen and twenty, having lived in a segregated ghetto, slave labor and concentration camps, a displaced person camp, and an army barracks, Mietek and Shlomo knew the game of bartering well.

Still, it was hard letting go.

The men felt close to the boys, who they'd adopted and nurtured all this time. Pee-Wee and Salomon had renewed spirit, able to imagine a future and forge ahead on their own. They asked Withers about the United States. He felt they needed hope and did not want to discourage them, so he spoke little of the prejudice that would confront him and his men when they returned.

"You'll be fine if you get to the States, one day," he remarked.

"One day," said Pee-Wee.

Mietek packed his canvas bag, neatly folding his tee-shirts, underwear, and socks. Spreading out his Army pants, belts and shirts, he counted them. Five pants, seven shirts, two jackets. Two pair of boots, two pair of leather shoes. It was more than he needed. Removing his cap, he sat down in his wooden chair, staring at his lined-up clothes. A second sack, stuffed with blankets, sheets and towels laid on its side, too full to stand upright.

Mietek thought back to his second month with the troop. They had left a nice barrack after orders sent their troop to a war-torn building. That's when he and Salomon knew the troop wouldn't leave them behind. It was the first time they didn't fear change. Most of the windows had been shattered, and the rainy night was damp and cold. Jim had come to his and Salomon's space—it wasn't quite a room—bringing extra blankets.

"Do you have enough?" he had asked them. "Are you warm enough?" And that's how their friends took care of them, over and over again.

Running his hands through his hair, Mietek felt gratitude, the kind that makes you want to help the world. He promised himself he would help others who needed it the most. He would do that.

Back at the inn, John Withers had asked his cooks to prepare a special supper, the boys' favorite. The kitchen was filled with the aroma of sautéed onions and gravy. Bratwurst slapped and sizzled in the cast-iron pans. One of the kitchen hands filled ceramic steins with dark beer, tipping them to get the foam just right, capping them with their pewter lids. One of the ornate steins depicted a man in brown leather lederhosen donning a feathered cap, dancing arm in arm with his *Fräulein*. Dressed in a red and blue dirndl and white blouse with puffy sleeves, she was reminiscent of a bar maid at a local pub. A work of art for a special night. Twenty-two of the men who had taken charge of the boys would eat together at a dining table, with all the fixings. Mounds of fried potatoes, bratwursts laid over sauerkraut, and baskets of oversized dinner rolls were kept in the warming drawer of the stove.

The lieutenant walked the kitchen and dining room checking that everything was in order. John was anxious. He knew he had to give Pee-Wee and Salomon the news. He'd received orders that his troop had to vacate the Grüner Baum Inn. This would be the boys' last night. They knew the day was coming, but everyone had held their breath in hopes of extending their stay.

A brass candelabra graced the center of the long dining table. John struck a match to light the five candles. The inn's owner had taken it out of storage and offered it for the occasion. John was pleased that he had such good relations with the owner and his family. He was proud that they'd built trust together.

Mietek ran a comb through his hair, wetting it to brush to the side. He tucked in his army-issued khaki dress shirt and straightened his collar. He picked up Shlomo in the next room. Stopping short before leaving for the inn, they made eye contact. They looked handsome in their uniforms. Shlomo pressed his lips together. Mietek nodded and took a deep breath. They were clean, well dressed, and healthy. They'd never take that for granted.

Pee-Wee and Salomon stopped abruptly when they entered the inn and saw that the dining table was surrounded by their friends. Candles flickered on the table, just like home. The soldiers pushed back their chairs and stood. They saluted the boys, holding their right hands at attention, a bit longer than usual. Pee-Wee and Salomon stood speechless. Their eyes filled up, but they fought their emotions. This was in their honor. How could that be?

Lieutenant Withers motioned the men to sit. "Welcome Pee-Wee and Salomon. Now if you boys don't mind, please come and sit next to me." Heads down, the boys did as he asked. They weren't used to being the center of attention.

The lieutenant nodded to the cook—dinner could be served.

Eyes wide, Pee-Wee and Salomon continued to look surprised. "Thank you," they said in unison to their lieutenant, and then to the men. "Thank you."

"I know you're ravenous. God knows you all have gigantic appetites," Withers said. He nodded to his first lieutenant Barboza, folding his hands.

"Bless this food, dear lord, we thank you for your bounty," began Barboza. "And bless these men who have sacrificed their livelihoods to bring closure to this ugly war. And lord, we ask you to look out for our little brothers, Pee-Wee and Salomon . . . thank you for all our blessings."

"Amen," Withers said. He picked up his stein, waiting for the others to do the same. "To your futures boys," he looked left and right, looking them in the eye. "You've taught us a great deal. About overcoming adversity, and about loving and cherishing family, to never lose sight of what you have. And we're honored to have become a family here. *Prost!*"

The men resounded the toast, cheering, whistling, stamping their feet for their young friends.

"Let's eat!" stated Lieutenant Withers.

"Hey, you gonna share those rolls or hog them all for yourself?" joked Dave seated next to Pee-Wee. "You're looking mighty spiffy tonight," he added, grasping the basket of rolls.

Jim sat across from Dave next to Salomon. Mietek loved these men. He loved the lieutenant, who he thought of as *his* lieutenant. These soldiers had gone over and above to keep them warm, fed, and nurtured. They hugged the boys. Patted them on the back. And every day helped them to become more confident. The men understood the intense, humiliating victimization that Pee-Wee and Salomon endured for years. These soldiers gave Mietek hope. Hope he could work toward a future, and hope he may get to the United States one day, because these people, Americans, were the most kind, most genuine.

Stories about their past year and a half had the men laughing.

"Remember when we had to hide you two and the officer came onto the truck, poking around?" said Jim. "We had to saunter to the back of the truck and sit on you boys, like sofa cushions." He couldn't catch his breath laughing. "And we were all scared to death. Can you imagine if we got caught? Real hard to find two white bony faces in our crowd."

"And remember the look on that German farmer's face when Pee-Wee walked over to him with a rifle slung on his back?" Jim sat up. "He thought you were gonna shoot him—you just wanted fresh chickens and ham! And you see his face when Pee-Wee handed him powdered milk and sugar? Your German is so good!"

Trays of assorted liquor chocolates, brownies, and nuts were brought out. The chef stood at the dining entrance and carried in a traditional German Black Forest cake. Whipped cream with chocolate shavings and cherries topped the dark layered masterpiece. The smell of brewed coffee wafted through the air.

Mietek breathed. It was a feast, the first he could recall since the New Year's Eve party at the Laks' home in Wierzbnik. Everything was perfect that night, as it was tonight. Family, friends, food, and a closeness like no other. A feeling of belonging, that he mattered, that he was loved. For just an instant, Mietek felt the goodness of that New Year's Eve, not the losses. Because tonight, he was with family.

The ringing of glass suspended his thoughts. Lieutenant Withers tapped on a glass with his knife.

"I'm sorry to interrupt the festivities," he began, "but I have an important message for all of you." He searched for the right words because he was a kind leader, one who led by example, never needing to raise his voice, always praising jobs well done.

Mietek knew that he was drawn to John for the obvious: it was John and his men who saved him. But it was uncanny how John was like his own father who also led by example, and it didn't take lectures to understand what was expected. Two men he admired, the second one he grew to cherish too.

Withers held up his head. "I received orders last evening that we're heading out, leaving the compounds of the Grüner Baum Inn. This will be our last night to dine together. We need to finish packing and load our trucks so that we can leave in the morning, the day after tomorrow." He hesitated, looking around. "I know this doesn't come as a shock to you, but we have a real date. Tomorrow … well, tomorrow it's goodbye."

Mietek reached under his chair. The time had come. The time he dreaded most. But he was prepared. He stood, waiting for the men to quiet. During one of his trips to Bamberg, he paid to have a picture taken of him which he mounted in a red leather album. He thought it would be the right gift for the lieutenant. How could he thank him for the past year? How would he remember him after he left to go home? He pulled out the album. "Thank you, Lieutenant Withers. Thank you for taking a risk on me and my friend Salomon.

We wouldn't be the same today without your help and support." He handed the album to John.

John flipped open the cover, peering at a picture postcard of Mietek in uniform. He read out loud, "To my friend, Lieutenant John Withers." He signed his full name, Mieczyslaw Wajgenszperg. John pushed back his chair and leaned over to embrace Mietek.

There was great reassurance in doing the right thing for the right reason.

John taught the boys much. And he had learned from them, too. He watched amazed as the boys recovered from the deep trauma of the war. They hadn't become bitter or dark. They didn't take things out on others. They had suffered the ugliness of oppression. Hatred, bigotry, and racism are always ugly. Somehow, though, the boys knew instinctively that the only thing they could control was how they responded to it, how they reacted. They brought light to darkness. And these boys, almost like sons, taught him how to move forward and keep a positive viewpoint.

"Thank you, Pee-Wee. Who'd have thought you would come along and change my own sorry perspective on life. Quite the kid," he cajoled. "You taught me how to put the worst atrocities behind me and remain a kind and decent human being. For that, I thank you." Then he whispered in Pee-Wee's ear, "I'll cherish this album, always."

The men cheered again, clapping. Lieutenant Barboza, Dave, and Jim stood up, walking toward the lieutenant.

"We have a little something for you to remember us by," began first lieutenant Barboza. He gestured for Pee-Wee and Salomon to stand. Dave and Jim brought out two identical albums they had held behind their backs. The rustic orange leather albums were secured by a leather closing strap. The men handed them to Pee-Wee and Salomon.

Mietek opened his album. He had to catch his breath. Their pictures were mounted on black cardboard pages separated by onion skin paper. In full uniform, the lieutenant's photo was affixed inside the cover. Then there was one of him and Salomon standing in front of the kitchen, Dave smiling inside the window. And Lieutenant Derry, Barboza. He palmed his hand on the table, holding in emotion. The photos had been taken over the past year. Withers wrote his mother's address in Greensboro, North Carolina, on the back of his photo. This would become their most precious possession. He promised himself he would keep the leather album with him forever.

Pee-Wee and John, circa 1946

One of the men drove them to Bamberg in a jeep. Handing them their suitcases, he pulled out two large burlap bags. "We felt these provisions would help you out," he offered. "Cigarettes, nylons and other stuff—they're pretty hard to come by here."

They placed the bags on the ground and saluted their friend. Holding back tears, they watched as the jeep drove out of sight.

Mietek wanted to block it out, like he had done with past separations, but he knew that these people were too important. This was a new stage of his new life. He and Salomon were ready to move on; they had to, it was time.

In December 1946, Lieutenant Withers and his men returned to the United States. Everyone had a piece of their time together locked deep inside their hearts. They had all learned life lessons from each other. None of them would forget.

"Taps"

Day is done, gone the sun
From the lakes, from the hills, from the sky
All is well, safely rest
God is nigh.

Fading light, dims the sight
And a star gems the sky, gleaming bright
From afar, drawing near
Falls the night.

Thanks and praise for our days
'Neath the sun, 'neath the stars, 'neath the sky
As we go, this we know
God is nigh.

PART THREE

CHAPTER THIRTY-TWO

Bamberg is one of those medieval towns often described as being *nestled among rolling hills*. There are seven hills, in fact, and each is home to an historic cathedral, some of which are over a thousand years old. Eleven bells toll in one of the cathedrals, all at the same time. Red tile roofs, steel gray domes, and majestic church spires form the tapestry of this storybook Bavarian town.

Today it's listed as a UNESCO World Heritage site, but at the time my father lived there, it was still reeling from the effects of war. Bamberg may have escaped Allied bombing—which is why, miraculously, the medieval bones of the city are intact—but a great many buildings were damaged when the Americans stormed the town with their tanks.

It was April 1946 when my father arrived. He felt at home along the old cobblestone streets and the charming half-timbered houses that lined them. The butcher, the baker, and the general store all felt familiar to him; the aroma of freshly baked bread brought to life cherished memories.

This is the story I grew up on. I know it well. Bamberg was my father's stepping stone to his new life and he loved to talk of his time there. He spoke about his friend Shlomo and their shared apartment, how they'd go out evenings and meet up with their friends, a mixture of townsfolk and refugees, like themselves. Then Shlomo got engaged. I always liked it when my dad got to that part. I imagined Shlomo getting down on one knee and asking Pola to marry him. He likely wouldn't have a ring to offer her, but in my young mind that was the most romantic part of the story: two young people finding each other after the hardship of war, promising to build a new life together. My father liked Pola, he thought she was warm and unassuming, and the three of them would get together at the end of the day and enjoy local brewed Rauch beer at the pub.

My dad had a deep empathy with people, an innate understanding of their character. "Judge by a person's character," he would say. "Not by their color or wealth, but by how they treat people." The words "of good character" were repeated often when I began dating as a teen. And so I learned that we, all of us, belong to one race, the human race.

Shops came back to life along the narrow cobblestone streets. Red geraniums layered with streaming vines draped over the window boxes. Mietek and Shlomo were adjusting to their rented room. They tried to make it home, and each morning the friends took turns going downstairs to the bakery, buying fresh croissants or almond pastries for breakfast. Evenings started in a smoke-filled pub near the old town hall, the Rathaus. Flanked by two stone bridges, the Regnitz River flowed through the underpass, which is why it was dubbed Little Venice. The views were striking. Mietek and Shlomo would hang at the arched bridge, listening to the water before entering the pub. The red-cheeked *Fräulein* automatically brought beers to their table. Many evenings, the friends ended up in an arm-wrestling match.

Shlomo's Pola came every other day to cook homemade dinners. After two months, they wanted a bigger place, an extra room to accommodate a dining area and make it feel more like home. After a few months in their neighborhood, they found a larger apartment, moving in with their clothes and their only furniture: a table and chairs they purchased with their own money. Both had saved their earnings from time spent with their troop. Their new place at 23 König Strasse was more welcoming, more comfortable. A fireplace adorned by an intricate mantel centered the main living room, and it was there they placed their table and chairs. Pola planted geraniums in their window boxes, and every week she would arrange wildflowers in a vase. The boys enjoyed these small feminine touches.

"Mietek, it's your turn to go to the market tomorrow," she said. "I'll need wine, vinegar, and onions to marinate the meat for sauerbraten and spätzle night." The young men were beyond happy. Homemade dinners were still a luxury.

As Polish-born Jews and orphaned Holocaust survivors, the boys had a lot in common. Nevertheless, by some inferred agreement, they kept quiet about their shared history. They respected the terrors and hardship of the past but didn't open up with each other. They didn't open up with anyone, in fact. Like many survivors, they worked hard to keep their memories locked away, to keep the ghosts of the past at bay. They weren't always successful.

Both boys were jobless. Germany was in bad shape. Everything—jobs, food, and housing—was scarce. Luckily for

Mietek and Shlomo, the locals coveted cigarettes, chocolate, and nylon stockings, of which they had a generous supply. These goods were their nest egg, their means to live independently until they found steady work. The boys hadn't seen their American friends in months, but each time they traded stockings for cheese or exchanged cigarettes for milk, they gave a silent smile and a little nod to the men of Troop 3511, fondly remembered as Company 3512.

In January 1947, Mietek got a break. Through his friend Hans Urleins he found a job working as an auto mechanic at his father's garage on Mittel Strasse, number two. Mietek had operated cranes, repaired machine parts, and worked with great precision under the Nazis. This experience—not to mention his perceptive, analytic mind—was of great use in the Urleins' family motor shop. They valued his problem-solving skills and honest character. They'd watched him in the shop and knew him to be a young man with a keen intelligence.

Mietek's work ethic stood out. His early roll calls followed by twelve-hour workdays were ingrained in his cells. This was good honest employment. Fair wages for a day's work. This was easy.

CHAPTER THIRTY-THREE

The middle child of five children, Margareta Rothlauf—Gretel for short—left her home at nineteen to study nursing in Bamberg where her family had arranged for her to live with her uncle. By 1944, she had graduated as a Red Cross nurse. The war was still pounding Europe and Hitler's army commanded her to leave Bamberg to tend to the German troops. Not wanting to serve in a war she didn't believe in, she *accidently* cut her hand and *allowed* it to infect. She was deemed ineligible to serve and returned to her home in Rattelsdorf.

The war had been hard on everyone. Fear dominated the lives of ordinary Germans. Gretel's younger brother, Hugo, had been forced to serve. He returned malnourished and barely alive. Her father had flashbacks to World War I and suffered chronic chest pain, a result of an injury he suffered during his service. Nevertheless, the Rothlaufs were more fortunate than many of their city peers because they owned a farm. Despite government pilfering of their meat, eggs, milk, and livestock, the family had managed to hide enough food to keep themselves from starving.

Gretel knew that the world was angry at Germany. At all Germans. She hated the war and the government that had imposed suffering on her family and her country, along with most of Europe.

Indeed, most of the world. She believed Hitler's regime had stained their beloved culture and traditions. A strong-willed child, she was always outspoken, but this time, her mother told her to keep her feelings to herself. It was dangerous to oppose the government.

Now twenty-one, Gretel was milking the cows on her family's farm for what she hoped would be the last time. She carried the milking stool to the corner, then walked out the barn door, heading for her house. Hurrying through the front door, she skipped every other wooden step, bounding up to the second floor of their farmhouse. She had a new life in mind. A new beginning.

Gretel had recently broken off her relationship with her fiancé, Rudolph. She was having second thoughts about becoming a farmer's wife, and when she'd learned Rudolph had impregnated another woman but still wanted her to marry, she saw her way out. "Absolutely not," she told him. "I'm going back to Bamberg to continue my studies. I've had enough of Rattelsdorf—and enough of you."

Adventuresome at heart, Gretel yearned to be free of village life with its oppressive religion and stifling routine. Her family attended church daily and twice on Sunday. Rattelsdorf's Catholic church was the center of their community and indeed their lives. But Gretel had made up her mind; she was leaving it all behind. Her uncle was happy to have her move back. Sophie, her best friend from Rattelsdorf, had also found work in Bamberg, and was only too happy to welcome her friend.

"I'm so happy to see you, Gretel. I missed you!" Sophie gave her friend a warm hug. "How are you doing?"

"Better, thank you."

Sophie hesitated before prodding further. "Do you think of Rudolph anymore? Still glad you left him?"

“Absolutely,” Gretel said. “I’ve left the past in the past, where it belongs.”

“He still wants you back, you know.”

“It’s over,” Gretel said. “Let’s not talk about him anymore … please.”

“All right, all right.” Sophie swung back around. “You won’t believe what I’ve decided—I’m going to run my own confectionery store once I save enough money. I think I’m pretty good at it.” She swayed her head side to side. “I love creating chocolate designs.”

She put her arm around Sophie’s shoulder, squeezing it. “That’s a great idea,” said Gretel. If it made Sophie happy to stay in town, she wanted to be supportive.

They arrived at the *bierstube* and found their friends sitting along the usual long pine table. Wood beams framed the pub and barrels lined the wall. Bamberg’s coat of arms, a knight in silver armor, hung over a thick wooden mantel. Gretel noticed two young men she’d never seen before sitting with her friends. She was always open to newcomers, to breaking out of the small-village mindset where everybody knew each other.

Sophie ordered them mugs of *rauchbier*, dark beer brewed in Bamberg, then the girls sat down next to their friend Hans.

“Ah, guten Abend Fräuleins,” he said. “I don’t think you know Mietek and Shlomo. Mietek works for my father at the garage. He’s one of the finest mechanics we have.”

Mietek’s deep brown eyes instantly captivated her.

“Hello,” she said. Hoping she wasn’t blushing, she made it a point to talk with him, flirting all the while.

Mietek thought Gretel was striking. Her long brown hair was swept back from her face with tortoise combs, allowing it to fall to her shoulders in waves. The style accentuated her prominent cheekbones, fair skin, and hazel eyes. Mietek appreciated her warmth and friendliness. And she was pretty. Until now, he had been so focused on establishing himself that he hadn't taken time to notice women, much less enjoy their company. But Gretel stood out.

The two new friends spent the evening getting to know each other. Talking about their friends, work, and the realities of postwar recovery.

As they left the pub, Gretel pulled Sophie aside. Pointing at Mietek, "See that fellow?" she said. "That's the kind of man I'm going to marry."

CHAPTER THIRTY-FOUR

For Mietek and Gretel, two young people who had lived through the horrors and privations of war, a pleasant night at the pub seemed like an elaborate luxury. No guards or guns, no bombs or air raids. Of course, reminders of the conflict were everywhere—rations, burnt husks of buildings, the specter of the missing and dead—but things were different now. A day was something to be lived, not endured.

Smells of stale beer and musty wood from overflowing beer mugs made the pub feel cozy somehow. Rounds of laughter rolled through the room, roaring louder as the evening wore on. No one felt alone here. Mietek and Gretel stayed long after the others had left. Mietek was attracted to Gretel's honesty and her beauty. But she was more than just a pretty girl. There was a depth to her eyes, a deliberateness to her walk. Her lilting German sounded like she was reading from a page of literature. She pronounced his name with a long e, *Meetek*.

Gretel was passionate about her nursing career. And she loved adventure. Mietek listened closely as she told him about a bike race she had when she was thirteen. Careening down a hill ahead of an older boy, her bike hit a rock, throwing her high into the air, rendering her unconscious. Her nose was bloody and broken and her family was worried about the extent of her injuries. It took weeks for her to heal, but she was strong.

Mietek liked this girl who didn't settle. He liked that she wanted more out of life and wasn't afraid to go after it.

For her part, Gretel was enamored with Mietek's drive and intelligence. She gravitated toward his quiet competence. Soft spoken and considerate, he didn't need to raise his voice to get his point across. He figured things out quickly. He treated everyone with respect and knew how to get along with difficult personalities. Something about Mietek's demeanor cast a welcome net and made people feel comfortable. He was just that kind of man.

Gretel had listened intently when Mietek told her that Shlomo had asked Pola to marry him. "When they were first getting together, I told him to spend more time with her at our place. You know, I'd make myself disappear more often." He hesitated, trying to figure out how much to tell this girl. "He needed to be sure this is the woman for him … and not just because she's a survivor, a Jew like him."

Gretel thought that Mietek was practical and compassionate—a good friend to Shlomo. But the discussion brought up her own angst. She hadn't told her parents about this boy. He was a Jew and she was Catholic. It just couldn't work out. Too many obstacles.

That weekend, Mietek visited Gretel at her uncle's house. Making himself useful, Mietek hung pictures and adjusted a couple of doors that wouldn't fully close. He could see that Gretel's uncle suffered from limited mobility due to his arthritis, so he stepped in to help without being asked. Two of the burners on the stove wouldn't work. He fixed those too.

When she asked if he thought she was selfish for wanting to move away, to travel and see the world, Mietek responded honestly.

"You have no idea what life will bring your way," he told her in his polished German.

"But no one in my family has ever left," she said.

"Go with your instincts. They're good. Happiness won't find you, you must go after your own dreams."

Mietek just knew what to say. He didn't question himself, like she did. His deep brown eyes, wavy hair, and handsome face drew her in. He was smart. He did math in his head. They were figuring out how to lay a carpet piece at her uncle's and Mietek called out square feet and dimensions in a second.

The couple met up most evenings at the pub when Gretel decided to show off her cooking talents. She got her uncle's approval to make dinner for Mietek one Friday night—the night her uncle played cards at his neighbor's. She planned to make a recipe that had been in her family for generations: *Bayrischer Gulasch*—German Goulash stew. She lifted her woven net shopping bag off the hallway hook and headed up the street.

"Guten morgen," she greeted the butcher.

"Grüss Gott," he replied.

"I need your best beef for my goulash dish. What do you have today?"

The stout butcher winked and went to the back room. Cradling rich red cubed beef in paper, he lifted it to show her. *"Nur für dich, Gretel."* Just for you, Gretel.

"Danke. Perfekt!"

He wrapped it up. She paid, grateful he charged her a lower price than he should have. After stopping at the bakery for a loaf of seeded rye bread, she picked up an assortment of liquor chocolates from the *Scholkoladenhaus*, a specialty candy store. Then she rushed home to clean. She wanted tonight to be special. What might life look like if they lived together. She shook her head, not wanting to think about it, reminding herself she was in fairytale land. Gretel set the table with crystal glasses and lit a candle. She pounded the beef cubes with a mallet to tenderize them. She pan fried the flour-dusted beef and added onions to the searing pot. Cooking the potatoes, carrots, and herbs filled the house with an enticing aroma. She took off her apron and changed into her beige embroidered blouse. After gliding on red lipstick, she pressed her lips together. Then she removed her hairpins, letting her hair fall to her shoulders. Stepping into her black skirt, she felt at home—at home expecting Mietek.

Mietek arrived promptly at seven. He had changed into his best starched shirt and dress pants. He kissed Gretel on the cheek and presented her with a bouquet of pink roses. Overtaken by the kitchen aroma, he shut his eyes for a moment. The familiar onion and potato smell brought him back in time to his last birthday at home with his family.

Gretel took the flowers and pointed to the beer stein on the dining table.

"Danke, Mietek," she beamed, placing the roses in a vase between two burning candles. "I love them." She raised her beer glass, and toasted, *"Zum Wohl."* To your health.

Mietek's eyes shone. It felt good to see Gretel happy. He got up, stein in hand, and wandered round the room. "Have you read any of these?" he questioned, referring to the books on her uncle's shelf.

"When I can between my studies." She got up next to him. He rested his hand on her shoulder. "I read that one." She pointed to Franz Kafka's *Die Verwandlung, The Metamorphosis*. "It was eerie. The main character, Grega, wakes up one morning and he's transformed into a huge bug. He's got to figure out how to cope." Gretel grinned.

Mietek was intrigued. "Do you think your uncle would let me borrow the book? Sounds interesting, I can almost relate…" He trailed off, realizing he was making a personal comparison to this bizarre plot.

"I've got to tend to dinner, Mietek. Make yourself at home." He continued to look over the other books, realizing how little he had read in the past few years. Gretel's call to dinner interrupted his thoughts. Grateful, he sat at the head of the table. She heaped tender brown meat and sauce with potatoes and carrots in his dish. He scraped the bowl clean, soaking up the last of the sauce with his bread.

The beer flowed. The conversation was effortless.

"I loved the dinner, Gretel." Mietek patted his stomach. "You're an amazing cook." He reached over, cupping her hand in his.

Gretel didn't budge. She loved the feel of his hand on hers. It was getting hard, not opening herself to him. Her last relationship didn't work out and she didn't like feeling vulnerable.

"You haven't told me much about your parents," Mietek said.

"What can I say? They own a farm with acres of land in Rattelsdorf. They raised all five of us to work with them, to learn how to manage the animals and the land. To their credit, they encouraged us to get an education—or a trade." She stopped short. While going to church every single day, she thought. She felt uncomfortable at the intrusion of religion, but now was not the time to have this discussion.

Gretel cleared the table and put out the tray of decadent chocolates. She poured two shot glasses of Jägermeister. The two of them moved to the living room sofa. Cheeks rosy, Gretel giggled and nestled closer to Mietek. He put his arm around her, feeling his inhibitions melt. He was unaccustomed to letting his guard down, but the softness of this young woman next to him was overwhelming. The sweet smell of her hair. Their eyes met and he kissed her. She kissed him back. He wanted her, she wanted more, but they stopped themselves. With a closeness neither had felt in a long time, they relaxed in each other's arms.

Gretel tenderly brushed his forearm where he had folded back his shirtsleeve. That's when she saw a trace of a tattoo. Gently, she pushed up his sleeve to reveal his number: A-19104. He didn't stop her. Tears rolled down her cheeks. She had learned some things about the camps after the war and knew that Auschwitz was the only camp that tattooed their tortured prisoners. How could this have happened? Such hate, such savagery? How could their crazed government destroy lives, destroy Mietek's?

"Can you tell me about this?" she asked.

"I lost my father there," he said, feeling unusually at ease. "He saved me to that point."

Gretel whispered, "And your mother?"

"They boarded her and my sister—" he couldn't say her name, "—on a train … to the Treblinka camp, where they … died." He hadn't uttered those words out loud in years.

Gretel allowed the moment to pass. She was shaken. She couldn't imagine the depth of his loss. To lose your entire family like this. How could you go on? Struck by his emotional and physical endurance, she yearned to ease the burden of his pain. She didn't know how. All she knew was that she wanted to take care of this beautiful, wounded man.

They became inseparable. Gretel helped him search for his family, utilizing the Münich Central Agency and the American and International Red Cross. Her work at the Red Cross, a tracing center for survivors looking for missing relatives after the war, was a tremendous resource. Gretel reviewed reams of paperwork, looking for the name Wajgenszperg. Finally, a name stood out. She brought Mietek to the Red Cross center and verified that the misspelled name was that of his uncle Henry who was living in the German city of Gauting, outside Münich. Henry was now a soldier with the British forces. Overcome with excitement, Mietek got permission to use the auto repair shop's phone. "How could this be?" Mietek's uncle said, shaken. He couldn't believe it was his nephew on the other line. "You must come to visit. This weekend. Come by train," he said. "It's just a half hour ride. I'll pick you up at the Gauting station."

The double shrill of the train's whistle signaled his arrival. Mietek stared out the window, trying to catch a glimpse of his uncle through the steam. He grabbed the bag with a box of chocolates and stepped off the train. A tall man with glasses, a derby hat, and a brown overcoat stood, hands in pockets, waiting. Mietek recognized his uncle, but Henry didn't recognize the twenty-year-old Mietek right away.

"Uncle Henry," Mietek exclaimed, flashing a broad smile.

"Mietek," he opened his arms, "I can't believe it's you!" They embraced, long and hard, as if they could rewind time.

"You look just like your father," Henry said sadly.

Mietek didn't know what to say to that.

"Let's get you home so we can talk," Henry walked ahead to his car.

"Are you in good health, Mietek?" he asked as he pulled away from the station.

Henry made coffee and set two cups on the kitchen table. His thick glasses brought Mietek back in time. He never forgot how he'd saved his life that day in the Starachowice ghetto.

Mietek shared his dream to immigrate to the United States. "You should go to Israel, Mietek, it's a free state now," Henry advised in their native Polish. "I plan to eventually go. Besides, we have relatives there. Your grandmother, on your mother's side. She lives in Tel Aviv. She left Poland for Palestine in 1935. You must remember her—you were almost seven. You should try to find her. This would be your chance to be with her."

Mietek had thought about going to Israel often. He wanted to connect with surviving family members—if there were any. Once there, he believed he could work toward getting papers for entry into the United States, his dream.

"You should know, Mietek, that if you decide to go, you'll be drafted into the Israeli Defense Forces," he said. "Israel needs every young soldier. Unfortunately, they've been forced to battle the Arabs right now."

Another war. Mietek looked at Henry, suddenly aware how much his uncle had aged. His peppered hair and white bushy eyebrows reflected his time at war. The men didn't talk about their losses, their wounds were still too fresh. They spoke about the future instead.

"After they established a State of Israel in May, the Arabs declared war, promising to annihilate all Jews the following day." He raised both eyebrows. "Unbelievable."

They shook their heads, astounded that even after the war, mankind couldn't get it right.

CHAPTER THIRTY-FIVE

Mietek had made his decision even before he got home. He would go to Israel. A new state. A new start.

But Gretel.

She had to come with him, of course … yet, she wasn't Jewish. Would it be dangerous for her in Israel? Would the Jews discriminate against her? Could she work, shop, lead a normal life? He couldn't risk hurting another person he loved. And he did love Gretel. Perhaps he should go ahead by himself and see if it would be safe for her to follow. Could he contact a relative in Israel to ask questions? The thoughts plagued him deep into the night.

He couldn't sleep. His future was at stake—a homeland, a wife—he wanted both. He needed both. He was used to making life and death decisions. Tough choices made in the moment under impossible circumstances. He had let his head rule then—his head and some raw instinct that came from deep inside. But this was different. This wasn't about survival. This was about happiness.

Happiness. A word he thought he had lost.

Mietek's heart raced as he knocked on the door. Gretel answered and invited him in.

He led her to the sofa to sit down. "You know I've talked about finding my family." He hesitated. "I've decided to make plans to go to Israel."

Her eyes filled up. She understood he needed to find his family. But the thought of being apart was torture. Now that she'd found him, how could she live without him?

Mietek held her close, stroking her hair, lost in the moment. He couldn't stay. This was his only chance to find his grandmother and his other relatives. Gretel kept her emotions in check. Mietek knew she was struggling to protect her heart. It worried him that she was trying to be stoic, just like he always had.

They spent almost all their free time together, knowing what was to come. But the time for his departure came quickly.

Mietek was growing anxious. Ticket in hand, he thought of the life that had taken shape near Bamberg. Withers and his men had given him hope and a home. Gretel made him feel things he'd never thought he'd experience in his life. He had fallen in love—head over heels, as the saying goes. As much as he wanted to be with her, he was driven by an intense desire to search for his family and make a life for himself somewhere new. He thought reuniting with relatives would help heal his raw wounds.

But would it?

A week later, standing on the train platform, the two young lovers shared a long kiss goodbye. Gretel shoved a paper bag in Mietek's canvas carry on, then she gave him a photograph. In it, she wore a two-piece gray suit over a crisp white blouse. Her hair was pulled back in her usual fashion, and her head was tilted, casting him a loving glance. She had written on the back, *Zur meinen liebe Mietek, zur erinnerung on schöne Stunden. Von Deiner liebe Gretel in Sommer 1948. (To my dear Mietek, in remembrance of our wonderful hours. From your dear Gretel in summer 1948.)*

Mietek felt a profound sadness that he thought he had protected himself against. He felt hollow by this latest, devastating loss. He settled into his seat, but the trip was lonely and long and he kept revisiting his decision, turning it over and over in his mind. Had he done the right thing?

He gazed out the window passing miles of barren land. Red painted barns dotted the landscape with hard-to-distinguish farm animals. He opened his paper bag from Gretel. Slowly, he unwrapped a salami and cheese sandwich on slices of dark pumpernickel bread. He could only think about her making this sandwich especially for him. A chocolate bar lay at the bottom, wrapped in extra napkins.

Clouds of steam obscured the station as the train screeched to a halt. Frankfurt. He needed to disembark and find his connecting train. Stepping out, Mietek checked the departure schedules and headed to the ticket window. He sat on the bench, outside the train depot. Reaching inside his pocket, he took out her photo. Her hazel eyes looked back at him. He knew what he had to do.

Two hours later, he took the last train back to Bamberg.

Mietek and Gretel were married August 22nd, 1948, in Bamberg by a justice of the peace in a civil ceremony. Mietek was twenty and Gretel, twenty-three. They left the following month on the Frankfort train headed to Marseille where they would board a boat for Haifa, Israel.

Gretel and Mietek, August 1948

CHAPTER THIRTY-SIX

The fishing boat pulled out of Marseilles' harbor with a blast of its horn. Mietek and Gretel sat quietly, hiding below on the orlop, the lowest deck of the ship. All one hundred fifty passengers huddled together, praying that the ship would set sail unnoticed. The temperature continued to rise in the claustrophobic spaces as the inspectors checked the Israeli-bound cargo and approved the ship for departure. Everyone let out an imperceptible sigh of relief as they left the French coastal town behind.

Mietek crouched next to Gretel in the unbearable heat. The responsibility of taking his new wife on this dangerous voyage weighed heavily on him. He was a veteran of oppression, but Gretel shouldn't have to suffer. She didn't complain, though, even when the temperature swelled to over one hundred degrees.

Late that first night, when the captain determined that the ship was out of sight of the mainland, the passengers were allowed onto the upper deck. Everyone felt the comfort of the cool evening breeze, the freshness of the salt air. Gretel and Mietek held hands and looked around them. She leaned her head on his shoulder. Finally, they were on their way.

"I'm not naïve," Gretel said. "I'm nervous, but I'm excited to make a fresh start with you." She smiled encouragingly.

"I mailed a letter to my Uncle Max, asking if we could stay with him until we can get to Tel Aviv."

She patted his hand. "It's going to work out, Mietek. I have no doubts."

The gentle waves rocked the boat, soothing the passengers to sleep. Their next stop would be Naples and once the ship passed another inspection, it would sail to its final destination, Haifa, Israel.

Mietek didn't have legal documents. Because he was stateless, and because he hadn't resided long enough in a formal DP camp, it was impossible for him to acquire a visa to move legally to another country. He was grateful the ZIM ships (a fleet of ships established by a Jewish agency) reactivated their mission to transport immigrants who didn't have proper papers. Up until 1945, they smuggled illegals into Palestine. Nevertheless, he believed that if he became a citizen of Israel, he could eventually apply for a visa to the United States.

Most of the immigrants were like Mietek: survivors of the Holocaust hoping to reunite with relatives in a state they could call their own. Gretel felt isolated from them, try as she did to understand their plight. When talk turned to the war and its catastrophic losses, she felt the gap between their experiences most acutely. Gretel's love for Mietek was pure, her compassion for survivors intense. But she didn't know how these people would regard her, a Catholic German. She felt uneasy, unmoored. But when she thought it was too much for her, when she couldn't go ahead with it, she looked at Mietek and knew the truth. Together they could go anywhere, they could withstand anything.

Mietek and Gretel stood on deck exhausted, but relieved, as the boat sailed into the port of Haifa. The steep cliffs of Carmel enveloped

Haifa's sprawling three- and four-story buildings. White houses jutted out of the mountain, balanced on the cliff's edge, all the way to its peak. The bright sun showed off the desert's white terrain and the long breakwater arched into the bay where sun reflected off the sapphire blue Mediterranean Sea. They were stunned by the beauty of the city. They were in the Middle East, now. It was a new part of the world for them. A new life.

Walking down the squeaking planks of the ship, Mietek scrutinized his surroundings. He'd contacted the Israeli consul about his arrival. Straight ahead he saw a cluster of greeters behind a roped-off area, holding up handwritten signs. To his relief, a big *W* caught his eye. *Wajgenszpergs*. Mietek made eye contact and raised his hand to the young man standing in shorts with a white linen shirt and sandals.

"Hello," the man reached over the rope extending his hand, "I'm Avi. Welcome to Haifa."

"Hello Avi," Mietek shook his hand, "We're so happy to meet you."

"Follow me please," he said in German with a thick Hebrew accent. "How was your trip?" He asked politely.

"A little rocky the last few days," Mietek replied.

"Ah yes, it can be. I expect you'll be glad to have your feet on dry land." The two men continued like that for a beat. Gretel was quiet, taking in her new surroundings. "Mr. and Mrs. Wajgenszperg, you arrived as Gretel and Mietek, but it's customary to change your given name to a Hebrew name when coming to live here. You're now Israelis—welcome to our country. We're proud of our heritage and our language. Your Hebrew name will connect you to the land of Israel.

"Mietek, you'll most likely be referred to as Moshe here, is that okay?"

"Moshe." Growing up he had friends named Moshe. It was familiar. He rolled the name around in his mouth.

"Yes, that is fine. Moshe."

"Mrs. Wajgenszperg … do you have a preference for a Hebrew name?" Avi asked.

Mietek whispered in his wife's ear. "I'd like Chana." She glanced at Mietek to write it down. He filled out her immigration form: C H A N A.

"Ah," Avi said. "Very nice. It means compassionate or graceful in Hebrew. I think that's a beautiful name for you."

Gretel loved the sound of Chana. She hoped it would connect her to this new land and its people. "Yes, I'm good with that."

"Can you sign here please? It will be your official first name and it's yours forever."

The paperwork finalized, the newlyweds introduced themselves.

"Hello Chana," Mietek said.

"Hello Moshe," she returned.

"Do you have a place to stay?" Avi asked. "I can help you make accommodations." Mietek provided Uncle Max's address in Telmont, Karkuri.

"Please," Avi said. "Allow me to get your tickets at the bus station. It's right around the corner."

"We appreciate that." Mietek was relieved. There would be no mistakes. Avi would make this happen easily.

Uncle Max owned a farm that had remained on Arab land after Israel was carved out of Palestine. He and his Muslim neighbors were caught up in territorial changes, but their deep-rooted friendships and mutual respect would not alter their history. They'd lived in harmony for decades, not willing to let newly drawn lines upset their homes and livelihoods.

The newlyweds arrived on the farm late that evening, carrying their few belongings.

"So, you're Mietek," beamed Max, speaking in Yiddish so everyone could understand. "I was so pleased to get your letter. You are always welcome here." He looked deeply into Mietek's eyes, adding, "You are a miracle, my son."

Mietek stiffened. He responded with a truth he hadn't yet acknowledged out loud. "It doesn't seem right that I'm the only one who survived."

Silence.

Max quickly changed the subject when his wife walked in. "This is Lea."

Mietek brightened. "Nice to meet you," he said extending his hand. Lea pulled him toward her and embraced him. Mietek introduced his new bride, "This," he said proudly, "this is my wife Gre—Chana!"

Lea ran her hand through her dark curly hair, brushing back her bangs. She gave a relieved Gretel a warm hug. The women wasted no time in getting to know each other.

"What a beautiful home you have," Gretel said, looking left and right. It was a one-story house, flat-roofed and simply furnished. They walked out back. "Your plants are gorgeous." She touched the edge of a cactus leaf, admiring the ruby red flowers.

"I enjoy working in my gardens. And these here are herbs that I use for cooking." She bent over clipping some woody rosemary shoots, handing them to Gretel to sniff.

She was surprised how quickly the two women connected. Gretel too loved to plant flowers and experiment with herbs. Inside, a huge bowl of unpeeled fruits centered Lea's kitchen counter. Gretel did the same in her home. It comforted her.

Uncle Max poured glasses of red wine. Lea prepared a fish dinner with potato latkes, and a cucumber salad.

"Please sit there, Mietek." Lea pointed to the head of the table opposite her husband, while placing the platters of food on the table.

Gretel appreciated the soft white tablecloth covered with colorful plates. "I can't believe we are here. Everything is so more beautiful and inviting than I imagined."

Max toasted his guests. "To your arrival in our wonderful state. *L'chaim*!"

Mietek took hungry bites of his dinner. "This is delicious, Lea," he said. "You are in the running with Chana—she's a great cook too."

Stories passed around the table. The state of Germany after the war, the devastation it brought to most of Europe. Max refilled the wine glasses, sitting back in his chair.

"I want to help you on this farm while we're here, Max," Mietek told his uncle.

Gretel immediately chimed in. "And so would I." She looked at Lea and Max. "I was raised on a farm. I feel very much at home here already."

"That would be wonderful." Max looked to Lea shaking her head. "Thank you both for your offer. Good help is always welcome. I promise we'll feed you well." He smiled.

Uncle Max and Mietek talked about Gretel's new Hebrew name.

"It's my grandmother's name, my father's mother. I'm honored she can carry it on."

"New beginnings and old connections. That is the best," Lea said. "You two must be tired. Let me show you to your room."

The young couple was thrilled with the cozy bedroom decorated with fresh flowers. Everything was fresh here.

"So Chana, how does it feel to be here?" Mietek asked.

"I'm happy Mietek, so happy. Lea and Max have made me feel at home. And you know what's surprised me? The desert—the land is beautiful. It's so natural, bright, it just feels calming."

He found her rosy cheeks and lilting voice adorable. She'd had a bit too much wine. As long as she was happy, he was at ease. He drew the drapes closed.

Chana turned down the double bed, setting her book by the nightstand. "We're here, Mietek. You made it happen."

"I couldn't have done this without you … Chana."

They kissed good night and fell asleep in minutes.

A loud boom woke Mietek and Chana at three a.m. Another explosion moments after that shook their bed. Mietek froze. He knew all too well the sound of cannons. This was close—too close. They were in the middle of the Arab-Israeli conflict. War was routine and peace was just a memory. Chana rested her arm across Mietek's chest, snuggling closer to him. "Shhh" she said, gripping his hand. His tense body relaxed. He had to calm his mind.

Uncle Max tried to ease the couple's anxiety over breakfast. "We're a new country—the Arabs are understandably upset. We've drawn a line, where before we coexisted for the most part." He finished eating an orange. "But I've gotten used to it." And they would too.

The next two weeks were something close to perfect. A hearty breakfast each morning, followed by a walk out into the beautiful plantation of orange trees. Mietek couldn't get used to the luxury of fresh fruit. Chana was transfixed by the beauty of the rolling hills. It was a pleasure to feed the roosters and hens in Uncle Max and Lea's chicken coop. Chana was in her element. Funny, but she had resisted becoming a farmer's wife back in Germany, and here she was married and working on a farm. This was different, though. She was happy to haul water buckets for the animals knowing that Mietek was working with Max picking oranges and tilling soil for new crops.

Still, this was not their final destination. They were bound for Tel Aviv. Mietek was grateful his uncle and wife opened their home to them to visit. Now he had to find work in the city. Finally Mietek got through to his uncle in Tel Aviv.

"What? Are you sure?" Mietek said. There was a pause. He thanked his uncle, hung up the phone and gazed at the floor. "I have bad news," he said.

Chana, Lea, and Max stopped working in the kitchen.

"My grandmother." He cleared his throat. "She died. Two weeks ago." They'd been so close—so very close. He lowered his head. Another loss, another death, another missed chance. Mietek would have to learn to live with this, too.

Chana immediately embraced him. Max and Lea dropped their heads.

"Please, sit down," Lea said. "I just made coffee. Come. Sit." They gathered around the outdoor patio table and talked about when Mietek's family was alive and together, sharing happier memories.

Mietek and Chana were incredibly grateful to Uncle Max and Lea for providing a safe home and an entry into Israel. Uncle Max arranged for their bus ride to Tel Aviv, and Lea packed some sandwiches lathered with hummus for their trip. After they held Max and Lea close, they thanked them for their kindness.

As their bus bumbled down the main road to Tel Aviv, Mietek grew excited. "The city is huge and full of life! Look," he said, pointing like a boy, "the buildings are short skyscrapers like the pictures of New York City."

Chana directed his attention out the opposite window. "And look, there's a beautiful park!"

Mietek was overcome with a warm feeling of being in a real city, a place where he might fit in.

Chana felt an immediate kinship to Tel Aviv. The city's modern buildings were so different from the historic architecture she was used to in Germany, but she fell in love with it all: the shops and apartments, the bustle of urban life. Their bus stopped, and they went to look for Mietek's aunt, Ita Rappaport, a relative from his father's side of the family.

Short and lively, with a big broad smile, Ita beamed when she saw Mietek. But as soon as Chana stepped off the bus, she turned away.

"Follow me," she said curtly and walked ahead to her car. Ita spoke only to Mietek during the thirty-minute ride. She talked about her son and daughter-in-law, about her first grandchild who had just turned two. She told him about the market she and her husband owned and how the oranges and dates they sold were the finest available anywhere. She told Mietek all this. To Chana, she said nothing.

This was Chana's first experience of intolerance here, but she knew it wouldn't be her last. Only fourteen when the war broke out, she was told only that her country was taking care of itself, fixing economic stresses, and working toward a national goal. They would emerge greater because of it. But she didn't buy it. None of it. What was so awful that it needed to be remedied with war? As for this German purity—no one in her family believed in it. In fact, as good Christians, they found it appalling. As the war raged on, her family, her village, and surrounding towns lived in fear. They were on the brink of starvation and bombs dropped everywhere. It was senseless. Evil. Millions of people had endured hardship and indignity—for what?

But she knew how she would be perceived by people who didn't know her. Intolerance was just something that she had to bear. And she would.

CHAPTER THIRTY-SEVEN

If anyone had a right to hate, it was Mietek. But he knew better. He had seen the devastation that callous judgment and bigotry could wreak. And he would live with it for the rest of his life. No one had the right to judge another because of race or nationality or religion. Respect. It was the only way forward. Mietek promised himself he would teach his children that lesson. His grandchildren too, God willing.

He had married a German. Most people had been accepting. Understanding, even. But such treatment from his own family. Mietek couldn't reconcile this behavior with his sense of right and wrong. Chana would not become a prisoner of intolerance, nor would he. Nobody would treat them this way.

Mietek had been looking forward to getting in touch with his mother's sister in Tel Aviv. His mother always spoke well of her and laughed recalling their childhood. Rifka Tzevyoni was a spirited child, always pushing limits. They had a special bond. Originally, he had intended to wait a few days until he and Chana were settled. He wasn't waiting any longer.

"Hello, Rifka?"

"Aye…"

"It's me, Mietek. Your nephew …"

"Oh my God, is that you?" she shouted in Polish. "Ah, Mietek, my boy! I am so happy to hear your voice!"

Mietek relaxed. "I was hoping to surprise you. I'm in Israel with my bride. How are you?"

"We are fine, you know, a meshugana family with many children," she said, laughing. "You must come see us!"

"We would really like that."

"When can you come? Can you get here on the Sabbath?"

"Yes we can, that's perfect. Thank you, Aunt Rifka. We're excited to see you and the family. What can we bring?"

"Just bring yourselves. We have much to talk about." Her voice lowered. "I miss my big sister … bring your mother's spirit with you, Mietek."

He took a deep breath. "She's always with me, aunt Rifka. Always," he said. "We'll see you Saturday."

As much as Rifka was thrilled to hear from Mietek, the call had brought up painful memories. Rifka and her mother had moved to Israel well before the outbreak of the war. Her hope for a new life in her new country had been ripped apart by the extent of her loss. As for her mother, Mietek's grandmother, she had never fully recovered from the death of Sonia and her family. Everyone except Mietek, that is.

Rifka opened the door, reaching out to embrace Mietek. She began to cry, holding him close. Turning to Chana, she took her hands, and kissed her left and right cheeks. "*Baruch haba*. Welcome, come in." The tearful reunion was joyous. Mietek was thrilled to see his aunt and uncle Leo again. Their four children circled the couple talking all at once. A cousin they'd never met, but one their mother talked about with loving reverence.

Their daughter Ida poured coffee into their finest china cups. She passed sweet breads and apricot rugelach around the table. Mietek talked about their harrowing journey to Israel. The kids loved it. "And we got sick from the waves," Chana added, "making sure we carried bags with us." Laughter filled the table.

"So where are you staying now?" asked Leo.

"It's a long story," Mietek responded, and shared the highlights of meeting his aunt Ita. You see, Ita doesn't—we're looking for a place of our own," he blurted out. Mietek glanced over at Chana. Rifka understood.

"Nonsense," Rifka said. Leo nodded. "You'll stay with us."

"We won't take no for an answer," Leo added.

Appreciation washed over Mietek. He looked at Chana. "We don't know how to thank you. We would love that." He pulled back his chair. "*Toda*, thank you."

The next morning, Mietek left Ita's key on her kitchen table. He took Chana's arm and walked out the door. They never saw Ita again.

Rifka and Leo were happy to add the newlyweds to their family. The bustling household was happy and noisy. What difference did two more people mean? Mietek's young cousins—there were four of them—ran in and out of the small flat, calling out to each other and to their parents. "Mama! Have you seen my sandals?" yelled Sara.

"You probably lost them again," shouted Ida. "Just put them in the same place!"

"I asked Mama, not you!"

Little Ida, who, at eleven, was all smiles and good-natured fun, quickly grew attached to Chana, following her around the house and especially the kitchen where they would bake Mandelbrot together, making it the old-fashioned way, rebaking the bread three times. The oldest boy, Aaron, helped his father at his grocer's business; the others had chores at home after school. Hugs were plentiful in this loving family. Teasing was routine. Over supper each night, everyone was encouraged to talk about their day, to share the best, and when needed, the worst. Problems were addressed together, with love. Always with love.

Mietek and Chana were settling in. Ida took Chana round the neighborhood and showed her the shopping areas and parks of Tel Aviv. Chana loved the color-rich foods displayed in rows outside the shops. Pomegranates, figs, apricots, kohlrabi, chickpeas, and assorted herbs dominated the market alleys. She breathed in the smell of fresh harvests.

Leo owned and operated a small business downtown—a grocery store which he was exceedingly proud off. Nestled between clothing, restaurants, and jewelry shops, he was near the heart of the Tel Aviv shopping district. The modest grocery was packed tight with fresh produce, fruits, cheeses, and sundries. Hebrew newspapers were stacked daily in front alongside magazines. One day, he took Mietek to an auxiliary storage area, where he came up with an idea.

"My nephew," he said, "look at this space. If you can see beyond the boxes and cans of tomatoes, perhaps this—"

"Yes!" Mietek knew what his uncle had in mind. Convert the storage area into an apartment. It was a tremendous solution to their cramped quarters. With the lease of the food storage area, Mietek and Chana would be on their own at last, in their first apartment. So what if the space at 47 Frischman had no windows and only two oversized commercial doors? The aboveground basement would do nicely.

Everyone pitched in, moving the grocery inventory to Leo's larger storage area, cleaning the place from ceiling to floor. The newlyweds were thrilled with their home. They bartered for a small stove. They inherited a mattress, some housewares, a table, and two chairs. That first night in their new home, Chana took great pleasure in pulling the table onto the patio—which was what she called *al fresco* dining—topping it with a home-sewn tablecloth and a candle. This became their mealtime tradition. She cooked her husband's favorite dinner of schnitzel, hummus, and pita bread. Mietek walked in, delighting in the wonderful fried-chicken aroma. He kissed her cheek, then her neck before taking off his military gear and leather boots. Chana lit the candle and poured a glass of port wine. They sat outside, enjoying the sweet evening breeze. Raising their glasses, they chanted in unison, *"L'chaim!"* A fitting welcome to their new home.

CHAPTER THIRTY-EIGHT

SEPTEMBER 1949

Chana worked at the Tel Aviv Hospital as a therapeutic massage therapist and loved her job. She was passionate about Israel, becoming a Zionist in her new home state. Mietek served in the Israel Defense Forces, the IDF, overseeing an air force commando unit in charge of the paratroopers' supplies. Together they earned enough to pay their expenses, without much left over for extras. They were fortunate. Israel was struggling to keep up with the steady stream of immigrants and jobs were scarce. But an extra was on the way. Chana was pregnant.

She was overjoyed with the news. She had conceived her first child on their one-year wedding anniversary and considered that a blessing. Mietek wasn't so sure. He wanted a family, but could he support both a wife and child? It was too soon. They weren't ready. Chana would have to quit work. How would he pay for everything on just one salary? Rent. Food. Clothes. And their son or daughter, a baby has so many needs.

But life goes on. His life was going on, and with it, a new family. Visions of his parents flashed before him. This is for you, he thought, your grandchild, your legacy. A miracle.

Chana continued to work at the hospital until late into her pregnancy, while Mietek continued to serve in the IDF. In the last week of April, she was intent to go back and tour the holy city. Mietek wasn't thrilled about the idea, but Chana had a mind of her own. She boarded a bus to Jerusalem the following day.

An overwhelming number of mosques lined the crowded streets. As her bus closed in on the Old City of Jerusalem, Chana fixated on the Temple Mount, awestruck by the elevated plaza and its incredible history. One of the holiest sites in the world, the Temple Mount claimed a place for three major religions, each of which dominated the space at different periods for thousands of years. Christianity, Judaism, and Islam converged here. To Christians, it's where the baby Jesus was presented in the Temple. It's where Jesus later prayed and taught. To Jews, the rock is where Abraham attempted to sacrifice his son Isaac before a messenger from God intercepted him. To the Muslims, the prophet Muhammad rose to heaven here. The Dome of the Rock crowns the Temple Mount, built as a shrine for pilgrims, and remains the oldest Islamic monument.

At the end of the bus trip, Chana visited a mosque, which for reasons unknown to her was operated by Catholic nuns. Moving slowly up the stone stairs, her feet swollen from the heat and baby weight, she arrived at the majestic, domed entrance. The ancient structure's ornate high ceilings were decorated in circular gold and blue designs, held up by massive marble beams. Chana caught her breath as she saw the snakes curled around the beams in the lower chamber. The sisters were enamored with her, a Christian with child, and suggested she move in and give birth in the mosque. Chana smiled to herself. *I'm a Christian, visiting a Muslim mosque, ready to birth my Jewish husband's baby.* The sisters continued to press and promise her safe accommodations. They believed that this would be a sacred event. A Christian birth in the walls of a mosque, near the holiest site in the world. Chana knew that she needed to be in a hospital for the birth, so staying wasn't an option; however, she felt so blessed at the offer, she thanked the nuns profusely. She would remember this visit for the rest of her life.

It was May 14th, 1950, when I arrived in a Christian hospital in Jaffa, the port city south of Tel Aviv. I was named Sonia Barbara—actually Sima in Hebrew—for my father's mother; Barbara for my mother's mother. It had been just five years since my father had been liberated from Dachau, five years in which he had recovered from the misery of war. He had been married for almost two years, and now he was a father in awe of his new baby.

My father would tell me later that he would count my fingers and toes, that he would stare at the curves of my ears and the bow of my lips. He would look deep into my eyes and when I looked back at him, he was sure I could see into his soul. I was a part of him. Part of his mother and father, connecting the past to the future. But amid all the joy and wonder, a darker emotion overcame my father. He could never forget his parents and the ugly reason they weren't here to share in his joy. And what if … it didn't bear thinking about. I should never see or live through the horrors that he had. I had to have a better life. That was up to him now.

The new parents recognized that their windowless home could no longer accommodate their little family, so they searched for a new place to live. It wouldn't be easy. However, one of the ways in which Israel responded to the huge wave of Jewish immigrants from Europe was with shikun settlements. Built for army soldiers, the lodgings in these communities were small—just a room and a kitchen. Mietek applied for a shikun but encountered too much red tape. Still, it wasn't long before he, Chana, and one-month-old Sonia were approved to join a community just south of Tel Aviv in Mishmar HaShiv'a to claim a home. The settlement, a moshav, was a cooperative which, unlike a kibbutz, allowed participants to own their homes. Founded in 1949 by former soldiers, this moshav was named in memory of seven guards killed near Yazur on January 22nd, 1948.

Now the family had an address: Shikun Chadasch #1. Their new home was idyllic. Mietek and Chana picked fresh oranges from the grove. Enjoying soy, olives, figs, and other sun-ripened delicacies, the family was always grateful to have food on the table. Chana loved cooking local Mediterranean foods and prepared traditional menus for the Jewish holidays.

The family got along well with the neighbors, despite Chana's German heritage. They became friends with another couple like them: she was Christian and her husband Jewish. Mietek was away most of the day, so Chana worked the land and took care of Sonia and the house. Once a week, she would take Sonia and catch the bus to meet Ida in Tel Aviv. Chana and Ida pushed Sonia in her stroller as the three of them walked to Kikar Disingof—Dizengoff Square.

A bright orange-and-red water fountain held center stage in the square. The fountain's exterior looked like an accordion, with three hatboxes piled on top of each other, the smallest at the top. The cement base had a white railing that guided visitors in a circle around the fountain. The square lured moms, children, and the elderly during the workdays. Lush green bushes and palm trees framed the background of the park, and small shops and food stands surrounded the fountain. Every time they visited the Dizengoff square, Sonia got an ice cream cup before they walked home.

On weekends, they all went to the beachfront promenade on the Mediterranean. Mietek took photos of Sonia sitting on the seawall, clutching her tiny purse, capturing the beautiful vistas.

"Look at me, Soniala, let's see a big smile," urged her Papa. This was the life he wanted for her. He just had to keep her safe.

Chana, Sonia and Mietek, Tel Aviv 1951

Sonia, Tel Aviv seawall, 1952 | Barbara Sonia, Tel Aviv seawall, 1999

CHAPTER THIRTY-NINE

The doctor had finished his examination. "Your nausea and light-headedness are most likely caused by working outside in the sweltering heat," he told Mietek. "You may be dehydrated, but it's my opinion that your years in the camps have compromised your health."

Mietek put his shirt back on. He had been feeling unwell for some time now; this came as no surprise.

"Your body needs a break," the doctor continued. "You shouldn't be working outside."

He had to make a change—but how? Unemployment was high and opportunities were limited. Israel was the most desirable option for displaced Jews seeking refuge, but the overwhelming numbers strained the country's economy. The government couldn't keep up with the pace of new immigrants. What life could they have here?

Mietek and Chana dreamt of going to the United States, but Israel wanted to hold on to its young people, so it didn't support the U.S. visa program. Hope came in July 1951 when the United Nations addressed the status of refugees and stateless persons. An international treaty was drafted which, when ratified, would address the rights of stateless persons such as Mietek. This would be the break he needed to get papers and be recognized as a person, to have the opportunity to move to America. He had ended his part-time job at the Tel Aviv Nigia transport office and would finish his military term in March 1953. Suddenly, the family's chances of gaining entry into the U.S. became much brighter.

Time for another decision. The young couple poured themselves a liqueur. Two drinks in, they agreed to move back to Germany and work toward their U.S. visas from there. Chana was a citizen. Mietek was a survivor. The German authorities had to provide support for stateless persons. It was now or never.

Christmas Eve, December 1954, and once again, my family was traveling. My most vivid memories go back to this time. I remember a loud whistle, followed by a surge of steam as our train screeched to a halt in Kaiserslautern station.

"Is this it, Mama?" I asked, clutching my doll to my chest. "Are we here?"

"Yes—and we're going to our new apartment." My mother said quietly. It was as if she had prepared for this day for a very long time.

Papa took my hand and guided me through the train's sliding door. "Come on, Sonia, jump," he said. It was a high step, but I landed squarely on the platform in this strange new place.

Only the lamplights illuminated the station. It was so tidy, so clean. Cities weren't like that. Papa took us with him as he processed the necessary paperwork, then he led us to a waiting car. My eyelids were heavy, but the world had changed, and I wanted to stay awake. Scared and unsure of what was happening, I yearned for my familiar room in Tel Aviv and for Mama's potato soup, a holiday staple.

"Papa, tell me again, why are we moving here? I forget."

He hesitated. "I have a good job here, Soniala, and you and Mama will make new friends."

"But Papa, the Christmas Angel won't be able to find us."

He and Mama exchanged a glance. "It doesn't matter where you live," he told me. "The Angel will know."

There were no holiday decorations in Tel Aviv, but when the driver stopped in front of our new apartment building, I could see Christmas lights through the windowpanes. Arched stones outlined the windows in earthy red. They were so pretty, the way they framed the lights, that I forgot to be homesick.

"Welcome to our new home," Papa said at 23 Turnerstrasse. Mama picked up her light suitcase, and I held tight to my doll. The driver followed with the larger luggage. As we climbed the stairs, I ran my hand over the smooth mahogany railing. The wood was thick, and the doors were tall. The apartment house smelled clean but old, like a library. Everything was so different.

"Sonia, close your eyes and take my hand." I reached for Papa's hand and heard the door open as a light breeze brushed my face. My heart raced.

"Open your eyes," Mama said. I could tell she was pleased with something, but when I opened my eyes to a fairyland—a miniature *Kaufladen* set up neatly on the living room table—I couldn't believe it. I ran to the play store and stared inside. Everything was perfect. Miniature boxes of food lined the shelves opposite a counter and cash register. A tiny record pad sat on the counter. Play money lined the register drawer. Such happiness. The Christmas Angel had found us after all.

CHAPTER FORTY

The red leather album had been moved from its usual place on the top of the bookcase. It was now within reach of my curious hands.

"Papa, who is he?" I asked, pointing to a uniformed man with kind eyes and a dark complexion.

My father hesitated.

"He's a soldier … he served in the war," he responded gently. "I was stationed with him."

At almost six, I assumed my father meant that they served together in the army. But there was something mysterious in Papa's reaction—a haunted look that, in turn, made me wonder why he got so serious.

"Where is he now?" I asked.

"I don't know, Soniala."

"Was he a nice man?" I asked.

"A very nice man," my father said. "And a very good one."

With that he closed the album and returned it to the higher shelf.

I didn't know about my father's secret year after he had been liberated from Dachau.

I didn't know he had learned to speak English from this soldier, who had told Papa that he could have a good life in America.

I didn't know that this man had been the origin of Papa's dream.

I only knew that this album and the man in the photograph were precious to Papa. And so, they were precious to me.

Mietek remembered what his American friends had told him.

"If you get to the States," John had said, "you'll be okay."

"Work hard," Dave said, "and you can get a nice home."

"Work harder," Jim had joked, "and you can get a nicer one!"

Now twenty-seven, Mietek wanted to make his dream a reality. He wasn't foolish enough to think that he could leave the past behind completely, but he wanted to try. He wanted to be a new man in a new country. He wanted to look forward instead of back. He wanted a future for those he loved. Hard work was never a challenge. Letting go of family was. Alas, he had done that, too. But he had a new family now, a wife and daughter. They needed to feel secure.

It was time to talk to Chana.

Mietek found her finishing the preparations for supper: hot pea soup with bacon sat steaming on the stove. She fussed with a grated carrot salad, and salami and cheese sandwiches.

"I need to talk to you," he said, kissing her on the cheek.

She couldn't wait for Mietek to come home. She couldn't wait for the end of their day—to talk to her best friend. Gretel lit a candle, smoothing the sunflower on the hand-embroidered tablecloth. She poured two steins of dark beer as Mietek sat down with a deep sigh.

"Where's Sonia?" Mietek asked.

"She played with the twins after school. They asked her to stay for dinner."

"Good. I was hoping we could talk, just you and me." He waited for her to sit. "Chana, it's time to decide," he said lifting his beer stein. "Sonia is ready for the first grade."

"And you think it's better to move when she is young. I agree with you."

Mietek took a deep breath. "I've been stateless almost half my life, Chana. Can you imagine being American citizens one day? A dream come true." His self-image of being an American flashed through his mind. Another dose of reality brought him back. "I'm worried for Sonia," he said. "This move could be hard on her … but she would have a chance for a better future, don't you think?"

"I think Sonia would do fine. And to be honest, I think it'll only get harder if we wait. Do what you need to do, Mietek," she said gently. "What *we* need to do … just not Canada," she reminded him. "It's too cold there for me."

Mietek smiled. "I've looked into ways we might get a sponsorship. It won't be easy. But I've been in touch with the Israeli law firm that forwarded my Israel Defense Force service papers."

"Ah, yes," Chana said, nodding. She recalled this law firm and the good work they did.

Mietek continued. "They told me about a Jewish group in New York City—HIAS. They sponsor Jews."

"So contact them, Mietek. Go ahead. Let's do this."

It would take many late nights and worried moments, but the Hebrew Immigrant Aid Society came through and secured the necessary paperwork for my family to enter the United States. On October 18th, 1956, we boarded a crammed ship for a twelve-day sail from Bremerhaven to New York. We said goodbye to family. We said goodbye to Europe, as my father checked his wallet to be sure his three hundred dollars was secure.

General W.C. Langfitt ship
Wajgenszperg family on board

CHAPTER FORTY-ONE

OCTOBER 29th, 1956

I will never forget the day the General W.C. Langfitt sailed into New York City harbor. The skyline came into view, appearing almost unreal, like a table model; the skyscrapers towered over the apartment buildings and stores.

Mietek stared. Was he dreaming? Dressed in his only dark gray suit, he removed his hat, placing it over his heart. *I made it, John. I made it here*. Awestruck, he spotted a stunning, larger-than-life statue appearing on the right.

"Who's that?" I pulled on my Papa's sleeve.

"She's the Statue of Liberty."

"What's that on her head?" I pointed, enthralled.

"That's her crown. Amazing, isn't it? It symbolizes the seven seas and continents," he replied in German.

Her right arm extended upward, thrusting the torch and flame as if toasting our arrival; the Statue of Liberty welcomed us all. Papa peered down at me.

"It's … the greatest city in the free world," he said, his voice cracking.

Mama gripped my hand tightly. Our ship slowed and prepared

to dock for the night. The Statue of Liberty stood vigil, as if to soothe us on our safe arrival. The sun was setting, streaking orange through the clouds, and casting a deep yellow reflection on the water. Mama brought Papa and me away from the rail. It was time for dinner and our last night on the ship.

Early the next morning a loud blast echoed through the ship's decks as we cleared our passage into the main city harbor. Marching band music filled the air. We all clapped and cheered as our boat docked.

"Do you see those buildings, Miriam? Look at how tall they are. And so many of them!" said a man to his wife.

"I never thought this day would come," said another.

"God bless America," uttered a woman wearing a fur collared coat.

Papa waited for the two straw crates, the size of small sofas, filled with all of our belongings. These crates, secured with huge, black metal latches, were labeled *Akron, Ohio*. But we weren't going to Ohio. HIAS had assigned us to the northeast instead. I had wanted to go to the place with the sing-song name: O-Hi-Oh! Mama was leery too, but Papa assured her that they had to trust the new circumstances. "These things happen," he told her. "It is all about finding work."

Standing in line to process our entry, we were advised by U.S. immigration officials to shorten our last name—a common practice for new immigrants. Papa agreed to "Weisperg"—it retained the beginning and end of the Wajgenszperg name.

No family or friends were there to greet us, but Papa searched the crowd for our HIAS representative. As we disembarked, we were asked to pose for our first photo in the United States in front of the sign on the side of the boat: U.S. Refugee Relief Program

Ship Chartered by I.C.E.M. (Intergovernmental Committee for European Migration). Clutching my doll, I stood next to Mama. We smiled and continued into the bustle of the crowd. Swells of people searching for family or friends jostled about.

"Joseph, is that you?"

"Over here Heinz!"

A stout woman waved. *"Ich bin so froh du bist hier!"*

"Sonia, don't let go of my hand," Papa said, holding me tight as we pushed our way through the congested dockyard. Groups of people found each other, hugging and kissing, and crying. But there was still no sign of our greeter. Mama was worried.

"Mietek, what if—"

"It's okay, *mein Liebling*! Don't worry. We are here. America!"

"Yes, but what if—"

"Look! Gretel, there!"

Papa spotted the handwritten sign: *Wajgenszperg*. It was to be the last use of our old name.

"Hello, I'm Danny. Welcome to the United States." Danny was tall and thin, wearing a brown-buttoned sweater over a white-collared shirt and khaki pants.

"Thank you for coming to get us," Papa said in broken English as he reached out his hand to shake Danny's, still catching his breath. "It's been a long trip. Do you speak any German?"

"I understand Yiddish, so feel free to speak German and I'll do my best," he replied in his best Yiddish. "I'll take you to your apartment. Stay close and follow me."

The aroma of roasting sausages wafted through the air. I looked around and saw vendors with small-wheeled carts lining the sidewalks. The sizzling sausage and onions were like a welcoming touch of home.

Danny drove us to our temporary apartment in the heart of New York City. The streets were swarmed with cars that constantly honked their horns. It was all shops and buildings—no parks or playgrounds anywhere. I couldn't even see the top of the towering buildings.

"We're forwarding your crates to Connecticut," explained Danny. Papa knew about our destination. That's where he would have opportunity to interview for a job. "Let me help you with your luggage."

He led us to the elevator, stopping on the twentieth floor. Danny walked ahead and opened the apartment's thick, brown lacquered door. It was a small three room flat. I would be sleeping on a cot. The cramped kitchen abutted an informal living room with a two-seat couch and chair. We were used to small spaces, but this—I was surprised—was this how Americans lived? After showing us around, he huddled with Papa to go over more details. After addressing all the particulars, he bid them farewell and left. Frozen for a moment, Mietek peered out the window. Skyscrapers jutted out everywhere. He was in the U.S. with his family. He had made it. We had really made it.

CHAPTER FORTY-TWO

We felt at home in New York. People came from all over the world—and they brought their food with them. Dark rye and pumpernickel breads, hearty lunchmeats, fresh vegetables, and fruits were abundant at the neighborhood delis and stands. New York City reminded us of Tel Aviv, only much larger. And like Tel Aviv, the city's parks and playgrounds were surrounded by shops and places to eat, and the waterfront outlined the city. Papa was the only one who spoke some English, but everyone in the city had a sixth sense for foreigners and found a way to communicate. Heads nodding and hands signaling, we navigated our way through the city.

Our stay in New York was short—a little over two weeks. Then it was off to Hartford, Connecticut where HIAS secured an apartment for us on Barbour Street.

"Such a blessing," were Mama's first words upon seeing her new home.

It wasn't just that our two-bedroom apartment had an eat-in kitchen and a cozy living room. The walls were beige and the rooms were sparsely furnished; only a blue living room couch added a touch of color. It was the kitchen that brought my mother to life.

"Mietek! Sonia! We have a stove and a refrigerator," she said with her hands crossed over her heart. "And I can use my new sewing machine on the kitchen table—plenty of space."

Within a week, Mama had unpacked our oversized crates. She was proud of her tablecloth and the lace curtains she had hung in the living room. Her Rosenthal porcelain coffee urn and cups were displayed on a silver tray near the dining table. A single flower in a glass vase adorned the windowsill. These small beautiful touches transformed our new apartment. The aromas of Mama's dinners made it home.

Papa was grateful. He got a job as an auto mechanic at Grody's Chevrolet dealership in West Hartford. America had been a dream for my parents for many years. Now it was a reality, and that meant countless details and responsibilities. Papa was used to having nobody to count on. He was used to having no safety net. And here, we were truly on our own.

In mid-November I began first grade at Barbour Elementary School. I struggled to communicate with my teachers and schoolmates. How would I know what to do? In Germany, I understood my kindergarten teacher's directions. The twins and Georg and I would run out at recess and have our jam-lathered bread together. We'd play games until the nuns called us in. Here, I stood against the playground chain-link fence watching the kids play. No one talked to me. They knew I couldn't understand.

A nagging aching stitch in my chest slowed me down. By the end of the school day, I would lay on our couch, pale.

Mama was concerned. I had been feeling unwell since we arrived in Hartford, so our German doctor had given me some medication and told my mother simply to give me time. But I was getting worse. My slight cough had become a constant hack. I was losing weight. Weighing less than fifty pounds, I couldn't afford to drop an ounce. Three weeks after starting school, I lay motionless on the living room couch. The pain had become unbearable. Mama called the doctor again. He listened to my chest, looked down my throat, and prescribed a different medication. Pale, weak, and still coughing, I was sent home from school the next day. Mama called the doctor again. She paced back and forth, clenching the phone, speaking loudly. This time she was angry.

"Sonia," Papa said to me. "You know how it hurts when you breathe?" he started slowly. "Well, the doctor wants you to go to the hospital so they can find out what's causing the pain." He hesitated. "You'll have to stay there until they figure out why you've been so sick. But we will be there *every* day!"

For the first time in my life, I saw my Papa's eyes well up. Nothing scared me as much as this. "I have to go and stay at the hospital?" I couldn't leave my home again. I couldn't leave my parents.

Mama brought out a small bag she had packed and handed me my *Puppe*—my doll. I did my best to comfort her on the way to the hospital, but when I was admitted to the stark white room at Mt. Sinai, there was no comforting me. Only a high, oversized round window let light into the room. I locked my hands around Papa's neck and wouldn't let go.

"You have to be strong, Sonia. I know you can do this," he said.

"Mama will be here every day and I'll come right after work. I promise." He helped me into the wheelchair that had been brought in for me. Then, turning to the nurse, he explained that I couldn't speak much English. My father's own English was limited and he struggled to keep up in the stressful situation. It was our social worker, Mrs. Newman, who interpreted for my father, explaining to him that I needed to be taken for a chest X-ray. His eyes intent, he watched as the nurse wheeled me down a long corridor.

The results of my X-ray were examined; a procedure of some sort was called for. Mama held my hand and walked with me to the operating room entrance. Harsh antiseptic smells overwhelmed the stark, silver space. White clad doctors and nurses smiled at me—a small kindness. They gestured to explain that they were going to insert a needle in my rib cage. Offering me a facemask just like theirs, they had hoped to distract me while they helped me up on a cold metal table. The nurse rubbed an antiseptic solution that smelled like diluted ammonia on my chest. Then came the largest needle I had ever seen. They inserted it slowly into my rib cage. I was fully awake for the procedure, in shock, and overcome with a piercing pain. A doctor drew liquid from my chest, leaving the long needle in place for what seemed like eternity. Slowly, the needle was extracted and the wound rubbed with cotton.

The procedure, thoracentesis, was repeated a few days later, but it never grew less painful. The doctors suspected pleural effusion, commonly known as pleurisy—a serious condition that arises from inflammation and fluid in the lungs. I lost more weight and was to remain in the hospital confined to my bed.

Mama walked to the hospital every day—an hour each way—and stayed with me as much as she could. Then she found an ally.

"Sonia, I met a very nice lady. She cleans here in the hospital and she would like to meet you. Her name is Miss Gertrude, and she speaks German." She brushed my bangs to the side. "She'll stop by when her shift is over!" As if on cue, Miss Gertrude walked into the room. Her white uniform sat tight on her short, stocky frame. Her light brown hair was pulled back into a tight knot, accentuating her round, jovial face.

"Guten tag," she said, walking right up to my bed.

Mama was thrilled to be speaking German again. "Miss Gertrude, this is my daughter, Sonia, who just got here three days ago."

"It's a pleasure to meet you, Sonia. Is that your *Puppe*?"

"Yes. I need her to stay with me," I responded, squeezing my doll.

"I see," she said, glancing at Mama with an understanding nod. "How do you like the food?" she asked.

"I don't like it much. I miss Mama's cooking." I looked her in the eye.

"Well, let me check if your mama can bring one food from home, would you like that?"

"*Na sicher.*" (Of course.) I bounced my head up and down. I liked this Miss Gertrude.

It was a relief for me to have someone to talk to after Mama left. She'd poke her head in my room and ask me what my favorite color was. Yellow, I said. The next day she brought in a yellow robe for my *Puppe*.

A day later, I heard a baby cry as the nurse wheeled me back to my bed. The parents leaned over a crib on the other side of my room, stroking the back of the baby dressed in a powder blue sleeper. The poor little baby wouldn't stop crying. I wondered what was wrong with him.

The nurse introduced me to the couple. Tall with dark hair—handsome, I thought—the father of the baby came over to shake my hand. It was a nice gesture since he knew that I didn't speak English. He pointed to the crib and used the word "son." The mother smiled and waved. I had company. And this little guy couldn't speak the language either. I understood how frustrated and alone he felt, so after visiting hours were over, I'd talk to him and tell him fairy tales. Sometimes I'd sing a German lullaby. He liked it, because he stopped fussing.

It felt good to have company. The baby's parents hovered over him and murmured in worried tones. I learned his name was Robbie. They'd include me in conversation as if I could understand. It felt good, like I had friends. They trusted me. I would gesture how the baby was doing—whether Robbie slept or cried or just stared at the ceiling. I felt a tremendous responsibility toward my little roommate. And I loved seeing his parents every day. Their presence made me feel much less alone.

Every morning, Miss Gertrude came to my room after breakfast. *Guten morgen* she would say. Then she'd ask me questions.

"Wie geht es dir heute?" (How are you today?)

"Ich habe Angst." (I'm afraid.)

"Hast du deine Puppe gebadet? (Did you bathe your doll?)

"Nein." Then she handed me a warm, wet washcloth and said I could keep it.

I was relieved to share my fears about needles and blood tests. I asked her when I could go home. Miss Gertrude shook her head and said she didn't know. Nobody knew. At least, nobody was telling me. Robbie's parents were kind. They sensed my fear and limitations, but I could tell they were grateful I was there. They walked in one day while I hummed a Brahms lullaby to him. It was naptime. Nodding their heads, they smiled and talked to me, even though I still didn't fully understand them. What I did understand was they accepted me, they appreciated me. Two days later, Robbie's parents came in with a small bag. The father walked over and handed me a gray, shiny, magnetic sheet and showed me how to use it. I could write and draw with a plastic pencil, and when I lifted the sheet, it erased the writing. I loved the gift. They were so kind. They kept speaking, as if they were explaining something while dressing their baby. When they finished, they wrapped him in a blanket, waved at me, blew a kiss, and took Robbie away. Sitting up in bed, I hugged *Puppe* and tried not to cry. I never saw them again.

After ten days in the hospital, my mother came with a red suitcase and packed my things. She helped me put on white tights and the navy blue dress she had knitted for me with red flowers embroidered near the hem. Elated to be out of hospital pajamas, I sat on my bed, coat in hand, making sure I'd be ready to leave when Papa arrived. I knew he never took time off from work during the day, but he was coming this morning specially to see me. I was thrilled when I saw Papa coming up the hall. He smiled when he saw me … but his smile didn't last long.

He bent over to kiss my cheek. "Sonia," he began slowly. "You're very sick … but we found a nice children's place on the seashore where they can help you get better."

"I want to go home!" I demanded. "I don't want to live in another place. It's almost Christmas!"

My parents tried to soothe me, but I was inconsolable. After a few minutes a nurse came in with a wheelchair and nodded; it was time to go. My parents led me to the waiting chair and placed *Puppe* on my lap. Papa held my hand. We walked down the hall toward the elevator with Mrs. Newman leading the way. I was sick, and I wasn't going home. I had tested positive for tuberculosis.

CHAPTER FORTY-THREE

The Waterford Sanatorium—known as The Seaside—was one of the first tuberculosis sanatoriums for children that opened in 1934. A majestic building, it was designed by Cass Gilbert, who also designed the U.S. Supreme Court building in Washington, as well as New York City's Woolworth Building. Surrounded by thirty-six acres of land, the three-story red brick structure stood isolated, overlooking the shoreline.

I was only six when I arrived at The Seaside, but I can still recall Papa's expression as he stretched out his hand, beckoning me to take it. Mama may have been my great nurturer, but Papa was my realist. I could tell by the look on his face that this was going to be hard.

Years after my illness, I would read about the intense and sometimes complex relationships survivors have with their children. Those who endured the horrors of the camps internalize a profound trauma that can be triggered by so many things, not the least of which is the sickness of their child. The fear of loss in the present brings back the profound loss of a repressed past. Now the survivor has to deal with terrors of past and present, as well as fears for the future. I have no doubt that was the case with my father.

It was a cold day when we arrived at The Seaside. Sunlight

skipped on the choppy waters of the Long Island shore. The icy coastal wind whipped at our backs as we made our way up the steps. We were glad to get indoors, where an attendant greeted us and led us to a large office. We sat, waiting, staring at a stack of neat documents sitting on a large, dignified desk.

A tall, well-groomed doctor entered the office. "Good morning, I'm Dr. Tombari," he said, shaking my father's hand. "I'll be overseeing Sonia's care while she stays with us. We'll begin today by filling out some forms." The color drained from my father's face when he saw the file the doctor's secretary placed on top of the desk. *Sonia Weisperg, Registered Number 29101*. The number that would become my identity in the sanatorium was so very close to the one tattooed on my father's left forearm: A 19104. His souvenir of Auschwitz.

It was a terrifying coincidence. And the worst was yet to come.

"Based on your daughter's results," Dr. Tombari told my parents, "she may be here for up to a year."

The doctor's words shocked my father. He stood motionless. How could this be happening? He loved two people in this world … and now, his only child was being taken away. He couldn't lose her. He couldn't. She had to get better.

"I know this is hard," the doctor said. "But we will do everything we can to help your daughter. She is very sick, so her diagnosis requires …" he hesitated, "I'm afraid Sonia has to be quarantined for now, placed in isolation. We have no choice. Her restrictions are part of the treatment."

It was too much. Mrs. Newman tried to keep up with translating but had to stop to grasp the disconcerting orders.

Dr. Tombari continued reading my file. He looked up and added,

"Sonia needs bed rest. She'll not be allowed to walk, even to the bathroom. It's all about getting her healthy."

Mama asked, "When can we visit her?"

Another hesitation. "Families can only visit on weekends," replied the doctor raising his eyebrows.

It was the worst day of my young life and the beginning of a nightmare year.

A trim nurse dressed in a crisp white uniform announced herself at my door. "Hello, I'm Marjorie McCarthy." A nurse's cap topped her strawberry blond hair. "I'll be your attending nurse today." She pulled a white mask over her mouth and picked up a clipboard. She read aloud as she wrote: b*ed slippers, bathrobe, brush and comb, two sweaters, one red dress, one pair patent leather shoes ... and one big doll-special.*

After taking my vitals, she introduced me to a shiny, metal chamber pot and had me pee in it. Another lady brought me a tray with tomato soup and crackers, a tuna sandwich, and orange jello. I wasn't hungry. Everyone who came in wore a white mask so I couldn't tell if they were smiling.

In the evening, nurse McCarthy came in before finishing her rounds. "I'm sorry," she said. "Doctor's orders." She strapped a huge cloth belt around my waist and tied the long straps to the bed rails. I couldn't move. Isolated, restrained, I clung to my *Puppe.*

That first week was filled with aggressive tests and hefty doses of medication.

Papa and Mama came to visit, laden with gifts. Mama sewed

doll clothes; Papa bought a journal I could draw and write in. I got new pajamas and a hand mirror so I could comb my hair. When Papa saw me strapped in bed, tied to the rails, he bolted, returning a moment later with a nurse who untied the restraints.

"Soniala, I am so very sorry," he said. "This will never happen again. I promise." He picked me up off the bed and held me close.

Mama was a stalwart. She wanted me to get better and so she adopted an attitude of *whatever it takes*. I knew she didn't like what was happening to me—to our family—but she accepted it. Papa was different. He may have agreed to the hospital protocols and the invasive tests, but he suffered under the weight of it all. For as much as he had already endured in his own life, he now understood how inadequate his own father must have felt trying to protect him. In this way he could feel all his own father had felt—and it was agony to him.

Within two weeks at The Seaside, I was moved out of isolation to the children's ward, a long room with about forty metal beds and children in each one. My father, especially, was relieved that I had other children around me. Oddly, the strict ward rules—fend for yourself, help others when you can—were not just familiar to him, but comforting. He could see by the camaraderie of the children that I was going to be okay.

But the tests that I had to endure kept my father awake at night. Worst of all were the gastric washing procedures, in which I had to swallow a tube inserted down my throat. A red tag tied to the bottom of my bed signaled that I was due for another of these painful processes. I asked my father to please stop them. He asked the doctors if there were other alternatives, but at the time, it was the only way to test for pulmonary tuberculosis.

My father looked up; I believe he called upon God to help me.

At last, some good news. On the week leading up to the Fourth of July, I was considered well enough to go home for a brief visit. Papa was overjoyed. Mama couldn't conceal her excitement. I could barely function, waiting for them to come get me. I had packed a few of my things, got dressed, and waited on the edge of my bed. My parents arrived to take me home to our Barbour Street apartment. I couldn't stop smiling.

We treasured our time together. We spent early afternoon at Elizabeth Park in Hartford, lingering on the banks of the serene pond, feeding the ducks. As we walked under the park's magnificent arches, Mama named the climbing roses in German. She spread a blanket under a tree, then opened our picnic basket and arranged our lunch, just like she used to do in Germany. Every minute was precious. I only had three days. How could I go back?

Papa talked about his new job at Royal Typewriter, and how he would like to get a job at Pratt & Whitney because it would give him the opportunity to advance. Mama worked at Royal Typewriter too. She could do that because I wasn't home. My parents discussed their overtime hours, something I couldn't quite understand. All I knew was that they were working hard, saving for our future. I was anxious for the future too. A future where I wouldn't have to go back to The Seaside, where I wouldn't be subject to the painful tests, the unrelenting homesickness. The drive back was torturous.

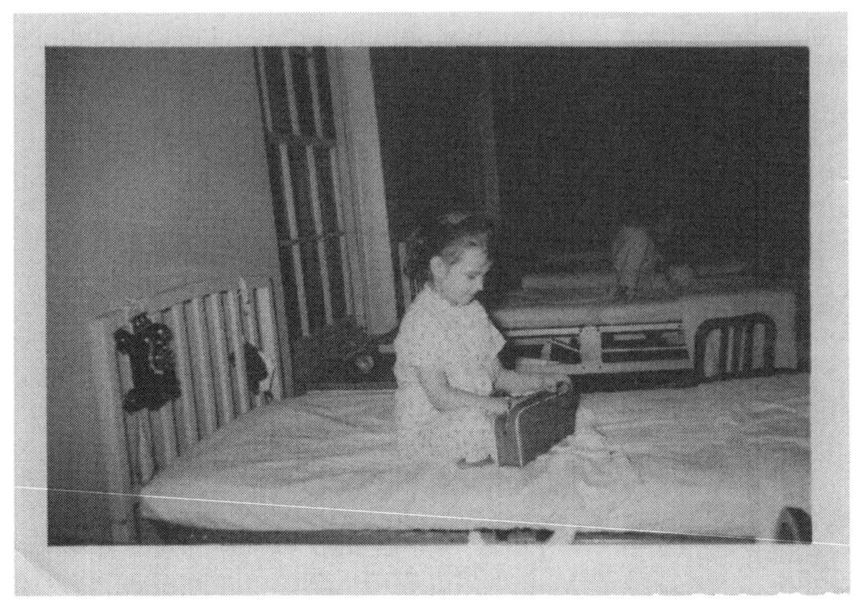

Sonia at Seaside Sanatorium, 1957

I found an inner strength during the second half of my year at The Seaside. I toughened up. My walking privileges, as they were called—another visit home—plus my bond with two girls at the sanatorium propelled me forward. My new friends began to call me Barbara, my middle name—I guess because it sounded less foreign. I was getting used to my new life. I was adapting. I attended classes and loved to learn. Working hard at my English, I found solace in books. I began reading and talking to the incoming children, helping them to cope with the devastation of being away from home. I understood their fear.

At last, on December 21st—another cold, windy day and a year after my admission to Seaside—I was discharged from Ward 201.

I had a hard time parting with my friends. They had become my family here and I knew I was going to miss them. But at age seven, I had learned to cope with change. I learned to adapt. I said my goodbyes to nurse McCarthy and to the staff.

We stopped in front of our car, taking one last look at the waves pounding the shoreline. It was time to go. I got to sit on the front seat and nestle between Papa and Mama, safe and loved.

I was called Barbara now. I had left Sonia behind.

CHAPTER FORTY-FOUR

The Seaside doctors were concerned about my long walks to school in Hartford, so my parents moved. They rented the second floor of a two-family house in West Hartford on Newington Road, closer to the best schools. I loved my room, the cornflower yellow wallpaper, and the window that overlooked our garden. Most of all, I loved being tucked up in my own bed, safe in the knowledge that my mother and father were down the hall, always there to look after me, just like it used to be.

I'd gained weight because of my restricted activities at Seaside. I missed my friends and was sad a lot of the time. My parents handled me tenderly, staying close. My father, more than anyone, understood the price of being separated from those you loved, of having your whole life upended. It would take time for me to recover not just my physical strength but my emotional strength, too. But I would soon be starting school and meeting new friends. That surely would help.

As a young girl, I'd look at my dad in his overstuffed chair, reading the paper, taking in the world events. He looked like any of my friends' fathers, but I knew he was different. My father never talked to me about what happened during the war. I may not have known the details of what he had to endure, but I knew that he exuded a strength, a quiet reserve that helped get me through my hard times.

It would be quite a while before I would understand the significance of his tattoo, but when I rested my head in the crook of his arm, I felt safe, loving the inked part of him too. Shortly after my release from the hospital, my father continued the process to receive restitution for his years as a slave laborer in concentration camps. My only clue was seeing the mail with distinctive international stamps from law offices in Israel, Germany, and New York City. He never mentioned he had to prove that his parents were, in fact, deceased and where they had been murdered. He didn't tell me that the only way to prove the circumstances of their death was through direct testimonies from other survivors. I cannot imagine how excruciating that must have been for him.

My father was attentive and involved. But he was never indulgent. He would ask me about school, listening carefully as I told him about how well I was doing in math and science, how I was struggling in English composition.

"Bärb," he'd tell me, "there's no reason you can't do well in every subject. You're a smart girl, you can do this." He always pushed me to do my best. I understood at an early age, education was a privilege.

My father's education had been cut short during the war, but he was a quick study and took night courses in electronics. He had left Royal Typewriter and got a job at Pratt & Whitney, as he had hoped. And now he had been promoted. My mother became pregnant when they bought our first house on Sidney Avenue in

West Hartford. My brother Edward was born the week before I turned ten. We were a family of four now; I was ecstatic. Settled for the first time in my life, I was thriving in my new elementary school. My English showed few signs of my foreign roots. I played piano and studied flute. I joined band, ran for a relay team, and was elected president of the student council. I loved school. It became the center of my universe. And Dad was proud of me.

The summer before I entered middle school, my parents and I became naturalized U.S. citizens, changing our name again from Weisperg to Weigen. Was our name less Jewish now, I wondered? All I knew was we celebrated and Dad was grateful. I didn't realize that my father had been stateless for over twenty years. No one talked about it. But he didn't stop grinning for a week. My father had made it. He and his family had become citizens of the greatest country in the world, the country introduced to him by his first American family: John Withers, and Dave, and Jim.

PART FOUR

CHAPTER FORTY-FIVE

APRIL 3, 2001

Dad leaned back in his leather chair, peered over his reading glasses, and flashed me a wide smile. It was after five, and we were finally alone in our office. The receptionist was gone for the day. My brother, Ed, had left earlier. We could finally take a breath after a busy afternoon tabulating and recording rent checks. Dad loved running his own businesses. For the past twenty-five years, he and Mom managed residential group homes, caring for people with special needs.

"You have a few minutes?" he asked, getting up from his oversized desk.

"I always have time for you," I assured him. I stopped shuffling papers into folders and reached out to straighten the frayed collar of his favorite shirt. "You know, Papa, you manage six properties, I think you can afford a new shirt," I teased.

He waved off my comment and passed me an index card. Dad put all his important notes on these little lined cards which he carried in his shirt pocket. *CALL MR. WICKERS* was written in his precise handwriting, followed by an out-of-state phone number.

"Papa, do you know a Wickers?" I asked.

He squinted, trying to remember. "I don't think so, *Bärb*." That's what he always called me, Bairb with an umlaut. Dad had been in the U.S. for over forty years by this time, yet he still hadn't lost his gentle Polish accent. "But an old friend from my hometown in Poland, Howard Chandler, phoned me last week. He pressed me to call this number and kept telling me it was important."

"Do you want me to check out the area code?" I asked. "You know I'm happy to call whenever you want."

He pushed his hands in the air. "Let's do it!"

"Now?"

"Why not?"

Dad was always cautious. And here he was taking a risk, not knowing anything about this person. What else could I do but agree?

A light breeze ushered in an earthy scent through the window, that wonderful smell of early spring in Connecticut. I had thought I might catch some daylight to plan my gardens at home—my escape from everyday obligations. But that could wait. This was obviously more important.

We agreed to use separate phones. I would call and Dad would pick up the extension once it started ringing. We locked eyes—whether to register the significance of the moment or just our general unease, I couldn't say for sure. But when I heard the phone ring in that unknown area code, I held my breath until a soft voice answered.

"Hello, is this Mr. Wickers?"

"Mr. Withers," he corrected me.

I introduced myself quickly so he wouldn't think I was a telemarketer. I had no idea who this Withers was, but I had to admit that I was curious about the man who had gone to the trouble of tracing my father all the way to Poland and back. Now that I had him on the phone, I didn't want him hanging up because he thought I was selling life insurance or replacement windows. "I'm Barbara Bergren, and I believe you're looking for my father."

There was a pause. "Is … your father Mieczyslaw Wajgenszperg?" he asked.

It had been a long time since I'd heard that name. It ripped right through me. "Yes." *How do you know?* I couldn't even ask the question.

Dead silence.

"My dad is sitting right next to me," I added. "But he has a hearing impairment, so if you don't mind, I'll stay on the line—"

Dad suddenly interrupted, "Are you related to Lieutenant John Withers?"

I stiffened, unprepared for his question.

"Yes," said the man on the line. "He is my father."

Dad lowered his head. "I know … John Withers," he whispered.

He sat motionless in his chair. At seventy-two, my father was still a good-looking man. His wavy hair had remained a soft brown, graying only at his sideburns. His eyes had depth, that's the only way I can describe them.

"Martin," said the caller in his deliberate, measured voice, "do you remember what the troops called you?"

"Peevee," my father answered without hesitation.

"That's right," the man said, sounding relieved. "Pee-Wee. I've been looking for you for over two years. I can't tell you how thrilled I am to hear your voice, Martin," the man continued. "I grew up on your story."

I was having trouble following this conversation; it was almost impossible to believe that it was real. Who was this man?

"Is your father alive?" Dad asked tentatively.

"Yes," said the man on the line. "But he's not here right now. My search for you is a gift for his eightieth birthday."

Floored, I clutched the phone hard. My dad knew this man's father, and yet I'd never heard his name before. How was that possible?

My dad sat up and the tension left his face. John Withers II said that his father lived in Maryland, outside of Washington D.C. John explained that he'd traveled through Europe and the Middle East looking for my father, only to learn that he lived in the United States. John quoted historical documents and books and authors that had helped him in his search.

I tried to wrap my head around the conversation. It was all too much. I glanced around the room. The white-laced window curtain framed Dad in that moment—his muscular forearm gripping the phone, his wide shoulders pronounced. Right behind him, an heirloom clock kept time as the gold pendulum swung back and forth. How fitting. All was as it had been just moments before, and yet everything was different. Dad was different.

Before the call ended, Dad promised to get back to John the following week. Pleasantries were exchanged. They hung up.

I raised my hands in helpless question. "Dad, what on earth?" I said. "Who is Lieutenant John Withers?"

Moving slowly, Dad stood up and walked past his desk.

"Are you … okay?" I asked.

Then he did something I will never forget. He raised his hand to the back of his neck, pulled the top of his shirt collar, and slowly lifted his head.

"He helped put me back on my feet, Bärb," Dad said simply,

then gazed at some faraway spot.

No words necessary. I stretched my arms, pulled him close, and breathed in the familiar scent of his spicy aftershave. I kissed his cheek. He kissed mine. He knew I understood that this was a missing chapter from his Holocaust experience. But now, I wanted to know the story, the whole story.

One phone call. One secret buried for over fifty years.

CHAPTER FORTY-SIX

APRIL 27th, 2001

Two dark-suited men with rolling suitcases dashed by us. A curly blond toddler dragged his teddy bear, his sister running after him. Her pink-flowered backpack just missed me. The parents were intent on finding seats together, herding all the suitcases with summer hats attached to the handles. An older couple stood mid-aisle, sipping Dunkin' coffees.

I wondered what we looked like, how my family appeared to the many travelers making their way through the terminal. We looked like everyone else, I supposed, pacing back and forth near Bradley's gate A-1 with our casual clothes and expectant expressions. But that was far from the truth.

"Do you think you'll recognize John?" I asked.

Dad nodded calmly, his words steadier than his nerves. "I think I will."

I couldn't begin to imagine what he must have been feeling. I had no context for this, no frame of reference. Dad was sixteen when he met Lieutenant Withers. Now he was seventy-two. A lifetime had passed. Dad hadn't shared much about those dark years. Ed and I knew the names of the camps, had heard others' stories, but

Dad still had a hard time answering the tough questions about his family, choking on the words, evading the memories, so we hadn't asked for more for fear of dredging up his tortured past.

It had been just over three weeks since that first phone call with John Withers II. And now here we were at the airport. Waiting.

Ed checked his watch. John and his wife, Daisy, along with their daughter-in-law, Maryruth, were due any minute. John II was expected later that evening. Dad would go with John, myself, and the Withers family to Water's Edge Hotel in Westbrook right after lunch. Afterwards, we planned to entertain at our beach house nearby.

The flight status board lit up. United Airlines flight 1988 out of Baltimore had just touched down. My husband Steve began filming; Ed readied his digital camera. We anxiously watched the passengers come through the gate. A young couple in matching UCONN sports team jerseys passed by us. A mother pointed to the baggage claim sign so her teenage son would head in the right direction. A brawny soldier headed to his waving parents. I clung to Dad, arm in arm, waiting to see John. The line continued, dwindled, but we didn't see anyone who might resemble the man he remembered. Dad remained calm. The last group emerged.

They spotted each other immediately. Walking toward one another, both men broke into broad smiles.

"Hello, Pee-Wee," said John. "Is it okay to call you that?"

"You can always call me Pee-Vee," Dad replied.

The men gave each other a long-awaited embrace. Still clasping each other's arms, they shared a moment—a moment of remembrance.

I felt my shoulders relax. To my amazement, John reminded me of Dad. Both were soft-spoken. Both were barely five foot eight and they shared the same kind brown eyes. They had round faces and high cheekbones, thinning hair. They both wore hats. John wore a beige cap. Dad had asked me to hold his navy captain's hat. John, eighty-four, looked much younger than his age.

Ed looked to me, we couldn't believe it—the similarities were amazing. We saw the index card tucked in John's white, short-sleeved shirt pocket. Dad also carried his notes on index cards stuffed into his shirt pocket. We were floored.

We had expected to see a dark-skinned family, but John Withers was light-skinned and his wife Daisy white by appearance, even though she was black. Maryruth, their daughter-in-law, was white. I guess that's why we almost missed them coming through the gate. Daisy had graying, light brown hair, bright eyes, and a distinctive nose. She was built a lot like Mom—full-chested with healthy curves. Petite Maryruth sported short brown hair and fair, Irish features. After embracing Dad, everyone hugged as though we had known each other all our lives.

Dad led everyone to his van. Steve had to return to work but would meet us later in Westbrook. Ed explained that Mom had leg pains that worsened this week and couldn't make the trip. She hoped to meet everyone at our house for Sunday's cookout. First stop would be in Middletown, for lunch.

Clanking dishes and loud voices filled the restaurant as the bus boys cleared tables.

"Table for six please," I asked the hostess. "If you have one away from the maddening crowd, it would be ideal." She led us to a quiet side table. Perfect.

We sat. My mind raced. We just met. We were together, but where would we start?

“Hi, I’m Amy,” our server interrupted. “Can I get you all something to drink?”

“Iced tea for me please,” I said as she proceeded to go around the table.

I wondered if everyone’s history was open for discussion. How did John Withers feel about his time during the war. How would my father go back to the details of his Holocaust history?

Maryruth dug right in. She peppered Dad with questions. “Martin,” she started, “Do you remember what it was like spending time with Father John after the war? Oh, we call him ‘Father John.’”

“Very well. He was a well-respected lieutenant. I remember the troop appreciated him and so did I.”

No sooner had Dad replied than she fired off more questions, trying to get to the heart of this spectacular reunion. But we were still getting to know each other, so we slowed it down, asking more about the present. It was as if all the years vanished. John turned to Dad during a lull in the conversation. “What have you been doing with yourself?” he asked.

“I run retirement homes,” he said with a smile. “Caring for the elderly and the disadvantaged.”

“I hope they’re better than some of the barracks we had,” Father John joked.

The Withers were warm and charismatic, bright and unassuming. Conversation came easily. John had served in the U.S. Agency for International Development in various countries. John II worked for the State Department and fondly spoke of his last assignment in Latvia. John’s other son, Greg, was in Colorado working for a chemical company in research and development. Daisy used to teach, but at eighty-one was enjoying retirement. Maryruth worked for the State Department and had worked for Madeleine Albright and other secretaries of state. Ed and I listened politely to their stories, but fidgeted in our seats, eager and anxious to know what had happened back in 1945. They asked Ed and me about our history; about our families. John sat back in his chair, grinning, when he learned that Dad had three grandchildren and a great-granddaughter.

We had thousands of questions and didn't know where to start. Perhaps at dinner time tonight, I thought. Yes, with a glass of wine.

Steve arrived that evening for our families' first dinner together. The Withers were only staying for the weekend, so each moment was precious. Already, there was a feeling of family.

Drinks were served as the seven of us settled in at Water's Edge restaurant. Dad was consumed with nostalgia sitting next to John.

"This man helped me recover after the camps," Dad said. "I had no place to go, and he was there for me." Dad and John talked as if the intervening years were mere days.

It was the perfect time. Ed reached into his bag and presented John with a gift, which he accepted. When he reached for his pocketknife to cut the wrapping tape, Steve and Ed and I shared a smile; Dad always used his pocketknife to open gifts and mail, too. John grinned when he saw the wooden plaque, engraved in gold, with the heading: *1945 Reunion 2001*. It opened ... *fifty-six years ago darkness ended, new life began*. Ed wrote the words to thank John for his bravery and kindness, helping Dad recover after the war.

The evening felt ceremonial.

My son Jeff joined us at the beach house the next day. Taller than the other men in the room, he bent over to bear hug his Opa. Finally, John II and Ed arrived. Our two families blended instantly. John II was a bit taller than his father, with a rounder face, donning metal-framed glasses.

"My brother Greg and I grew up on our father's postwar story," John II explained. "My father didn't talk about combat or planes raining gunfire and bombs near their camp. He told us about two Jewish boys seeking refuge." John II recounted what his father had told him, how his troop welcomed the boys because they understood racist mindsets and the scarring abuses.

I felt such joy. I knew my father harbored many secrets, but this one shone a beautiful light. It comforted me to know that a group of men took him in, eased his pain and brought him back to life. It answered part of my lifelong question—how did my dad get past the Holocaust atrocity? How did he find the will to go on and not end up a bitter, angry man? John Withers was a big part of the answer. He and his men had extended kindness to my father when he needed it most.

Knowing how much Pee-Wee and Salomon meant to his father, John decided that searching for the boys would be a fitting tribute for his father's eightieth birthday.

"Deciding was the easy part. Going about it was harder than I thought," he said. "I searched documents in Israel and Germany looking for Martin and the other boy they called Salomon. I only had your dad's full name to research. That led me to your father's record in Bamberg, stating he emigrated to Israel in 1948."

John explained how Salomon had stumbled into the army camp

and into both of our fathers' lives. He believed his father thought of them like brothers after their time together. The boys shared history—although that topic was off-limits for discussion—they created a bond. A bond his father honored with reverence.

Sensing my discomfort, my father turned to me. "Bärb, you know that photo of me with my friend Shlomo—Shlomo Joskowicz, the one where we posed with his fiancée? Well Salomon is the name the soldiers gave him."

I knew the picture well. In fact there were many of Shlomo with his soon to be bride, with the inscription of 1946 dates. I thought that they had met in Bamberg after the war. I had no idea they were both survivors. Before I had time to contemplate this new relationship—this year the two survivors spent together in the safety of their American comrades—John told us that Salomon had died some ten years before.

Dad pursed his lips. I think he felt guilty that they had lost touch. They corresponded for a time, but both got caught up with raising families, building their new lives. And now he was gone. A piece of heartfelt history gone with him.

Dad prepared drinks while I made sure all the finger foods and snacks were laid out. Everyone was talking at once, until Dad, in typical fashion, raised his glass to toast.

"Welcome everyone. It's an honor to have you all here. I would never have believed this day would happen. Never. Thank you, John. *Salut!*"

Dad reached for his reading glasses and pulled out his old leather-bound photo album from a shelf under the bar. No sooner had he placed it on the countertop than John opened a satchel and pulled out his faded red album, a gift from Pee-Wee and Salomon, and placed it next to Dad's. They'd each carried them across three continents for the last half century. They flipped open their albums.

My father stared at his first photo. Twenty-eight-year-old Lieutenant Withers' round brown eyes suggested a wistful look into the distance. John had written his name and address in the States on the back. Because of that photo, I always thought Dad had served in an army, with no clue where or when. Now I knew the story was much different. John's first page displayed seventeen-year-old Dad's smiling picture, donning an army cap; both photos were circa 1946. He had written in English, *To my friend, John L. Withers*, and had signed his full name on the back, Mieczyslaw Wajgenszperg.

Steve videotaped while Ed snapped pictures of the two albums.

There was something I needed to know. "John, what did our dad look like when you met him?"

John hesitated. "I recall seeing their smiling faces, big eyes, and gaunt bodies. I was startled that they were so young. They recognized authority, and in this case, that was me."

Now John II asked about Pee-Wee's time with his Dad.

"He was like a second father," Dad responded. "He understood, really understood, what I'd been through." He paused. "Those soldiers were like our family. They protected us, included us in everything."

Bit by bit, Dad opened up about the aftermath of Dachau in 1945 and '46. It exposed a deep wound from the past. John and his troop had helped him during the most vulnerable time of his life.

Meeting the former lieutenant John Withers was a life-changing event for our family. Both families were captivated by our unfolding story.

I reexamined my busy life, feeling a higher sense of compassion as if, for the first time, I had witnessed humanity at its best. But the credit went to John's son, John II—for his extensive search to find my father and reconnect the two men.

Martin and John— meeting again after fifty-five years

Reunion Dinner

Left to right: Daisy, Martin, Edward, Steve, Barbara, Maryruth, John

Martin and John with their photo albums

CHAPTER FORTY-SEVEN

"Are you ready to hold her, Papa?" I asked.

"You bet." He straightened up in the vinyl hospital chair as I positioned the swaddled baby in his arms. Lips pursed, my father smiled, holding the infant-like fragile porcelain. That familiar, soft, adoring look swept over his face. A look I'd come to appreciate—it always made me feel special, like I was the only one who mattered. Now it would be for her too.

"Meet Ashley Sonia Klara," my daughter called from her hospital bed. "What do you think Opa?"

"She's beautiful." And she was. Perfect skin, beautiful eyes, cute button-like nose. He stared. His first great-grandchild.

I kissed his forehead, brushing his feathery hair to the side. I sensed her name would hit him hard, that this tiny, miraculous girl would bring him back to a time he'd tried to keep locked away. Eyes welling up, he cradled her near his heart.

Our first grandchild had been born on January 1, 2001. Our daughter had become a mom while finishing her senior year at the University of Connecticut. Jeff, our son, was working at Mass Mutual in their large corporate markets division. Ed's son, Christopher, was now the second youngest, and entering first grade. The grandkids adored their Opa and embraced the Withers family who had no grandchildren of their own.

Our daughter and her fiancé had decided to wait and marry a few months after little Ashley's birth, which is how the Withers' family came to be at the wedding.

Kimberly married at the First Congregational Church in Westbrook, near the beach house, on July 28th, 2001. John and Daisy, along with their sons and daughters-in-law, John II and Maryruth, Greg and Carol, all came to share in the special day.

Everyone danced together at the Water's Edge reception hall overlooking Long Island Sound. Martin shared the spotlight with John. After the father-daughter dance, Kimberly danced with her Opa while I twirled on the floor with Father John. She brushed against me and we exchanged dance partners. Jeff circled the room with John's wife Daisy. The newlyweds' happiness filled the room, and with it a sense of gratitude for the profound connection between past and present.

The next morning, Dad insisted on inviting all the wedding guests to breakfast at the resort. He and Mom were proud to host. Tired from the previous day of celebration, everyone was still eager to gather and enjoy the connection with family and friends. Mom and Dad's pride showed as they welcomed the guests. They were in their early seventies now. They understood the significance of seeing their granddaughter marry, welcoming their great-granddaughter into the family, and having their close family all together. Now there were six more—our extended family included the Withers.

CHAPTER FORTY-EIGHT

2002

Seagulls screeched while circling the marina outside our beach house. It was July 19th, a calm, cloudless hot day. The Withers family was expected later in the afternoon. John and Daisy, along with their son John II and his wife Maryruth, had accepted an invitation to stay with us at the beach house. John was drafting a book about his father's story. Dad was to be an integral part of 1945—a pivotal year. This visit was social, to enjoy family time, while John II took the opportunity to interview Dad for his manuscript.

Dad set his newspaper down on the cocktail table and walked out the sliding-glass door. High tide covered the sandbar while waves lapped gently against the beach house seawall. Grasping the iron railing, I watched him look out over Long Island Sound. He had stocked the bar and checked off his to-do list. Everything had to be perfect.

Just a week earlier, we celebrated Dad's seventy-fourth birthday. Mom had made her famous potato salad and Ed had courageously boiled lobsters. I had carried out his birthday cake while all the kids sang, all the while laughing over our not-so-perfect voices. His smile that day radiated calm. In those precious moments, I knew he'd felt an inner peace—his family was all together, all twelve of us.

Dad stayed with the Witherses and cooked breakfast the following morning. Steve and I drove back to Westbrook; I felt it important to be there when John II asked Dad questions about his past. John II had started interviewing before I arrived and had asked Dad to sign some letters requesting archival information from both German and Israeli agencies. Instinctively, I asked to see what Dad was signing. He was the smartest man I knew, and I knew John II to be a man of integrity. Nevertheless, Ed and I vowed to always protect him, so we examined the paperwork. It passed our scrutiny—of course.

John II and I stole away outside. We heard the waves slap against the seawall—it was high tide. We reminisced on how fascinating it was to see our fathers' history unfold. How we were making new memories.

"Did you know that your dad had only seen pictures of black people before he met the soldiers of 3512 Company?" asked John.

Dad met people of many races in the camps, but it hadn't occurred to me that he had never known a black man. "Gosh, no. I guess I never really thought about it."

"That really struck me. Your dad had no preconceived ideas about race. In part because of his lack of exposure … perhaps in part because of his youth."

It was profound to hear John talk about my father this way. I only knew our own family viewpoints.

As if he heard my thoughts, he continued, "Martin had met some dark-skinned people, specifically Turkish prisoners of war and Central Asian soldiers, who had served in the Red Army."

I stood still, taking it all in. John continued.

"Did you know that a Uzbek prisoner tore his bread ration in two and gave half to Pee-Wee?"

I was taken aback. How did I not know this? At the same time I thanked God for such kindness.

"Your father had encountered Poles and Jews who were indifferent or uncaring, yet here was this man, Asian by birth and Muslim by faith, sharing what little he had with a young Jewish boy. I think your father knew then—as he always knew—that it was a person's inner qualities that mattered, not his racial or religious designation. Certainly not his nationality."

I thanked John for his research and his stamina. For uncovering the truth.

The midafternoon sun beckoned us for a break. We headed back inside.

Coffee cups in hand, Father John took me aside and shared that he had been diagnosed with prostate cancer a couple of years before but was thriving on the medication his doctors prescribed. He felt the Veteran's Administration was doing a great job treating his illness and advising him on his options. He looked so healthy at eighty-five years of age. It felt good to know he trusted me, that he trusted our family.

John always made the person he was talking to feel important. He complimented you. "Oh Barbara," he would say, "aren't you so smart? How did you know to research that?" And he never missed an opportunity to make everyone laugh. I appreciated that he was comfortable opening up to me.

John's stories of a young black man living in the South were captivating. He grew up in a house with his parents and siblings, but when a cousin's father met with tragedy, his parents invited them to stay at their home. It put a tremendous strain on the family. The house was crowded and there wasn't enough income to cover expenses. John resented having to share his private space. There was no place to read in peace. Worse, he hated himself for feeling resentful. That's just not what good people did.

The Withers wanted to know more about Dad's businesses. My father explained how he'd acquired and managed the six properties but didn't mention that he worked all the time. Steve and I shared our college stories with John II and Maryruth. Our last night dining in Essex's Griswold Inn felt like a party.

"You have to join us for an opera evening," John said after he learned that Jeff hadn't attended one. "I mean it. Take a couple vacation days, come and stay with us."

"Only if you let me take you to a baseball game," Jeff said.

"You have a deal." John lit up.

We ate well, drank happily, laughed continuously, and hugged a lot.

No meet and greets, no wedding arrangements—we just spent time together. One blended family.

John and Martin with grandsons Jeff Bergren and Chris Weigen

CHAPTER FORTY-NINE

It had been two days and the fever hadn't broken. Dad finally admitted to me that he was having hand tremors. When Dad spoke up, you knew it was serious. He didn't want to be a bother. I immediately called Dr. Dauod, the surgeon who had repaired Dad's hernia the year before. It had been his first operation. He would soon have his second—removal of his gallbladder.

Mom was no longer able to help with Dad's care. The pain in her lower legs seemed to have gotten worse. She was struggling with mood swings now and in denial about her condition. Worse, she refused to seek treatment. Her strong personality wouldn't allow anyone into her private world—that included her husband.

I drove Dad to the hospital for his scheduled operation on the morning of October 24th. He looked pallid and gray. I was worried but remained optimistic because gallbladder surgery was considered routine. Staying close to him, I believed my presence would help him feel in control of his surroundings. He always refused medications that might alter his mind. Of course—he had to keep his wits about him during those years in the camps. He wasn't allowed the luxury of being sick. It was a matter of life or death.

"Your chariot awaits you, Mr. Weigen," said a nurse pressing the brake on the mobile bed. It was time. I walked with him, kissed his forehead, and let go of his hand. Anxiety overwhelmed me when Dad was wheeled into the operating room. To keep my mind busy, I set up work in the waiting area, diving into my client's financial forecast. Surgery was expected to take one to two hours. After almost three hours, I stopped. Something wasn't right. I found a nurse and asked her to check on Dad. Time passed slowly. Finally, Dr. Dauod called the waiting room. He looked tired.

"Sorry it took so long," he began, pulling off his surgical cap. "Martin's gallbladder had partially ruptured and the colon and liver were wrapped around it. Our findings necessitated a more extensive surgery then I had anticipated."

"Is he all right?" I asked, frantic.

"Yes, he's in recovery right now, but two veins didn't come off the gallbladder, so we had to sever them. They bled, so your father needed a blood transfusion. He's very weak."

I sat down. Was the blood clean? I'd read articles on blood donor contamination.

Dr. Dauod shook his head. "We removed the biggest stone I ever saw in all my years of practice." He handed me a photo. I was taken aback. "It was the size of a pear," he said. "I had to take pictures." I stared at the huge shiny object. How could he have lived with this, never complaining?

"I can't believe he let this go so long," said the doctor. "He had to be in tremendous pain."

The next two weeks in the hospital were a nightmare. Ed and I took shifts while Steve and the grandkids filled in the gaps. The morphine knocked Dad out and he began hallucinating.

"Barb, I'm at the hospital," Ed relayed over the phone. "Dad tried getting out of bed at five this morning. The nurse called me so I could talk to him. He said a taxi was waiting to pick him up."

"I'm on my way."

Ed went to the hospital every morning. I went in for some lunches and always after work. We were both in and out every day trying to manage Dad's care. It was chilling. We had never seen my father lose control. Never. I went into research mode and discovered that the meds he was on often overwhelmed older patients who couldn't metabolize opioid drugs. When I asked if anything could be done, I was given an offhand response—"Oh, he's just *sundowning*." More research. Apparently many elders get confused late in the day after the sun goes down—hence the term sundowning. It was just one of the many questions that educated me in the attitudes hospitals employed with older patients who are often dismissed and not taken seriously. I was appalled.

I needed to save my father from this trauma. These drugs were overwhelming his mind. He fought it but lost this battle. He tried to get up, removing his IV. The staff restrained him. That's when I lost it. It took me back to when Dad saved me at Seaside.

I hovered to see what went on during the day and night. I talked to nurses. The few who cared were helpful. Noise and commotion were believed to exhaust older patients' systems. Ed and I learned that we had the right to get a one-on-one aide based on his condition. We fought for it and won. The restraints came off. That evening, I walked into his room. The aide had overhead lights on, the TV blaring with a game show on. Dad's arms were quivering; he was clearly not resting. It was almost time for the shift change. I lowered the lights, turned off the TV. Leaning over Dad, I whispered to him, "I'm so sorry. No more noise. You rest and get better. I need you. I really need you, Papa." And I waited.

Guilt kept me on edge. I couldn't stay overnight. Hospitals made me anxious, and I knew if I didn't sleep, I couldn't take care of Dad. I couldn't work. I'd be useless.

At eleven o'clock, his night aide walked in. She was young and bright. I had to bring Dad to life for her—I needed her to care about him. We talked. She got to know him.

"Please, keep his room dim and calm." I looked to Dad, his fisted hands trembling. "And no TV—can you do that for him please?" I pleaded. "The meds are overwhelming his system." I choked up. "He needs rest … he needs calm."

"I'll be sure to keep his room quiet," she said in her lilting Spanish accent. She sat next to his bed and took Dad's hand in hers.

I smiled, relieved. As I got ready to leave, Dad called out, "Bärb!"

I stopped dead at the door. He was sedated, yet he knew I was there. He hadn't said a word in days.

Walking back to his bed, I brushed his hair to the side. Cheek to cheek, I kissed his head. "Tonight will be different, Papa—there'll be no noise, no extra light. It will be quiet, peaceful … I promise."

And it was. This aide was an angel.

He woke up the next day and asked to go home.

John Withers and his son called to find out how Dad was doing. I had been afraid that they could tell from my voice that he was still in danger.

"He's so strong, he'll beat this," said John in his soft, familiar voice. As always, he tried to comfort me. I was grateful for his strength all over again.

Thankfully, after two weeks, I picked up Dad to bring him home. He gradually recovered, although he wasn't used to living on a slower schedule. Not surprisingly, he remained strong and didn't ask for any help. Ed and I watched him closely, helping him recover. We both thought he'd gone back to the office too soon, but we realized that work was part of his rehabilitation, he needed something to do. He needed to keep busy.

More cards and flowers arrived from the Withers family. John II called again to check on Dad. Ed and I promised to set up time to visit them in Maryland once he felt better.

Time with Dad was always precious.

CHAPTER FIFTY

As one of the first African Americans hired by the United States for the Agency for International Development, John L. Withers served as a Foreign Service officer. Even after he retired, he was invited to State Department events. In May 2003, he and Daisy were at a Foreign Service dinner party in Washington, D.C. As John listened to the diplomats detail their latest assignments over dinner, he decided to share his World War II adventure.

John's folksy-but-eloquent storytelling sparked everyone's interest. "My men had wanted to keep the boys," he told them. "Funny to look back on it, this notion of men and boys. But the two kids who stumbled into our camp looked so young … thin and terribly sick. We couldn't think of them as anything but boys."

He explained how diseases among the former prisoners of war were rampant, that he risked dishonorable discharge if Pee-Wee and Salomon were ever discovered. I wish I had been there that night to see the reaction of the diplomats upon hearing his story. But one thing's for sure—they would have no trouble understanding the connection between the Jewish boys and the black soldiers. Hostility and discrimination are things you don't easily forget. Bridging that gap had been the bond that conquered all.

John continued, talking about the reunion with my father. "We recognized each other instantly. Was I really standing face-to-face with Pee-Wee? A grown man with his family?" You'd have to be pretty jaded not to be touched by John's account. It was an emotional moment around the table, a reminder of the healing power of kindness amid the most terrible racism and abuse. One of the guests was particularly impressed. "That's a great story," he said. "Would you be willing to share it? With your permission, I'd like to make a call to a friend of mine who may be interested in having you speak." He handed John his contact information and asked for his in return.

Stories spread. Good stories spread fast. John and his son were invited by one of their local organizations to share the account of their reunion with Pee-Wee, as the Withers family still called him. The modest group of about thirty people was enthralled with this tale of bravery and grace. It wasn't long before John II got a call from Tom Hamburger, a political reporter for the *Wall Street Journal*.

Accustomed to covering stories about the government, Tom was swept away by what had happened some fifty years earlier. He wanted to know more. John, always eager to share his father's story, was thrilled by the possibility of a wider audience for this unlikely friendship. He and Tom met over lunch. The two men hit it off, but by the time the coffee came around, they understood that this wouldn't make a political article. Still, Tom wasn't ready to let it go. That's when he called his friend, the feature writer Bryan Gruley.

Bryan was working on a project for the *Journal* that would monopolize his time for the next few months, but he was drawn to the story. Two weeks later, another meeting was arranged. This time, Tom asked John II to join him and Bryan for lunch.

Like his father, John II was an exceptional storyteller. He knew what to focus on, giving the men details of the war history, keeping it on point and adding humor in just the right spots. Bryan was touched by the tale and asked to meet John's parents.

On May 28th, Bryan drove to John and Daisy's home. Anxious to meet them at last, Bryan was charmed right away.

"Hello and welcome," said Daisy in her uplifting, slight Southern drawl.

"Hello and thank you," Bryan returned. Right away he was captivated by the beautiful home with its Southeast Asian artifacts. A gold elephant tapestry hung over an easy chair. "That's stunning," he said.

John reached his hand out to welcome Bryan. "Just a little something we brought home from Burma when we lived there."

Daisy led them to the dining table. "I've got tea and some sweets. Won't you come sit down? Or would you rather have coffee? Oh John, can you get the cream please?"

"No, no, please. This is already too much." Bryan felt right at home. Something about this place was … just warm, inviting. As a couple, John and Daisy exuded an engaging energy, an ease as they worked together, welcoming him.

"I've heard a lot about you, John," Bryan started. "Can you tell me a little about yourself?"

"Not much to tell, really," said John in his soft-spoken way. "I was born in Greensboro, North Carolina. You know, we were part of the segregated South."

"I know you went to school here. Where did you go to college after high school?"

"I was fortunate to graduate from North Carolina A&T College."

John thought for a moment. "That was in 1937."

Daisy finished for him. John never boasted. "He received his Master's in Economics from the University of Wisconsin in 1941. He so wanted to work toward a doctorate degree." She nodded to John.

"Well, luckily the GI bill became available while I was stationed overseas during the war." He hesitated and went off topic. "Can you believe my son took a sabbatical to find the Jewish boys as a gift for my eightieth birthday? It had been our nighttime story since they were young."

John didn't like talking about himself and gracefully transitioned to April 1945. His rank of newly commissioned second lieutenant had placed him in charge of supplies in a black unit.

"It was tough on my men," he shared. "Despite the army's singular mission, blacks and whites were segregated in the service." He paused. "We were all fighting for the same cause, but still considered outsiders.

"When I got orders to dispatch enormous amounts of food and aid to a base near Münich, I didn't realize that the American Army had just liberated the camp. I also didn't know everyone was scrambling to manage a human catastrophe. No one was prepared for the sick and dying prisoners of war they found behind the iron gate of Dachau." He shook his head. "My men were in shock. I'll never forget their reaction staring into the face of evil. They stopped joking. They stopped talking. They wouldn't even play their usual games at night."

"How did you react when you met the two boys?"

Describing the risk that Martin, dubbed Pee-Wee, took leaving his DP camp, John was clearly impressed with his courage. "And the other boy, Salomon, he did the same thing. Can you imagine? After all they'd been through, risking their only chance at a livelihood?" He grinned, "I was really torn. There were these smiling young faces that I knew were tortured boys."

Bryan asked, "What made you change your mind to keep Pee-Wee and Salomon?"

"They had these gaunt, innocent faces; they were sickly and just kids," John responded. "I was surprised. From what my soldiers had said, I had expected war-hardened men."

Bryan and John talked back and forth like that for a while. *How did you communicate? How did they get on with the other men? How did you hide them?* For every question John answered, two or three more followed. To say that the story resonated with Bryan would be an understatement. He was fascinated—fixated. He needed to meet this Pee-Wee.

I'm sure John II could sense my reluctance over the phone. Would Dad consider being interviewed for the *Wall Street Journal*? He navigated the process and, delicately, I pushed back. "I'll certainly share this with Ed and my dad," I said. "I promise to get back to you soon. Clearly we need time to digest this."

I've always assessed situations before jumping in: the pros, the cons, the aftereffects. I learned from a very young age to deliberate my decisions. This one could be life-altering. An interview would put a tremendous weight on Dad. It would force him to remember his time as prisoner of war, his slain family, our family. He wasn't a spotlight kind of guy. He survived by staying in the background, and this interview—with a *Wall Street Journal* reporter no less!—would be front and center.

In talking it over, Ed and I came up with all sorts of questions. What was the objective of the interview? Was it just about John and Dad? John's part is heroic, but Dad's Holocaust experience would anchor the story and it had never been told. The interview would highlight John's role in helping two young Jewish boys trying to recover from their Holocaust experiences and would provide recognition for the risk he took after the war. But our greatest concern was the emotional risk to Dad. It would force open old wounds. We knew this was Dad's decision, not ours, but we figured it was a pretty safe bet that he wouldn't want to go down that path, much less broadcast his horrific past to the world.

We figured wrong.

Ed and I picked a day that week to see Dad. I left work at Blum Shapiro early enough so we could meet at the office for our talk. Our office conference room doubled as a dining area where we worked, socialized, and toasted special evenings together. In typical Victorian style, the fireplace mantel centered the room. We displayed special vases, sometimes a photo of the family. The blue swag curtain emphasized the high ceiling. Dad kept a bottle of Port in the closet, so after our office employee left for the day, he poured three glasses of wine as we sat around the table. Dad asked about his grandchildren—Jeff, Kimberly, and Chris. Ed and I assured him they were all doing well.

"And how is my great-granddaughter?" he asked proudly.

"Fine." I smiled. "Talking up a storm." He beamed. His kids and grandkids were everything to him.

Dad lifted his glass to toast the children's health. This was part of his routine whenever we got together.

Finally, I paused and looked at Dad. "John II called me this weekend … John Senior shared your story at a meeting near Washington, D.C. It seems you're in the capitol spotlight these days." I rubbed his arm. "John got a call from a writer at the *Wall Street Journal*."

Dad tilted his head, squinting his eyes in question. Ed and I rolled out the request for interviews with both men. We shared the details as Dad sat back in his chair, arms folded, thoughtful.

"If this helps John, I'll do it."

Ed and I were speechless. We hadn't come to talk Dad into doing the interview. In fact, I felt I should talk him out of it. What happened to all the years of secrecy—listen to your surroundings, don't talk, don't tell. I'd grown to automatically assess religious affiliations of people I met. School, work, play. It was their way of keeping me safe. At Blum Shapiro, my burden was lifted working with Jewish partners. I was safe to share my dad's history, my Israeli roots, my Jewishness. Prior to high school, I was the good Catholic, and it was okay to have a German mother. No one knew the rest. I'd lived like that my entire life. Now, Dad was about to go full public. He'd always stayed under the radar, always. Both my parents suffered discrimination—Dad on the largest scale, and Mom was often ostracized for her heritage.

"You realize Bryan will ask about your Holocaust years," Ed declared.

Before Dad could say a word, I interrupted, "Please! Think this through, Dad. You'll be asked personal questions—about your family. And we don't know what may go to print. It's an international paper." But I realized quickly, once this interview began, what I feared the most—I couldn't protect him. I couldn't keep him safe.

He looked at me, he looked at Ed. "Don't vorry children … I can take care of myself."

But we continued to talk about all the things that could happen during the interview. Was he really ready to share details of his past? Whenever we approached the subject, he had choked up. When we asked about his parents and his sister, he'd always shut down. We'd always backed off. This would be risky. This would be public.

But Dad had made up his mind.

CHAPTER FIFTY-ONE

My heart was pounding. This was *the call.* But right away, Bryan Gruley's voice put me at ease. I found him to be friendly, casual, and deliberate—a good combination. We made small talk about his assignment at Florida State University, an investigative piece about undergraduate drinking on campus. And we shared family details. His parents owned a summer home on Lake Michigan, mine on Long Island Sound. But that was just the warmup. Soon he was telling me how he became interested in my father's story. I could tell he was sensitive to Dad and his history. John II had done a good job prepping him.

"You know, I've heard a lot of war stories, but I've never heard anything like this," he said. "Talking to John, I felt a depth to their relationship—a closeness and reverence toward your father. Frankly, it blew me away."

That's how I felt, too.

"Bryan, I'm sure you know, but this is very hard for my father to talk about. I have to say, I was a little shocked when he agreed to the interview."

"You want to protect your father. I can appreciate that."

"Good. Thanks." I was stumbling over my words. This was all so new. "This is nothing personal, but when you come out to meet

Dad, I just want to make sure you know that my brother Ed and I will always be with him."

"I completely understand. I'm sure I would do the same if I were in your shoes."

I breathed a little sigh of relief.

"If it's all right with you," Bryan continued, "I'd like to come out in July. Does that work?"

"I think so," I hedged.

"I'm free the weekend of July twenty-fifth. How would that be for you folks? I'm thinking we could meet for dinner when I arrive so we can spend some time together. You know, getting to know each other."

"Great idea," I said as my mind flashed through July dates. Dad's seventy-fifth birthday party on July 20th was all I could think of. "I'll talk with Dad about the date and have him pick a restaurant."

"Can we set up the following day to start the interview?" Bryan asked. "I'm planning on about four hours or so."

Whoa! This was my reality check. I couldn't even imagine Dad being questioned about his past, never mind for four straight hours! Maybe Bryan didn't quite understand how delicately we had to tread. "I think that's too much." I hesitated. "You know, this is his first time sharing details …"

But before I could finish, Bryan said, "Absolutely. We can do it over two days. How does two hours each session sound?"

Bryan was personable and professional. He knew what he wanted. More to the point, he had respect for his subject and his story. I agreed.

It was all happening so fast. I felt nervous, anxious, wondering what would come out. I couldn't even watch a Holocaust movie without imagining what Dad had been through. Never mind hearing him open up about his own story. I feared learning more details of his past.

He could still walk away. Maybe I should suggest that he pull out. But would that upset him? Would it make things worse? Since his stint in the hospital, I worried constantly about his health. Could reliving the deprivations of his youth in the camps come back to haunt him physically, haunt him emotionally? I didn't want to find out.

But what I didn't know was Dad was losing weight.

Pacing around Bradley airport's receiving area, I was once again meeting someone I've never met before. He said to look for a tall guy with glasses … but there were a lot of tall guys with glasses! It wasn't long before a tall, handsome man with an athletic build made eye contact. He looked to be in his forties, and he walked with an air of confidence. And he wore glasses.

"Barb?" he asked, extending his hand for a firm handshake.

"Boy—are we good!" I smiled. "Amazing, we had no problem finding each other."

As we walked to my car, I told Bryan about our evening plans.

"We're meeting at The Butterfly," I said, "a Chinese restaurant up the street from our business. It's one of Dad's favorites."

On those rare occasions when Dad and I found time, we would meet at The Butterfly for a drink after work. I leaned on him when life became overwhelming for me. The last time we were here, I confided about Jeff. "I'm worried Dad. He's working long hours and struggling with his relationship. He won't talk about it, needs to do everything on his own—a lot like you." Dad assured me he'd talk with him. I ordered another glass of wine. He was not only my rock; he counseled the kids. And now, this time, I would be his. At least I would try.

Bryan and I walked to the parking garage. "Funny, I met John here in April. And two years later, after seeing my father with him—their deep friendship, you just can't imagine how that made me feel."

"I can't wait to meet your dad. What's he like?"

This one was easy. "He's unassuming, has an incredible memory, wears a hearing aid, speaks with an accent," I said, tilting my head with a smile. "He's one of the greatest men to walk this earth."

Touching the center of his glasses and pushing them up on his nose, Bryan laughed. I thought he understood my protective love for my father. Tread lightly. I was starting to relax. It was my job to assess Bryan and call my brother with a report before meeting at the restaurant. The report would be favorable. Bryan listened. He adapted to Dad's needs. And I was starting to like him.

We arrived at The Butterfly at six. Ed had arranged for a table toward the back of the restaurant. After much handshaking and polite chitchat, we ordered a round of drinks. Bryan had a great sense of humor and everyone was getting more comfortable now. Ed and I watched Dad interact with him; they were lost in their conversation, talking easily, like friends. Bryan was earning our blessing.

CHAPTER FIFTY-TWO

JULY 26th, 2003

I brought Dad a second cup of coffee. Sunlight spilled through the oak branches, dotting the deck with spattered light. Bryan had piloted Dad back to his hometown, Wierzbnik, and exposed a treasure trunk of history. Real events I didn't know about. The house he grew up in, where he played, his love for his sister Klara.

Bryan knew how momentous this all was. "You've carried this around with you for a long time, Martin."

"After the war, I never really went back. I never wanted to think about it. I never talked about it. I just tried to leave the past behind me. My children even didn't know. I was not strong enough … not to break down to tell them all of this. I think talking to John about the war changed my mind. You know, whatever they want to know, whatever I remember. It's time."

Bryan continued writing all this down in his spiral notepad. Ed was capturing every treasured word on videotape. I tried to protect his heart.

The interview opened up Dad's life as a child. We met his family, felt the transition they endured into the war. Witnessing the October 27th Selection Day through Dad's eyes was torture.

No one spoke. No one moved. It was a raw moment.

Bryan guided Dad through the Starachowice slave labor camp period, finally ending this first interview.

"So how long were you in the Majowka camp?"

"Until July 1944," Dad shut his eyes for a moment. "That's the time they loaded us onto trains to Auschwitz."

Auschwitz, if ever there was a word to make me stiffen, to put all my senses on alert. The air grew heavy at this point—at least it seemed to. I didn't dare make eye contact with Ed for fear I'd lose it. The name itself conjured up black-and-white photos of innocent families arriving to be torn apart, likely murdered. How on God's earth did this happen in our lifetime?

Most disturbing to me was that my father, the man who loved and guided me through life, was one of the Jews who witnessed the reality of Auschwitz. It remains incomprehensible to me.

CHAPTER FIFTY-THREE

AUGUST 2003

I was shopping for drapes at Macy's when my cell phone rang.

"Hi, Barbara, it's Bryan Gruley."

I repositioned my phone closer to my ear. What could he be calling about?

"How are you, Bryan?" I asked, surprised. It had only been a few days since he left Connecticut.

"I'm fine, thanks for asking. I'm back at Florida State University researching my other article. More important, how's your dad doing?"

"He's doing all right," I responded.

"I can't get your dad's story out of my mind. I mean, it's just overwhelming what he went through."

It surprised me to realize I was still standing in the middle of the curtain aisle. I hadn't moved from the display of lined drapes. I took a breath, trying to focus. "I know, Bryan," I said. "The interview uncovered all sorts of feelings for Ed and me too. You did a great job."

"I'm trying to figure out how Martin got through this and lived to tell about it."

I wondered what my role was here. Did he need more specifics? More clarity? Then I realized he needed to share his feelings and come to terms with listening to a witness share some of life's worst crimes against humanity. I just needed to listen, so I did. Dad's unfolding history had affected Bryan. It disturbed him, just as it disturbed the friends I'd shared the story with. They usually got quiet, assimilating the significance of his reality. It made me feel good he was so moved, and I was grateful for his keen interviewing skills. I thought he might draft the story with more empathy.

We talked about Dad's steady determination and the upcoming second interview, scheduled for August 23rd.

"Great to hear from you, Bryan. We're looking forward to seeing you in August," I said as we hung up the phone. He was handing us the keys to unlock Dad's remarkable past. We were lucky to have him.

No way could I continue shopping. I put my phone away and left the store.

Something was different. Ever since the interview with Bryan my father seemed a little changed. Sure, when I asked him how he was doing, he'd say he was okay, but I didn't quite believe him. Not completely.

"Papa, tell me the truth."

"Well, I'm waking up at night, but you know me, when I fall asleep, I stay asleep." He tried to make light of it. "I'm thinking back, remembering what we talked about with Bryan. I haven't thought about it in a long time."

Those words unraveled me. I understood too well the way night intruders could mess with your mind. I've had my demons visit me when I close my eyes. I realized if I was asked to share my time at The Seaside, I'd be forced to open that chapter, the one I had blocked out for decades. The last thing I would wish on my dad was having six years of the Holocaust intrude on his sleep. I felt helpless.

I called him back. "Papa, you don't have to do another interview if it's causing too many bad memories."

"I'll be all right," he said, "I have to finish this. You know, I have to do this for John."

He was a man of his word and wouldn't consider backing out of a promise, especially one he made to John.

CHAPTER FIFTY-FOUR

AUGUST 23rd, 2003

We believed the worst was behind us. We had listened to Dad as he detailed where he grew up, the house he lived in, the shops in their market square. We saw Wierzbnik through his eyes and learned so many things we didn't know. Dad's uncles came from Warsaw and Krakow to watch his soccer tournaments; his father was the president of the soccer league. He became animated sharing his time about his family's summer vacations and rowing on the lake. I loved that part.

Then came the darkness of the camps. "In our situation, we camp prisoners had to come together. We provided hope for each other. We also tried to build up the naysayers—the cynics—and at the same time, yourself. We never liked to talk about the reality and lost family, it just made the situation worse. Hope. You had to have hope."

Another beautiful August day ushered in the second interview. Any tension from rushing that morning melted away when Dad stood next to me overlooking my flower garden; the last towering pink coneflowers waved back and forth in the gentle breeze. Coffees in hand, Bryan, Steve, and Ed joined us outside.

We were in good spirits. Sitting down on the same chairs as the first time, Bryan propped open his spiral pad and began to read his notes.

"So, Martin, where were we when we last left our heroes? You had just met John Withers. You and Salomon were in his office."

My father repositioned himself in the chair. He was uncomfortable with the word "hero." Not me. I was used to seeing him that way.

Dad chuckled as he described how he and Salomon hid from Army officials, how the troops protected them. He lit up when he talked about his last encampment in the village of Staffelstein—he pronounced it in true German, *Schtaffelschtein.* He told stories about their time living at Grüner Baum. It was their last stay with the troops and his favorite place. I gleaned that it was where he felt most at home. My father recalled one afternoon when the men played baseball. He caught a ground ball, hesitated—and threw it to the wrong base. John was cheering them on the sidelines and broke into a barrel laugh. Before he knew it, Dad and the team had stopped playing they were laughing so hard.

"Evening meals brought everyone together. Like family. We joked and looked forward to playing games before sunset, before they played 'Taps.'"

Soon the boys spent time in the nearby town of Bamberg, preparing for their independent lives.

"The war is over. How did you feel Martin?" Bryan asked. "Getting ready to move on?"

"At that time, I was just coming back to the reality of life." Dad hesitated, lost in thought. Lost in the past, perhaps?

I rubbed Dad's shoulders. He understood the nature of suffering in a way I never could. I guess that's what he was trying to protect me from. He went on, recalling happier memories, such as how he learned English: "Good morning, Mr. Withers. Good evening, Mr. Withers." Dad referred to the soldiers by their first names, but John was always "Mr. Withers." I realized Dad revered John and was encouraged by his attention. But it was with the other men—the soldiers he worked and played with—that he felt most at ease.

"It was our home," Dad continued. "Even in the back of the truck—it was a home. In the morning, we had our breakfast; when it was cold, we had plenty of blankets. They were very concerned and would ask if we wanted more. They'd ask twenty times. The supply sergeant came to us, 'Need more? Warm enough?'"

Another pause. Gratitude washed over me. God bless them, I thought. Dad mentioned a soldier named Dave. Here he spoke about a lot of the men, but Dave was special.

Then Bryan asked about the day he separated from the troop.

"It was sad for us. That was our family. That's all we had. At that time, Salomon hadn't found his sister yet, so we didn't have anyone … that goodbye is a moment I didn't want to have happen either. That's one of the things I didn't want to remember. I blocked it out."

Bryan turned psychologist. "After spending four to five years in camps, one camp after another, losing your family, ending up in a different family—how did that change you inside?"

Dad took a deep breath. "I always said, never blame the majority, blame the people who are responsible. With hate, you can only create more hate. Try to transform yourself and understand the situation in which some of the people were. Try to make sure to transform the future of humanity, not to let it happen again." He paused. “But I said, I was eleven when the whole thing started. I committed a crime. My crime was, I was a Jew.” He threw his hand up, staring straight ahead. He paused.

“You have to forgive. You have to understand. There are some people who are hiding behind the truth. But the majority, they are honest people. They never wanted to see it happen. How it changed me? I don’t think that I ever hated anybody, but I did try to start to understand, and convert it to a situation of mutual understanding.”

We all just listened, hanging on every word. My father was the most compassionate, most gracious man I knew.

He continued, “Some people did things which they weren’t aware of at the time. Some were forced to it, some just did it for the pleasure.” He was looking directly at us, when he said this. His hands were folded—a small signal of composure—but the emotion on his face was evident.

“How it changed me? I only knew I was fighting to survive.” He paused. “I did.” Lips pursed, he stopped speaking and lowered his eyes as his mind hovered over the dark corners of his past.

Bryan broke the silence. “Let’s take a break.” Gratefully, everyone stood up.

Hovering over Dad, I leaned in and whispered, “Let’s have some lunch. I’ll put sandwiches out on the dining room table.”

He smiled up at me. “Dat sounds good, Bärb.”

Everyone was grateful for the break. I put out a small platter of sandwiches, and we talked about the weather and the garden. Ed might have mentioned a feel-good story he saw in the local paper.

Just small talk—exactly what we needed. Then it was back to the interview.

"How did staying with Withers prepare you for the rest of your life?" Bryan asked.

"First, I learned to love those people." Dad responded, meaning Withers and his troop as a whole. "Some of them probably never had a proper home, but they were full of heart and always willing to give.

"That's the time that they gave me a lift, put me on my feet. They showed me freedom and how to look into the future." He became very animated. "Ironic, many of those men were denied freedoms."

Dad looked at us, suddenly in the present, transitioning to sharing the impact on his life, on his children's lives. "I tried to teach my children to differentiate between good and bad, to be judicious. If you have a question, sit down, evaluate it again. And if you don't know, can't make a decision, then discuss it with somebody you trust." He paused. Caught up in the moment, caught up in his emotion. "My children, my grandchildren, I'm very proud of them."

He looked at me, then Ed. Taking out his handkerchief, he wiped his eyes for the first time.

I got up and hugged him, kissing his cheek. "Nobody's as proud as Ed, me, and your grandchildren," I whispered in his ear, rubbing his back. Then I wiped away my own tears.

PART FIVE

CHAPTER FIFTY-FIVE

2003

Our exhilarating summer ended with problems on the home front. Mom's leg pain had escalated and was really slowing her down. Worse, she was showing signs of decline. Previously independent, high energy, and ready to help her family—anyone, really—she had receded into her own world. Mom was becoming selective in what she heard, responding only to what made her feel comfortable. I just couldn't get through to her anymore. When I asked if she would consult a doctor for care or if she'd let me help clean the house, I was met with an absolute, resolute, *no*. I didn't realize it, but she was covering up cognitive and emotional changes she herself didn't understand. Unfortunately, her delicate mental state made it impossible for Ed and me to include her in Dad's care decisions. She accepted our assessments passively. It broke our hearts to watch our strong mother lose her ability to make her own life choices. Still outspoken, she used her rebellious strength to cover up her gradual memory loss.

Dad maintained her routines at home. Before leaving for work every day, he cleaned their patio table and chairs. Mom loved nature, so he moved her favorite chair closer to the sliding door, making sure to top up the bird feeder so the blue jays and cardinals would make their daily visit. If she wasn't up to cooking, he brought dinner home, laying out the food and telling her about his day. This was their time to talk, to reconnect … to act as if things were normal when they were anything but. Dad would never give up on my mother, so they lived in a world of pretend, as if time hadn't stolen her illustrious spirit.

Early in September, while working in his office, Dad admitted he had abdominal pain. He offered no objections to a doctor's appointment, thank goodness. He underwent his first colonoscopy. Then the phone call. Colon cancer. The tumor was large; the doctor recommended surgery. Ed and I researched the ugly diagnosis and drove Dad to his appointments. We did our best to help him through this new world of cancer. After many discussions, we agreed with his doctor, the same one who removed his gallbladder, that surgery was the best option. It was the end of September. The operation was scheduled for October 30th.

The first day of October was brisk, without a cloud in the sky. Ed and I drove Dad to St. Francis Hospital's imaging center for a CT scan. After parking the car, we each took one of his arms and tenderly walked him to the clinic.

"What's your hurry?" Dad asked. "Take your time." He wore his captain's hat and smiled at us, looking left at me and right at Ed.

We talked to staff before the procedure. Dad had to drink a "pink juice" before his scan. While the cocktail traveled through his system, we enjoyed some time together, chitchatting and joking.

Like mother hens, we guided Dad to the imaging room. I was relieved this would not be an invasive test. The procedure done, Dad came out, speaking calmly, assuring us he was fine before going to change. Ed and I worried about the test results, but at the moment, we were elated just to be with him. It had been a long day. Finally, the doctors cleared Dad to leave. We walked back the way we came, through the parking lot where the sun hung low on the horizon, reflecting off the brilliant yellow leaves. Framed in that moment, enveloped by sunshine, Ed and I turned our heads at the same time and kissed Dad on his cheeks.

Dad insisted on going to work. We drove him back to the office, his second home. He was adamant that Ed and I leave him. Payroll and employee schedules needed to get done. "Why can't this wait?" I asked him. The schedules weren't due for a few days. It was as if he knew a deadline loomed. Reluctantly, Ed and I left after five. He stayed late, finishing his work before heading home to Bloomfield.

Around eleven that night, a distraught Mom called to say Dad was running a high fever. Ed picked me up, and we raced the half-hour drive. Turning up our parents' long driveway, the headlights illuminated the big, white colonial home, stark against the night. We hurried to the front door, pausing a moment between the grand pillars framing the entrance. We turned the key and ran upstairs to the master bedroom.

Dad's fever had spiked. He was delirious, but still trying to calm us. "I'm okay, don't vorry," he stammered.

I kissed him on the forehead and told him we would call an ambulance. I couldn't believe that just two hours before he had been sitting in his office, working. What had happened?

In less than twenty minutes, the ambulance arrived. Ed and I assured Mom that we'd keep in touch with her. The paramedics got Dad on a stretcher and sped to St. Francis Hospital. Ed and I followed close behind, hearts racing.

It was a busy night at the ER. There were no cubicles available, so we stood watch over Dad while he lay in his hospital bed parked in the hallway. The tests the attending physician ordered showed that a bacterial infection had caused Dad's fever, evidently a common side effect of mobile catheters. Ed and Dad had earlier decided on using the mobile catheter which was supposed to make it easier for the doctors to check Dad's levels and—hopefully—clear him for surgery. I felt guilty, angry and pained. Shame on the nephrologist for not advising us on what could go wrong. Had we been rushing too much? How did we miss this?

Looking up from Dad's report, the nurse delivered another blow: the CT scan showed that the cancer had spread to his liver.

We were speechless. This was devastating.

That night, watching as Dad slept, we tried to make sense of his test results. We were grateful that we had medical power of attorney and could make key decisions on his behalf, be Dad's voice. At daybreak, he was admitted to the intensive care unit. The test results came back with more bad news: the bacterial intrusion resulted in sepsis, a serious blood infection.

Stay strong, I told myself. Stay strong, Bärb.

After two days in the ICU, and with the help of medication, Dad fought through his high fever and stabilized. Now he had to move to another unit. Fearful because he would lose his one-on-one, round-the-clock care provided by the exceptional ICU staff, we knew that we had no choice. The other hospital floors and care centers couldn't compare.

Family came every day to see Dad. Jeff left work and came at lunchtime. Steve came from work. Kimberly came afternoons, and her husband visited in the evening. One day they brought Ashley. Their Opa had tremendous love and support—Opa, grandfather, Papa, Martin, Dad.

Ed and I were navigating treatments and the aftermath of sepsis, which had become compounded by breathing difficulties. Every other day, Dad was moved to different floors to accommodate his health fluctuations. Thanks to one nurse, we learned days after his admission that some of the prescribed drugs were known to repress the respiratory system. She noticed that we were scrambling to keep up with the changes in Dad's condition every single day and made sure to keep us informed.

I had lost ten pounds in the week and a half since Dad had been admitted to the hospital. Steve had just left on a business trip to Bermuda, so I was on my own. Breaking for lunch at work on Wednesday, sitting at a table in the outside courtyard of my office, a Blum Shapiro partner, Bernie Cohen, saw me resting my head in my hands. "What's wrong?" he asked.

I told him about Dad.

He looked at me and said, "I know the best colon specialists in the state; I do their tax work." He went to his office and contacted Dr. Sam Banarjee to oversee Dad's care.

That afternoon, I spoke with Dr. Banarjee and he agreed to see Dad the next morning. Clearly, he was doing this only as a favor to Bernie, but I explained to Dr. Banarjee that his primary care physician had given up on him and had called me to consider hospice care. *Hospice!* Dad was running his own business a week ago, in charge of his life. I realized that sepsis was hard to treat, but

Dad was alert and mentally back to normal once his fever broke. I just wished I had thought of having a colon cancer specialist oversee his care at the onset. I didn't know. God forgive me, I just didn't know.

I was outraged at the primary physician's lack of coordination of specialists who worked on his case. I informed the care team that Dr. Banarjee would care for Dad's colon cancer. This change, of course, created confusion with the doctors. It was a circus.

I didn't care. I would do anything for Dad.

EVENING, OCTOBER 15th

A major thunderstorm accompanied by high winds raged through the state. I met my friends, Carol and Ronnie, for an early dinner in Cheshire. Since they worked in healthcare, they could give me much needed advice on how to coordinate with Dad's doctors.

The wind howled, thunder cracked, and lightning skipped back and forth across the sky as I drove to Hartford following dinner. Clutching my steering wheel to keep the car steady, I felt empowered after our talk. Carol and Ronnie agreed that changing the primary care physician was a good move. We would have a fresh start. I couldn't wait to see Dad.

The tumultuous weather left the streets of Hartford deserted. I arrived at the hospital and was glad to see my son-in-law in the room with Dad. He left us alone. Sitting up and ready to talk, Dad seemed in good spirits, but his right leg was red and sore; he could hardly move it. He'd begun dialysis and had lost more weight. He couldn't get out of bed; the last two weeks had taken their toll on his body.

I began with my daily ritual, massaging his back and neck, planting a kiss on his cheek, and whispering in his ear, "I love you, Papa."

"I love you too, Bärb," he said smiling, turning to kiss my cheek.

"Sit down," he said. He always wanted everyone around him to be comfortable.

I poured him his favorite Poland Spring mineral water and pulled up a chair.

"Have you been able to sleep?" I asked, leaning forward. His medications and various ailments often kept him awake, and he couldn't focus enough to read or watch television.

"No," he said. "Not yet."

"Why don't you take the night medication? It will help you sleep." But I knew he wouldn't.

"You know I don't like to take anything I don't have to, Bärb."

I knew why.

"The doctors are meeting with Ed and me tomorrow morning to go over your care plan," I said. "I just met with two of my friends and I want to figure out all the issues going on here."

"Bärb, I don't want dialysis right now. Not every day."

"I understand." I looked at his sore leg and thought about all the complications that had ravaged his poor body. "I'll make sure of it."

I saw the disquiet in his eyes. "Bärb, we'll just get the information from the doctors in the morning and then decide what to do, one step at a time."

I tried a smile. "Guess what?" I changed the subject, an attempt to get our minds off all the health problems. "Bryan Gruley's article on Florida State University appeared on the front page of the *Wall Street Journal* yesterday."

Dad smiled. "Congratulate him for me and save me a copy."

We talked, laughed, and appreciated stories about the children and grandkids for two wonderful hours. Pouring him another glass of mineral water, I set down his cup and leaned over to hug him. A sense of peace prevailed. We had forgotten about the health obstacles for a little while and just enjoyed being with each another. I was grateful.

MORNING, OCTOBER 16th

I woke up early the next day in a rush to get to the hospital for a meeting with Dad's care team. Since the doctors did early morning rounds, Ed and I had missed getting updates firsthand and had had little chance to discuss how treatment would proceed. I believed there had been a great many errors that had put Dad in the hospital and wanted—needed—to set things straight.

Juggling my briefcase, purse, and medical notes, I headed for Stop & Shop to get a special yogurt for Dad. His nurse had told me he'd had a hard time swallowing his pills, and she'd filched a creamy yogurt from the staff refrigerator which helped him take his meds. He had also developed thrush, a reaction to the medications, which made it hard to swallow. This nurse had been one of the angels in our lives who made a difference. I had promised to bring the yogurt the next morning.

Rushing to the supermarket, I received a call from my staff

accountant saying the Excel program I'd sent him that morning wouldn't open. I had worked like crazy to have the program to him in time for a critical deadline. Now he couldn't open it? I turned around and rushed back to my house, started the computer program, tested the worksheet, and re-sent the file. With a prayer, I headed back to the grocery store in high gear. Nearly ejecting myself from her car, I arrived at Stop & Shop, frantically searching for the aisle and scanning the yogurts. I found "the" yogurt and nearly pushed the customer ahead of me out of the way to pay. Every second counted today.

I arrived at St. Francis' inadequate parking garage where I maneuvered my car into a miniscule spot. I was beyond panic. Grabbing the yogurt and my notes, I sprinted to the entrance, wondering if I should take off my heels to pick up speed. Finally, I arrived at Dad's floor, sweaty and out of breath. The doctors were huddled outside his room. I waved at Ed and rushed past everyone, needing to see Dad first.

He was in bed, having a hard time catching his breath. What on earth was wrong? I yelled for the nurse. I didn't want them to start the meeting without me, but Dad needed help. A nurse came. I pointed—he was gasping for air! I knew I had to leave his room to see the doctors. I reluctantly left him in his bed.

The care team gave Ed and I the update on Dad's condition: his creatinine and blood urea nitrogen levels were off, meaning his kidneys weren't working well enough to perform the surgery. I clenched my fists at my side. But that was the reason he wore the damn mobile catheter, and they'd ordered three kidney dialysis treatments! To further complicate matters, they told us that the urologist had performed a procedure near the urinary tract. This sensitive process could be done two ways; one was invasive, the other less so. I had been relieved that the urologist could do the less invasive one; however, he had punctured a valve. I rolled my eyes heavenward. Mother of God! Dad was strong, but he had sepsis, kidney problems, colon cancer, and respiratory distress. Now the doctor had created more problems. I didn't understand … I'd had a miraculous evening with Dad the night before.

Dad's nurse came out of his room visibly upset, asking the doctor to go in immediately. Dad needed a breathing tube inserted through his nose. They wouldn't let Ed and me in the room because the procedure was grueling. Did these decisions make sense? It was all happening so quickly. Ed and I looked at each other, wondering if this was the right thing to do, whether there was a choice, whether this was another mistake or if there was anything anyone could do. We couldn't keep up with all the information.

The doctors told the nurse to transfer Dad to intensive care. Ed and I couldn't see him for a few hours. I stood bewildered, head shaking, devastated. I felt helpless. Like my dad, I didn't admit that, ever.

Ed and I stumbled off down the hall together. Alone in the waiting area, I wadded up tissues into a ball. Ed coughed into his hand. He glanced at me. "I'm going to my doctor, Barb. I can't shake this cough." He had been feeling sick and run down for several days. I wanted to stop him, to tell him, "No! Wait! This is a critical day!" But I nodded, trying to understand, trying to keep all the threads of my family's health together.

As Ed left, I felt faint and had to sit down.

My world was spinning out of control. I had to stay strong, just like Dad always did.

CHAPTER FIFTY-SIX

AFTERNOON, OCTOBER 16th

I was looking for a private corner in the hospital hallway when a need to find the chapel suddenly overcame me. I had tried to locate it before, but the building was a maze with new additions everywhere and I just gave up. This time, I followed the signs and when they disappeared, asked for directions.

Finally, I found the narrow hallway leading to the chapel. My cell phone rang. It was a dear friend and business associate, Cindy, a registered nurse. She heard the worry in my voice as I described my day and Dad's condition.

"Barbara, sometimes there's nothing more we can do," Cindy said. "You have to know when to let go."

Her voice was soothing. I knew her to be strong and smart, giving her honest advice. But I wasn't ready to let go. I thanked her as I came upon the chapel door. I ended the call. My instincts felt stronger. I knew I had to have a conversation with God.

As I entered the room, a sense of peace surrounded me. A man was near the altar, mopping the floor. He politely left. My eyes rested on the simple white cross centered at the front of the chapel. Two tall green plants flanked the cross. It was quiet.

I looked up and whispered, "Dear God, I need your help. Please look in on my dad. You know, he's my best friend, my mentor. He's the anchor for our family. Please help me do what's right. Take over, and whatever is supposed to happen, please guide it, guide me." I pursed my lips, lowering my head.

A sense of awe overwhelmed me. I knew the decision was out of my hands. I just knew. With all my heart, I gave it up to Him. Eyes closed, hands folded, I allowed my spirit to hover. I can't fully explain that afternoon, but I experienced a sense of something bigger than me. I thanked God, made the sign of the cross, and walked out.

My first call was to Jeff. I had to give him a head's up to be ready to leave work for the hospital. It was good to hear his voice. Jeff was most like Dad—brave, smart, and kind.

I found my way back to the hospital floor. One of the young hospital doctors, who I had learned was of Polish heritage, had been kind enough to answer our questions earlier that week. Now he was looking for Ed and me. I explained Ed was at an appointment, so the doctor asked me to follow him into a small office and closed the door. I prayed he would tell me that Dad was getting better … please!

"Barbara," he began, "your father is a very sick man. As doctors, we can do a lot, but sometimes we are helpless and can't fix the problems. This is one of those times." He was gentle and took his time explaining how Dad was declining, guiding me toward acceptance. I wished Ed were there, but I had to brave this information alone.

It was too much. Emotion overcame me. "My father's a Holocaust survivor and shouldn't have to suffer anymore." I rarely shared that information, but I felt like I was having an out-of-body experience.

"If I thought we could do more, we would," he said. "You have to make a decision. His respiratory system is compromised. He probably won't make it through another day. If his respiratory system fails, you need to decide if you want a do not resuscitate order issued."

"Can't we do more?" I asked.

My head spun. My heart pounded in my chest. But this kind young doctor sat with me, taking the time to explain. It was time to decide if we would artificially resuscitate Dad, and, if so, to what end? By the time he finished talking, I had the overwhelming feeling again that this situation was out of my hands. People say we humans have a defined number of "end of life" exit clauses. I had once read that people could die one of six times. Dad had survived so many. Was this the final day?

Lowering my head, I whispered, "I'll talk to my brother, Doctor. We'll get back to you." The young man nodded. I left the office, went to the nearest window, and stared out at the trees, clothed in brilliant autumn colors. My instincts told me to let him go. I felt a sense of peace about it. He wouldn't suffer, but how could I do this? *I can't let him go—he's part of me. I tensed, wishing desperately. Ed, where are you? We need to talk!*

As if on cue, he came around the corner. Thank you, God, I needed relief. I pulled him aside and told him what had just transpired. Wanting to find another way, I reminded him about what the doctor said. I also told him I had a strange feeling that we should let things happen naturally. Ed stepped back when I finished. Face drawn, he paced, distraught. He checked the clock.

It was midafternoon.

What would Dad want? I kept asking myself. He's a fighter, but his poor body had been compromised in so many ways, I didn't want him to suffer anymore. After going back and forth, we considered allowing nature to take its course, but first we had to see Dad. The hospital staff eventually allowed us into his room. A huge breathing tube had been inserted into his nose, taped onto his face. Heavily sedated, his eyes were closed. It was so hard to understand—what had happened here? How much of this could have been avoided? A short time later, we agreed to let things progress naturally.

But still I had the thought—maybe he could pull through?

Mom had not been to the hospital since Dad had been admitted almost two weeks earlier. The pains in her leg were acting up and she couldn't make the trip. Now she had to come.

Mom was reluctant, but I told her she would regret this for the rest of her life if she didn't. Then I called my daughter Kim, telling her to come. I redialed Jeff and explained why he should leave work now. Taking a deep breath, I phoned Steve in Bermuda. He bemoaned the fact he couldn't be there with us. He loved Dad like his own father.

At around four-thirty, our small family huddled in the waiting area. Jeff, Kim, Mom, Ed, and I stood pensive. Ed and I tried to prepare them when we shared the doctor's update. Jeff and Kim adored and respected their Opa; they always appreciated his sage advice and generous love, and the family was together to be there for each other.

As we entered Opa's room, Mom was taken aback at the breathing tube. "What have they done?" she asked over and over.

I asked her to stop, to please stay in the moment. She did.

We stood around his bed and kissed his forehead, one by one. The respirator beeped, but the interval between breaths grew longer and longer.

When it was my turn, I kissed him just as I had every day. "I love you, Dad," I whispered. "I love you."

The beeps from the machine continued to slow. No one said a word, but I sensed we were each frantically struggling inside. I noticed Dad straining to open his eyes. That was haunting—the meds had knocked him out, but his incredible strength came through. I saw him try to speak with his eyes. He was communicating with them.

I whispered in his ear, "You can let go. Be with your mother, your father, and sister again." My daughter had shared that thought with me, and it was the only comfort I could think to give him. I knew that the hardest part of his survival had been their loss. I believed the only thing keeping him was us, his family—he didn't want to let us go.

Dad continued straining to open his eyes. *Oh my God!*

Then his breathing machine stopped beeping. He passed at 5:35 p.m.

I kissed him one last time. The greatest man in my life. I had believed him to be immortal. I knew I would never get over this. Life would never be the same. As we left his room, I remembered his words from the interview with Bryan. "You must never take everyday things in life for granted." And I swore I never would.

CHAPTER FIFTY-SEVEN

OCTOBER 20th

I wasn't ready to say goodbye.

I stood at the podium, glancing at my notes.

"There are no words to describe my father. He had a *silent power*. He made you want to be your best. How lucky was I to be his daughter?" I paused and took a breath. "Above all, Dad cherished his family, his children and their children. He is Opa to Jeffrey, Kimberly, Christopher, and Ashley. He raised a family and nurtured mutual love, respect, and trust, and created a safe place to belong. I don't know if he was done, but he established that safe place for us. Because his was stolen from him. I realize more, as time goes on, the significance of having that special place.

"He was our guiding light." My voice broke, then strengthened. "*Never judge others!* That was his lesson to us. We love you, Dad, and we'll always celebrate your life."

A few years ago, I gave him a plaque for his other birthday. He loved it. I read it out loud:

"We cannot direct the wind,
But we can adjust the sails"

You did that Dad, my wise teacher. You'll always be my hero.

CHAPTER FIFTY-EIGHT

"My name is John Withers, and I have known Martin I think longer than anyone in this room, including his wife, Margareta." He smiled, charming everyone right from the start, as usual. Then he became more serious. "I had the honor and pleasure of being his friend. As he came out of Dachau, Martin was a young kid. Our all African American, segregated troop took him in. They made him a little brother. He brought truth. After Martin spent some time, this one little kid changed the attitude and actions of these big, tough, Southern, uneducated black fellows from Mississippi and Alabama. The men would be careful what they said around him. They stopped complaining. Criticism stopped because they saw that no job was questioned, no job too difficult for Martin."

John paused and became philosophical. "Martin touched on all facets after the war; anti-Semitism, the cruelty and horror of Nazism, he touched upon segregation because he was with our segregated unit and we had to hide him. In a small strange way, he affected and was affected by all of the events of American and world history.

"Martin believed in a philosophy which I wish could be adopted all over the world—not to judge by groups—ethnic, religious, national—only by individual acts, that was important. That's the reason he had such a successful life and overcame obstacles. He believed not so much in words as in actions. I'm sure if he had turned his thoughts into poetry, he would leave this thought with his children and grandchildren:"

And then Lieutenant John Withers recited,

"When these golden days are gone
For you I shall continue on
You are thread of life to me, you are my immortality.

"I would like to close with this: Martin liked the words to this as it very much helped him improve his English. He liked to sit around the campfire, listening. In memorandum, I'd like to share them with you:

Fading light dims the sight
And a star gems the sky, gleaming bright
From afar, drawing nigh
Falls the night.
Day is done, gone the sun,
From the lakes, from the hills, from the sky
All is well, safely rest,
God is nigh."

Silence pervaded the room after John Withers finished reciting words to "Taps."

CHAPTER FIFTY-NINE

I entered a state of grace after Dad passed. There's no other way to explain it—I had never experienced that feeling before. I wanted to do everything right, help everybody, be of service to all. I felt love toward everyone. Reading about mourning loved ones, I'd learned that Tibetans pray for forty-nine days until the soul gets established in the next "heavenly" phase. Dad's spirit, the essence of commanding love, hovered around me. I was sure of it.

The day after Dad's burial, Steve and I stepped out onto our bedroom balcony. He watched me closely, worried how I would cope without my father. We were trying to make small talk, commenting blithely on how tall the trees were in our backyard forest. Out of the blue, a dragonfly swooped down and landed on the railing. It was beautiful. The wings were a brilliant indigo laced with strands of lustrous green. Suddenly, three more dragonflies landed right next to it, and all four aligned in perfect order, as if they were together. I was taken aback. They were less than two feet in front of me, and they didn't move.

Steve was just as surprised. We stood there, staring.

After a few minutes, Steve looked at me and in a hushed voice said, "It's your dad, joined by his family; he must be telling you he's all right."

Steve's not terribly spiritual, but he believed it. I believed it too. I never had a dragonfly attraction, but suddenly, I understood their significance. I remembered seeing them in gift shops, as garden ornaments, and brooches pinned to women's jackets. Now they had meaning for me. It would be the first of many inexplicable encounters.

Two days after the burial, I returned to work for a half-day at Blum Shapiro. Telling me to take as much time off as I needed, Lori Budnick, the partner I worked with, was concerned. I told her that I needed to work or I would lose my mind. Anne, the firm's marketing director, encouraged me to take it easy as well. She had been helping me navigate the *Wall Street Journal* process.

After work, I drove to Bloomfield to spend time with Mom. Once fiercely independent, she continued to struggle with memory lapses. It worried me. She had relied on Dad to fulfill her day-to-day needs. Now I was relying on her, leaning on her to fill my void. I arrived at her house, checked to make sure she had food and eyed all the things that needed to be done. Fresh coffees in hand, we sat down at the kitchen table. Her mental state had become so delicate that I only brought up topics I knew she would be comfortable discussing. Her favorite was our time in Israel. I held up the picture of she and I standing together in our garden when I was barely three. It was a time Mom and Dad were so in love, a time full of optimism, when it was just the three of us. I was overjoyed to see Mom's face light up. I longed to have my mother back, to fill my overwhelming sense of loss—loss of my secure life with Dad at its center and loss of my nurturing, strong mother. Mom didn't leave her house much, so I brought meals and Ed checked on her constantly.

A week later, Bryan Gruley called me. He had completed his article about Dad and John and wanted to share his draft with me. Bryan wanted my approval before running the article by the editor; he also let me know it could change once the editing team reviewed his draft. The *Wall Street Journal* only allowed verbal previews, so Bryan summarized his draft over the phone. I tried hard to concentrate and take it all in. It was a story about two heroes and how they had inspired each other. It was everything I wanted to hear. The story had been cut short by Dad's passing, but I had come to trust Bryan and gave him approval to move forward. He hoped the story would run in November because the upcoming holidays made it harder to get print space for publishing feature-length articles.

I thanked him and hung up the phone, feeling blessed.

Thanksgiving was just a week away. I knew I couldn't host the holiday at our home this year. My eyes welled up with tears every time I looked in my dining room because I saw Dad's chair at the head of the table, lifting his glass to make a toast before we said grace. Tradition was important. I felt it my responsibility to carry on the rituals my parents had forged for me and our family. My parents enjoyed their growing family every holiday—they'd deserved it. They hadn't had parents to rely on in the States. Now there were eleven of us.

I phoned John and Daisy Withers to wish them a happy holiday. I needed to hear John's voice. Then, for the first time, I asked Ed if he could host Thanksgiving dinner. I was both thankful and touched when he agreed.

CHAPTER SIXTY

NOVEMBER 24th

Bryan had beaten the Thanksgiving deadline by two days. He called to give us the news, sharing the story's title: "For Lt. Withers, Act of Mercy Has Unexpected Sequel." The article would run on November 25th, 2003.

I stopped, struck. I was taken aback by the word "Mercy." Dad had never begged in his life! The word didn't suit Dad's character nor his life's philosophy. That was the opening line? How could this happen? I'm sure Bryan noticed my hesitation, but he had another call coming in so he said he'd phone me back. I was grateful for the break. I needed to process my feelings.

It was after 9:00 p.m. I called Steve, who agreed to call Ed to come over. We had to talk about this in person.

Ed arrived five minutes later, grinning as he entered. "Happy birthday, Steve!"

"Thanks, Ed, never a dull moment here." Steve added logs to our fireplace and then handed us each a drink. We settled into the family room as I reviewed what Bryan Gruley had said.

Looking at Ed and then Steve, I said, "Let's be calm about this. Remember, we're all emotional because Dad's not here. It's only been a month since he passed."

Nevertheless, we agreed over the wording being wrong. Dad was *never* a victim and the word "mercy" was unsettling. As promised, Bryan called back, and together we explained our feelings about the headline. I could tell Bryan was caught unaware. He wanted to help, but explained changes were *never* made to *The Wall Street Journal* at this juncture. The article had gone to print, but he would try to see what he could do.

"What do you think of replacing *mercy* with the word *kindness*?" Steve suggested. We all agreed that felt right.

"Congratulations, Steve," said Bryan, "You're a headline writer."

I was grateful that we were still protecting Dad, even now.

The three of us were anxious as we waited. It was late. Commiserating with each other about everything, we were a mess. A log crashed to the fireplace floor, casting a burst of light, a warm glow over the room. I just stared into the flames, exhausted.

The phone rang about an hour later. It was Bryan. The headline was already printed, he explained, but he was able to get "Kindness" into some editions. In other words, part of the country would see "Mercy" and other sections would see "Kindness." I knew he was trying hard and I could tell it bothered him that we were upset. We thanked him for his efforts and his loyalty.

I could try to sleep now. Ed left for home close to midnight.

Tuesday, November 25th, 2003, Bryan Gruley's article on Martin Weigen and John Withers ran on the front page, left column of the *Wall Street Journal*. The story continued on page twelve, accompanied by photos of Dad and John and our families.

The story was substantial and well-written. It was very different from the draft Bryan had read in late October; the story was more from John's viewpoint and about Dad's wartime history. It didn't seem to capture the essence of the man Dad had become or show his love and devotion to family. The story was a tribute to his past, but the original version had been focused on both heroes. I reminded myself that our family was in a different place now, mourning Dad. Perhaps the story had appeared too soon? Dad wasn't there to witness the fruits of his labor. This moment confirmed what I already knew—I had to pass on his story. I needed to pay it forward to convey Dad's lesson regarding humanity. His lesson not to judge others by their skin color, religion, or beliefs. His lesson on kindness. He'd taught me to keep my head up, always. There was no room for bitterness after enduring life challenges. His story *had* to make a difference in the world. It just had to.

I spoke to John Withers later that day. Delighted for him that at age eighty-four, he had received recognition for his brave act and kindness after the war. I knew that was what mattered to Dad. That was why he had agreed to the interview and it was where I'd found solace.

The day was bittersweet. It felt as though I was trying to enjoy myself at a party that lacked its guest of honor.

Steve, Ed, and Jeff went to drugstores, grocery stores, and gas stations, trying to pick up as many copies of the papers as they could so we would have original prints for the family archives. We started getting calls from friends. The feedback was overwhelming as people honored our two heroes. The themes of love, loss, religion, and race hit home for many. This was a moving story, despite our disappointment about feeling that Dad's character wasn't fully portrayed. Many expressed how surprised they were to learn about

Dad's past; few knew he was Jewish.

The *Wall Street Journal* published letters to the editor from all over the country. People had been moved. A woman in Texas sent a handwritten personal letter to Ed. She felt this story reminded us all about people's love and kindness. Those sentiments seemed to be the common thread. People craved a kind human-interest story and were inspired. Dad's legacy was one of embracing diversity as well as dealing with adversity. Most said they had cried.

John Withers and his son were asked to speak at Jewish organizations. They requested that Ed and I participate, but emotionally, we simply weren't ready to make public presentations. We gracefully bowed out but were happy that they would continue to share the story. The world looked up to these men and their tale of perseverance and friendship.

Dad and John would forever be my two great heroes.

John and Martin, 2002

EPILOGUE

READER'S DIGEST

A dark cloud hung over our family as we turned the calendar to 2004. It was hard to start a new year without our wise guide. We had survived the holidays by focusing on the children. I buried myself in work, glad the busy season kept me at the office for long hours.

On the bright side, Jeff was dating Ellen, and I sensed that they were falling in love. Ellen was beautiful inside and out, and she and Jeff were a great couple. Kim had moved into a new home and hoped to have another baby. My granddaughter, Ashley, was flourishing in preschool. Life was moving on.

Steve and I flew to the west coast of Florida whenever our schedules allowed. Our family joined us for a long weekend; my friends, Lori, Delia, and Elena came for girl time. Our days grew hectic because we had purchased a condo that needed a complete overhaul. We had to make decisions on all aspects of a new kitchen and flooring for every room.

But when evening came, the big sky showed off brilliant shades of orange as Nature's brush painted the sky. Steve and I set our beach chairs on the shore, cocktails in hand, and we'd watch the blazing sun drop slowly, and, once at half-mast, it would disappear in seconds. Waves gently washed up as the sky glowed red. It was in this spot, at this time, that I felt at peace.

Having lived near water most of my life, I knew I was meant to be here. Looking up our Florida coastline reminded me of seeing Tel Aviv from Jaffa, my birthplace. The new home became my private sanctuary where I began to heal.

In early May 2004, I sat in my West Hartford office looking over my work plan. My assistant buzzed, saying there was a woman on the line who wanted to speak with me. She introduced herself as a writer for the *Reader's Digest* and asked if I would be willing to do an interview on the phone. They were publishing a condensed version of *The Wall Street Journal* article about Dad and John. I was cautious. I knew firsthand about the twists and turns of journalism.

But as we spoke, our conversation flowed and she sounded kind. This was my opportunity to address my perceived omissions from the article. It felt right, so I agreed. She verified facts of the story and asked more questions about Dad. I explained the change in the *WSJ* article after Dad passed. Toward the end of our conversation, she asked if she could call again after she drafted the article to go over final details.

"Of course," I said, feeling a sense of responsibility. I had to get this right.

I stared out the window—what just happened here? I didn't realize the magazine was planning to publish this condensed article until the call came in today. I phoned my brother. Ed had been reeling from managing the business without Dad. He was always in a hurry now, but we had an understanding that we would always keep each other in the loop to minimize surprises.

After I shared the *Reader's Digest* call, we both agreed; if it was done in good taste, it would honor Dad and John and send the right message. A message about humanity—the best and worst of humanity.

Two weeks later, I received another call from the woman at the *Reader's Digest* asking how Dad had passed. Her question took me by surprise. What had been his diagnosis? I hesitated. How could I explain? I didn't have a clear answer. So many problems had merged at the end. His diagnosis was colon cancer, but sepsis was the primary catalyst to his cause of death. I did my best and I appreciated her sensitivity. Her questions brought me back again to the moment, the time, when I lost him. Eyes closed, I choked up.

In late May, I received a box of *Reader's Digest* magazines. Kate Hudson adorned the cover of the June 2004 issue and I quickly found the article on page 135, credited to Bryan Gruley from *The Wall Street Journal*. The introduction and the headline read, "After five decades, an old soldier and the man he saved find each other again, *Reunited*." I turned the pages in wonder. I loved that they had both photos of Dad and John from 1946 and began the story in the present. Although it was a condensed version, Bryan Gruley had worked with *Reader's Digest* to add some of the material that had been cut from the *WSJ* article.

The truth suddenly struck me, overwhelmed me. She had listened, Bryan had listened. The article was a wonderful tribute to both my heroes. I loved it. Our family loved it. The Withers loved it.

I looked up, whispering through a smile. "Dad, you good with this?"

It's fine, Bärb, I heard Dad in my head. I could picture his kind eyes and gentle smile. I was engulfed by a sense of calm.

ACKNOWLEDGEMENTS

I sensed a divine intervention during the time I wrote this story. Books appeared, documents surfaced, the time was right. I met people from all walks of life who directed me to persons and places, guiding me to uncover details to tell this story.

It is with overwhelming gratitude that I thank the late John Withers for his heroic act and for the honor of meeting his spirited and loving wife, Daisy. An extraordinary thank you to John Withers II, without whom this story would never have come to life. Many thanks to his wife, Maryruth Coleman, for her insightful questions, and his brother Greg Withers and wife Carol for their kindness and support. Our enduring friendship lives on.

I am forever grateful to Regina Laks Gelb, my father's neighbor and friend who provided details of Starachowice's daily life and memories of their time together. A survivor along with her two sisters, Anna and Chris, she shared rich history about her parents and my grandparents, and her keen revelations of the war. Thank you for translating the Judenrat document and for allowing me and my family into your and Victor's home for wonderful meals and history lessons. We cherish our friendship. You helped bring this book into focus.

Thank you to writer Bryan Gruley for your outstanding interviews and sharing in Dad's history.

To my extraordinary editor Brenda Copeland. Thank you for working with me to elevate this manuscript to new heights. Author Dawn Metcalf, my appreciation for holding my hand to eliminate some darlings, while bringing others to life. And thank you to my friend, spirit guide and copy editor, Elizabeth Petry, I am grateful. A Catholic, a Jew and an African American respectively. Each of you shared your perspective and advanced this story. You have been a dream team!

To my devoted, lifelong friends, without whom I would not have completed this writing journey. My soulmate, Lori Garon, I'm forever grateful for your wisdom, your unwavering encouragement, and your love. Patti Tyson, my outstanding alpha reader, thank you for listening, consoling and inspiring me. Elena Stathis, my wise friend, you knew early on that this story had to be told.

To my wonderful friends and colleagues who guided me while I found my way, I am grateful for your patience and kindness. I'm blessed there are so many of you. A special thank you to Anne Elvgren, Lori Budnick and Cindy Bober for helping me navigate through my father's final days and embracing his story.

To my fabulous Florida friends. Thank you for listening and guiding me through the emotional hard times of writing this war story. My Clearwater family, I'm overwhelmed with your kindness, your consistent encouragement, and our walks on the beach. I'm grateful to each and every one of you. Michele Shannon, you were there for me from the start.

My second generation family, all of you, thank you. Always patient, always supporting my Holocaust study endeavor. Charlene Wygodski, Bonnie Stein, Yael Schauder, Halena Herman, you've helped me share this story and spread the word. I'm forever grateful.

My second generation conference buddies, you opened up a new world for me.

And to my Connecticut writer's group, where chapter by chapter, it all began. Thank you Joan Shapiro for guiding and advancing our writing endeavors. I'm grateful for the friendship and support of writers Erin Doolittle, Elaine McMahon, Donna Smith, Terri Klein, Ellen Karamidas, Jennifer Pacquin. I'm also grateful for my author friend and guide, Hanna Marcus. I love you all.

Thank you Rabbi Jeffrey Glickman and Mindy Glickman, for welcoming me to Temple Beth Hillel and expanding my world of Judaism. To my temple family-you know who you are. I'm so grateful you embraced Steven and me, bringing new light into our lives.

A heartfelt thanks to my brother Edward Weigen for archiving tons of photos and researching war documents. It's a gift to share our love for Mom and Dad, and to keep their memories alive over a glass, or two, or so … of wine. Thank you best nephew, Christopher Weigen, I still need your media help. And to Elaine Smith for cheering me on.

Ellen Carey Bergren, my smart daughter-in-law, always available for counsel, urging me on. Thank you so much. And to Debbie Bergren, always like a sister to me.

And finally, thank you to my amazing children. My son, Jeffrey Bergren, your love, wisdom and kindness enrich my life every day. My daughter, Kimberly Bergren Rambo, your sweet heart, keen mind and constant support motivate me. I love and cherish you both.

Love to my remarkable grandchildren: Ashley Sonia Klara Rambo, you've been a part of my writing venture since you were a little girl, Zachary Rambo, and Alexander Bergren—you are the light of my life.

And to my husband, Steve Bergren, your patience and love supported my writing habit. You made sure I didn't give up. Thank you for always believing in me.

SOURCES

The following resources were integral to details surrounding World War II, concentration camps, and depicting Starachowice under Nazi occupation. Christopher Browning's *Remembering Survival* was not only a classic book of Starachowice's Holocaust history, it was timely in my research quest.

Christopher R. Browning, *Remembering Survival, Inside a Nazi Slave-Labor Camp* (W.W. Norton and Company, Inc., 2010)

Louis Weber, Publisher, *The Holocaust Chronicle* (Publications International, Ltd., 2003)

Dr. Marcus J. Smith, *Dachau: The Harrowing Hell* (SUNY Press, 1995)

Elie Wiesel, *Night* (Hill and Wang, 1958, translation 2006)

Primo Levi, *Survival in Auschwitz* (Touchstone, 1996)

Helen Epstein, *Children of the Holocaust* (Penguin Books, 1988)

Żydowski Instytut Historyczny, *Minutes of Judenrat*, (Warsaw, Poland, 2002)

Translation of Wierzbnik chapter testimonies, *Encyclopedia of Jewish Communities in Poland*, Volume VII (Yad Vashem, Jerusalem, available by JewishGen, Inc. and the Yizkor Book Project)

Bryan Gruley, *For Lt. Withers, Act of Mercy Has Unexpected Sequel* (The Wall Street Journal, November 25, 2003)
http://isurvived.org/InTheNews/WSJ-folder/wsj-article-112503.html

Bryan Gruley, *Reunited* (Reader's Digest, June 2004)

Made in the USA
Middletown, DE
19 January 2020

83422870R00227